SMALL BUSINESS
BIG
OPPORTUNITY

Systematize Your Small Business, Create Personal Freedom, and Live the Entrepreneurial Dream

BEVERLEE RASMUSSEN

Brookswood House PUBLISHING INC.

Small Business, Big Opportunity

© **Copyright 2023 Beverlee Rasmussen**

All rights reserved.

Printed in Canada

No part of this publication may be reproduced, stored in, or introduced into a retrieval system, or transmitted, in any form, or by any means (electronic, mechanical, photocopying, recording, or otherwise), without the prior written permission of the publisher. Requests for permission should be directed to admin@systembusinesscoach.com or mailed to 3963 205B Street Langley, British Columbia V3A 2B2.

ISBN: 978-1-9993807-4-8 (Paperback)

ISBN: 78-1-9993807-5-5 (Hardcover)

Printed by Brookswood House Publishing Inc.

Vancouver, BC

Canada

www.brookswoodpublishing.com

For all courses, inquiries, or orders visit www.brookswoodpublishing.com

or email admin@systemsbusinesscoach.com

1st Edition

PRAISE FOR SMALL BUSINESS,
BIG OPPORTUNITY

"Every small business owner yearns to have a business that fuels joy and stability, not fear and overwhelm. *Small Business, Big Opportunity* unlocks the secret to profitable growth: a clear, practical and actionable framework to systemize your business so that you focus on what you are best at: delivering great service to your favorite clients. I will give it to every client moving forward!"

—Pamela Slim
Award-winning author of *The Widest Net, Body of Work*
and *Escape from Cubicle Nation*

"This book is the guide and support small business owners need! Powerfully written with Beverlee's experienced insights and expansive knowledge, *Small Business, Big Opportunity* brings practical wisdom for small business leaders of every industry."

—Dr. Marshall Goldsmith
Thinkers50 #1 Executive Coach and *New York Times* bestselling author of *The Earned Life, Triggers,* and *What Got You Here Won't Get You There*

"This book is very much on target, and the way leaders create, embed, and evolve culture is well captured."

—Dr. Edgar Harry Schein
Swiss-born American business theorist, psychologist, and professor at the MIT Sloan School of Management

"An absolute game-changer! *Small Business, Big Opportunity* is a must-read for any entrepreneur tired of spinning their wheels. Beverlee Rasmussen's expertise shines through as she provides actionable strategies to streamline operations, empower your team, and finally make sense of your numbers. This book is your roadmap to small business success."

—Kermit Jones, Jr.
CEO, Kamel Press

"A must-read for any business owner who is committed to turning their business vision into a thriving reality and for business coaches who care and are ready to help those entrepreneurs. Beverlee deeply cares about the success and well-being of business owners and her book masterfully lays out the roadmap using systems thinking to build an organized and profitable business. Practical insights and actionable strategies you will find here aren't just textbook theories - they come from a place of genuine concern and understanding."

—Povilas Petrauskas, MCC
Founder Akademija Infinitas

"The practicality of the book is simply outstanding, making it akin to a comprehensive manual tailored specifically for entrepreneurs. What truly sets the author apart is her genuine empathy and dedication towards the well-being of small business owners, shining through in every chapter."

—Leo Liu
Founder CEO at Wendao International Group
Board of Director at International Coaching Federation (Toronto Chapter)

"Beverlee captures the essentials for any small business to start, scale and grow. She's brilliantly captured in a few pages a success system well worth its weight in wisdom."

—Crystal Gregory
Founder CEG Coaching

"She had me at the first story!! And kept me interested even as a micro business owner. A practical, useful and often entertaining resource for small business owners written by someone who understands both the heart and soul of the small business owner and the breadth of the skill set needed to succeed. Beverlee has a rare and valuable background which results in a special kind of credibility and a combination of grit and kindness in her approach. This is a great read, cover to cover or read the chapter summaries (so you know what you don't know) and then dive into the chapter that you really really need first."

—Adele Fedorak
Story Practitioner, adelefedorak.ca

"As an experienced entrepreneur with over a decade of building small businesses, I found this book to be an absolute treasure-box. Each chapter provides invaluable insights that continuously motivate me to enhance and refine my company. If I had come across *"Small Business Big Opportunity"* at the beginning of my journey, it would have spared me from countless headaches and propelled me much further ahead. This book is a must-have for anyone in the business world looking to grow and succeed. Highly recommended!"

—Armin Ruser
Founder AHA Factory GmbH

"I love the premise of this book for a few reasons – it tells stories, and I love Beverlee's; it IS small business focused; it's heartening, or inspiring / a bit of both; it provides hope to those who may be floundering in year one or two of business."

—Dawn McCooey
Business Advisor Victoria British Columbia

"Unveiled the secret to my business's success. Offers invaluable insights. A must-read."

—David Summers
Founder, Urban Energy Group

"Finally, a book that speaks to the heart of small business struggles! *Small Business, Big Opportunity* is a beacon of hope for entrepreneurs drowning in overwhelm. Beverlee Rasmussen's insights into leadership, operations, finance, team, and marketing are a goldmine of wisdom. This book is a must-have for anyone serious about their business's success."

—Vanessa Tveitane
Project Manager Community Futures BC

"I've had the opportunity to use Beverlee's work with various business clients. Whether you're a new entrepreneur or a seasoned business owner, Beverlee's easy-to-use tools and techniques provide a systems approach to business development that will assist in a successful start-up or expansion. I recommend anyone interested in developing their business knowledge and skills to utilize these strategies."

—Glenys Reeves-Gibbs
Small Business Coach

"Small businesses are the lifeblood of our economy, but let's face it – many small business owners are drowning in a sea of tasks, priorities and feel constantly overwhelmed. That's where *Small Business, Big Opportunity* comes in. Drawing from real-world experience and written by someone who's been in the small business trenches, Beverlee lays out a no-nonsense, practical and actionable framework to help you take charge. Read this book, put the framework into action, and you'll find yourself with better control over your time, improved profits, and a fanbase of happy customers. A must read for any small business owner!"

— Urs Koenig, CEO Radical Humility Leadership Institute,
former UN peacekeeper and author of *Radical Humility*

To Brent, you came into my life and took my breath away, you are the one I was waiting for. Thank you for fulfilling your promise of something better.

I could not have done this without you.

OVERVIEW

Imagine a world where all small business owners have the skills, tools, and confidence to contribute to a healthy world economy, creating secure, meaningful employment while maintaining personal prosperity and freedom.

If only it were that easy. Small businesses account for 90 percent of all businesses globally and employ 70 percent of the world's workforce.[1] The role of the small business owner cannot be underestimated—as goes the small business owner, so goes the economy. Yet 51 percent of small businesses don't make it to year five.[2] The owners of the surviving 49 percent struggle to build (and keep) a profitable business. They tend to produce inconsistent results for customers. Often, they cannot pay their employees or themselves what they deserve. Instead of feeling proud of the company they've created, some business owners feel trapped. Start-ups and corporations get help from venture capitalists or grant programs; Main Street small business owners don't—especially not during years three through eight when most have a viable business, several employees, and more struggles than they expected.

It's time the engines of our economy—small business owners— receive the help they deserve.

Small Business, Big Opportunity: Systematize Your Small Business, Create Personal Freedom, and Live the Entrepreneurial Dream offers that help. This practical and complete guide to documenting and designing business systems empowers small business owners to free themselves from day-to-day operations and earn consistent profit so they can give back first to themselves, then to their family, their community, and the world.

1   International Labour Office, World Employment and Social Outlook: Trends 2022. (Geneva: International Labour Office, 2022), https://www.ilo.org/wcmsp5/groups/public/---dgreports/---dcomm/---publ/documents/publication/wcms_834081.pdf.

2   Eileen Fisher and Rebecca Reuber, The State of Entrepreneurship in Canada—February, 2010. (Ottawa: Industry Canada, n.d.), https://www.ic.gc.ca/eic/site/061.nsf/vwapj/SEC-EEC_eng.pdf/$file/SEC-EEC_eng.pdf.

This book is a radical shift from popular authors, speakers, and trainers who've never built, run, and sold a business. Their well-intended advice neglects the owner's personal aspirations and emotional needs. Every small business owner feels the pressure of their responsibilities. This pressure often turns into anxiety, fear, and doubt, taking its toll on the owner's health over time. No book, course, or seminar before *Small Business, Big Opportunity* has helped business owners replace those negative feelings with hope.

Small Business, Big Opportunity approaches small business owners with empathy and understanding. The author herself started, grew, and sold a profitable small business in a down economy. She's also helped hundreds of other business owners get organized, become profitable, and be financially free. Her book distills twenty-five years of small business success into a single volume, representing ten thousand hours of coaching and three thousand small business assessments. Small business owners will learn every key business system from structure and staffing through sales and service. As a result, owners can achieve goals on autopilot and build a profitable company worth selling or passing on to the next generation.

Small Business, Big Opportunity targets the world's combined five hundred-plus million small business owners to set them up for the success they imagined when they first started their venture. Written by an award-winning small business owner turned world-renowned small business coach, its pragmatic yet friendly style is illustrated with inspirational real-life small business success stories throughout.

TABLE OF CONTENTS

Tells the story of an overworked, underpaid entrepreneur who designed systems to finally earn the freedom that motivated him to start his business in the first place. Shares how the author went from being an under-appreciated travel salesperson to building, systematizing, and selling her own travel agency in a down economy. Reveals there is still hope for every struggling entrepreneur to create time, money, and lifestyle freedom, especially during the toughest years of building a business—years three through eight.

Establishes that strong leadership is the prerequisite to business systems. Explains how the owner's personal motivation provides sustained energy to reach long-term business goals. Teaches how to set, benchmark, and achieve tangible goals. Shows how to identify the owner's core values and design them into every business system. Helps owners summarize their business offering in a simple promise. Explains how to write a shared vision statement that maintains employee morale and aligns every business activity to a shared mission.

Reveals the secret to taking back control of a business from daily operations chaos and ensuring consistent profitability—shifting from tactics thinking to systems thinking. Explains how to document existing systems, how to design new systems from scratch, and which systems to start with so owners are freed from daily operations. Lays out simple steps to compile all systems in a policy and procedures manual.

Breaks down mindsets about money that keep owners broke and unhappy. Introduces a simple finance system to "know your numbers," stay (or become) profitable, and make informed decisions about product development, purchasing, sales, and more. Explains which financial records to track and how. Reviews in plain English the three financial statements every owner needs. Interprets these statements as directions to increase revenue, profit, and equity while decreasing expenses and liabilities.

CHAPTER 5.   HIRING: BUILDING A TEAM YOU CAN TRUST   65

Introduces organizational charts and position agreements into the small business ecosystem. Explains how to write position agreements (and therefore job descriptions) to maintain company-wide standards and prevent confidentiality and noncompete breaches while also giving new employees confidence in their role. Teaches owners to manage a company's biggest expense—staff—with a step-by-step system for recruiting, vetting, and interviewing qualified candidates. Helps business owners remove bias and emotion from both hiring and firing.

CHAPTER 6.   TRAINING: DO IT YOUR WAY   91

Lays out simple steps to onboard new employees and set them up for success. Explains how to reverse engineer top performance from employees using the policy and procedures manual. Offers practical tips on creating a culture of continuous improvement in a small business. Busts the myth that policy and procedures manuals eliminate creativity and shows small business owners how to create a learning organization.

CHAPTER 7.   TEAM: SOLVING PEOPLE PROBLEMS   103

Teaches small business owners to methodically gain personal freedom by building and organizing their team to replace the owner's role in the business. Explains how to let staff know what is expected of them, which will result in a great place to work, fair compensation for both the owner and employees, and a predictable customer experience. Shows how to document processes while creating an environment where people want to come to work each day. Provides guidance on forming productive business partnerships in which all parties receive equity or compensation appropriate for their respective financial and time commitments.

CHAPTER 8.   APPRECIATIVE INQUIRY: MAKE MEETINGS MATTER   115

Expands on effective small business leadership philosophy. Teaches owners how to maintain an almost metaphysical state of presence in every conversation. Teaches appreciative leadership (AL), a model of company ownership that involves building trust, staying curious, and following through on what was discussed. Gives examples of AL in which customers, employees, and vendors feel heard and understood in a judgment-free relationship with the business owner. Introduces appreciate inquiry (AI), a mental model that empowers owners to reframe challenges as opportunities, brainstorm possible solutions, and strategically work their way out of messes. Offers a proven method for discovering which key performance indicators to track to ensure progress toward the right solution.

Reveals the number-one reason mistakes get made in business—the owner thinks other people know what's on their mind. Addresses common miscommunications in a small business and how to prevent them going forward. Teaches owners effective communication strategies such as active listening.

Introduces and explains the great culture paradox—despite existing as a shared experience, culture is the direct consequence of an owner's attitude and behavior. Provides owners an easy-to-use survey to get culture feedback from employees so they can participate in positive change. Teaches how to shift a culture of blame to one of praise. Offers relatable examples of small business owners who've emulated the most successful employee experience upgrades of the Fortune 500.

Introduces the customer life cycle and describes in detail the first two stages—attract and convert. Explains how to go from common and ineffective our-target-market-is-everybody marketing to a product-market fit (niche). Offers branding guidelines to create consistency, facilitate brand recognition, create a positive identity in the marketplace, and manifest a personality that stands above and is distinctly different from competitors'. Teaches the four Ps of marketing—product, price, place, promotion—and how to get them right. Addresses common marketing FAQs, such as how to capitalize on holidays and other seasonal opportunities as well as maintain profitability during typically slow months.

Reviews the customer life cycle and describes in detail the last two stages—close and delight. Explains the difference between marketing and sales—getting leads versus getting them to buy. Guides owners through a value proposition exercise to clarify customers' reasons to buy (and buy now). Gives examples of following up with leads without annoying them. Offers a customer experience checklist for in-person and online shopping to make it easy to buy.

CHAPTER 13. GUARDING YOUR CUSTOMER SERVICE STANDARDS   189

Teaches small business owners how to define customer service standards so they can differentiate their company from their competitors. Shows how to develop systems to go above and beyond for customers and minimize negative experiences, creating deep and lasting loyalty. Explains how owners can enhance and support their small business's reputation through fulfilling Maslow's hierarchy of needs, such as putting in place customer privacy and security systems to fulfill the need for safety. Shows owners how to retain existing customers and generate sales via word-of-mouth referrals by providing a consistent customer experience.

CHAPTER 14. REWARD: FINDING YOUR FUEL   203

Reminds owners why they need a personal reward beyond profit as compensation for their hard work—to achieve personal satisfaction and fulfillment. Teaches owners how to build a personal reward system to achieve a motivating personal goal (such as meaningful time off), achieve the reward, and enjoy the reward guilt-free.

CHAPTER 15. BE PREPARED FOR CHANGE   211

Distinguishes the two types of business change—planned and unplanned—and how to best prepare and respond to both. Shares practical insights into dealing with external change such as economic shifts, industry trends, and new regulations as well as internal change such as a key employee's retirement, loss of a big account, or a nonrenewable lease. Helps owners reflect on recent significant changes, what went wrong, and what worked so they can feel better prepared for future change. Presents a proven support system to help affected employees deal with emotions, provide all stakeholders the opportunity to contribute, and ensure both customer and vendor loyalty. Introduces learning organization theory to small business owners so they and their employees can perceive change as an opportunity, not a threat.

Shares dramatic yet relatable examples of owners building wealth at the expense of their health, then spending that wealth repairing their health. Inspires owners to take better care of themselves and provides practical entrepreneur-friendly strategies to structure healthy habits, choices, and experiences into their day. Helps owners visualize their ideal healthy lifestyle and create a step-by-step plan to transform their environment so they, their family, and their employees benefit mentally, physically, socially, and spiritually. Extrapolates personal wellness habits onto organizational health. Reviews the nine areas of organizational health and how to optimize each.

Presents a small business paradigm shift—build a company to sell it; don't run it then shut it down when you retire. Teaches both new entrepreneurs and seasoned owners how to strengthen their business before selling, how to calculate a company's worth, and how to negotiate with prospective buyers. Shares useful lessons and actionable insights from the author's sale of her travel agency.

Lays out the path to build true wealth—build, sell, repeat. Tells compelling stories of small business owners in white-, gray-, and blue-collar industries who cashed out of a first business and started a second (and third and fourth, etc.) using the money from the sale as well as the operations systems from the previous successful company. Teaches the fundamentals of writing and executing a living business plan so the business stays on track and is able to mature into a sellable enterprise. Answers common questions about ownership, structure, and financing to get a company off to a profitable start. Highlights the most underused ways to protect cash at all costs as the company grows. Helps owners get out of start-up mode quickly and growth hack their way to sustainable revenue.

Praises the generous entrepreneurial spirit. Offers useful tips for connecting with local and regional influencers in both government and the private sector to influence the community, create lasting positive change, and leave a legacy—all while converting relationships into referral opportunities.

Introduces the Type E (entrepreneur) personality. Celebrates the distracted, daring entrepreneurial brain in all its uniqueness. Reframes perceived success barriers such as ADHD and risk-taking as creative genius traits that owners can leverage for success. Encourages owners to be OK with themselves, their situation, and their place in the foundation of the economy. Reminds business owners what is possible when they design and follow systems in every department of their business.

Leaves small business owners with tangible hope—hope that their dreams can come true, hope that they will find a way out of a mess and into a brighter future no matter how bad things might look. Recommends business coaching as long-term support to clarify direction, set higher and more meaningful goals, and live their life the way they'd always imagined. Reminds small business owners to build their dream one practical system at a time, creating prosperity and freedom.

CHAPTER 1

FREEDOM

Letter from a Freedom Seeker

Dear Beverlee,

Every entrepreneur has their reasons for trying to start their own business. For some it's money (no doubt), a sense of purpose and independence, an all-consuming idea, or a way to do it better or differently. For others it may be to help, serve a greater purpose, or be part of something bigger than they are. For me, it was freedom; financial freedom for sure, but more for a sense that I was the captain of my own ship, charting my own course and deciding what I wanted to do, when, and with whom. I wanted to be accountable to myself.

When I first started my business, this was a pretty clear dream, and it was easier to achieve than I had originally thought. So naturally I wanted more. I wanted to make a difference. I wanted my company to be better, different. I wanted staff and customers who loved belonging to a company that looked toward continuing improvement and betterment of its staff, relationships, and systems. Secretly, I wanted to build a little empire and get the recognition and accolades that go with that.

The business started growing—more money, more staff, and shiny new offices. It all happened organically at first. Word-of-mouth referrals led to new customers being slowly added to our growing client list while we kept the existing customers happy. People around me noticed changes, too, I'm sure. Nicer car, bigger apartment, bigger bank account. It was my dream come true.

I was miserable.

I was plagued by sleepless nights, anxiety during the day, mental and physical exhaustion, and a constant nagging feeling that I didn't belong. I felt I was an imposter. I didn't know why I was doing this anymore, and I sure wasn't having fun. Freedom had flown out the window long ago. I was focusing on just making it through another day. What I would have given for just a regular nine-to-five job at that point. I was in over my head.

A colleague who also owned a business suggested a business coach. I admit I scoffed at the idea at first. I had serious reservations about letting somebody else look behind the curtains. After all, I was an imposter. What if they confirmed what I already knew? I'm out of my league. I relented, though, and my colleague put me in touch with a business coach named Beverlee Rasmussen.

I'll never forget that first meeting with Beverlee. She listened to my story, took notes, and asked questions. She drew boxes on paper and inventoried my abstract ideas and feelings, turning them into concrete objectives. After that one meeting, what had been a giant ball of knotted ugliness now had definition and contrast with a beginning and an end. All the problems and issues were still there, sure, but I could grasp them now and go on the offensive. I had something to work with. I had goals, and they had a timeline that could be measured!

Beverlee was able to get me to express in my own words why I was doing all this, a purpose I'd forgotten long ago—freedom. Forget the business for a moment. She helped me find the handholds I needed to grab on to my life. She taught me how to think systematically and empowered me to create my own systems and processes. More importantly, I could measure my success and finally score what I felt were wins.

Turns out I am good at this. I always have been. I'm not an imposter. I belong here. I just needed somebody to help me bring freedom into focus and keep it in focus. Where I once had a compass that gave me general direction, I now have a GPS system with laser-point accuracy. Beverlee acts as my reference point, a lighthouse in a sea that's always changing—a beacon that I can look to for truth, honesty, and peace.

Here we are five years later, and Beverlee and I still talk every Thursday. I look forward to our discussions just as much now as I did when I had all of these seemingly insurmountable obstacles.

My income has more than quadrupled, and my business has won awards for both growth and profitability. My staff has tripled, as has the number of customers in my portfolio. I am happy, and I am free. I now believe in myself as much as Beverlee always has, and for that I am very grateful.

Thank you, Beverlee.

—Andrew, Business Owner, Freedom Seeker

Completely Naked

"What do you think about partnering on a second location?" I asked my boss.

She laughed at me. "Where are you going to get the money from?"

I felt my face get hot. What gave her the right to talk down to me like that? The fact that I was a single mom? She was married to a wealthy businessman, wore fancy clothes, and drove an expensive car. I wasn't, didn't, and could not. That didn't mean I was not capable.

What would *it take for someone like me to start a business?*

And that's how I ended up on this journey. That very day, I started paying full attention to the answers to that question. I looked over my boss's shoulder as she prepared to open that second office. I calculated how much I needed to open my own travel agency—to see if it was even possible. Rent, office supplies, commission to agents, utilities, subscriptions. *Check, check, check, check, check.*

Having been a top agent with a huge clientele for so long, I knew I could sell well over $800,000 a year on my own—probably $1 million with some help. Out of the eight agents in the office, I was producing 27 percent of all sales—that's one out of every four calls for me, one out of every four pieces of mail. The time and attention it took to manage that volume of business was beginning to cause tension with my boss and the other agents. When I proposed a baseball tournament in Florida that would bring in $250,000 in additional sales, my boss wanted more of the action. She wanted me to take less commission on that project but still do all the work. That was the tipping point. She wanted the best producer in the agency to take a pay cut? As the sole provider for my family, I was already just getting by.

I'd wanted to hire part-time help using money from my commission because I was starting to fail. I couldn't keep all the balls in the air. I was too much in demand. When you reach capacity, you start to slide backward, and you can't keep your promises. Back then, we hand delivered paper tickets and went over itineraries in person. It was labor intensive. I was starting to screw up, forget things, and not have enough time to get back to people. I needed help.

And that was just at work. Being a single mom with no child support, no shared custody, and no partner to help me, I often had to bring my first son, Joe, to work with me after hours. One night he got bored waiting for me to finish and pulled out a few plugs before I could stop him, resulting in the data lines of every travel agency in town going down for three days. My boss banned him from the office. It was brutal. From then on, I had to get creative about getting my work done. I hired babysitters and went into the office late at night. I swear, I tried every day care and preschool in town looking for a place where my kid would be happy and safe. Just before his fourth birthday, I got a call from his latest day care.

"Ma'am, your son fell from a play structure. And . . . well . . . he broke his leg."

I had high standards, and my child was my first priority. At the same time, I longed for a life partner. Someone to spend time with, to share the financial burden, to be a role model for my son. Somehow, I found time to socialize, but back then, every date was a bad date. I was frustrated. I went to see a psychologist, who asked me a defining question: "What if you never find anyone good enough?"

That was what I needed to hear—*I* had to create the life I wanted for me and my son. It was up to *me* to earn more money so he could go to college someday. It was up to *me* to pay my mortgage and feed my family. The only way I could see that happening was to have my own business. That way I could hire help, sell more, earn my freedom, and be the mom my son needed me to be.

Norm, one of my travel clients, owned a TV repair business at our local strip mall. The economy wasn't great at the time, so a lot of spaces at the mall sat empty and available. When I mentioned opening my own agency, he grabbed the phone to call his landlord. Bright and early on a Friday morning before work, I sat across from Mr. V. (one of the wealthiest men in the country) and pitched my plan to open a travel agency in his strip mall.

"Even if I hire part-time help and only sell what I'm selling now, I won't have to share my commission, putting me further ahead," I said. "Then again, I'm quitting a forty-thousand-dollar-a-year job, taking on two thousand dollars a month in rent, and remortgaging my home. I'll find a way to make this work."

"I like your passion. Your tenacity . . . your determination," Mr. V. said. "I want to help you. I think you've got what it takes. Tell you what—I'll give you five months free rent, my lawyer, my accountant, and all my company's travel business to help get you started."

"Wow, that's . . . that's so generous of you," I said. "No, thank you. For now, at least. My banker recommended I start out with more money than I think I'll need. No one will give me money if I run short. I need about twenty-five thousand dollars more to be safe before I jump into anything. Over the next six months, I am going to earn that money. Then we can talk again."

"I see," Mr. V. said. "To tell you the truth, I want a tenant sooner than later." After a long stare, he looked away, opened the middle drawer of his massive desk, and took out his checkbook. He scribbled for a moment, then tore out a check and handed it to me. "Here."

Twenty-five thousand dollars.

"Pay it back when you can. Five percent simple interest. I want you in here next month."

I now had everything I needed. It was time to give my notice to my boss.

The breakup wasn't pretty. I was accused of stealing customers and talking trash about my coworkers. Not true, of course. The rumors and gossip unnerved me anyway. I couldn't sleep. I started to second-guess my decision. What did I know about running a business? I knew I was a great travel *agent*, but I certainly wasn't prepared to become an agency *owner*.

There was no looking back.

At 8:00 a.m. on April 11, 1993, the first day in my new office, I pulled into the strip mall parking lot. I cleaned, hung posters, and moved in office furniture. After several hours, I was all ready to go—except for my license from the International Air Transport Association (IATA). I couldn't legally open without a license. For ten long days, I sat there holding my breath, waiting for the phone call, unable to open my doors.

At lunchtime on day ten, I got the call. "You have been approved, Ms. Somerville. Here is your IATA license number." It was time. I took a deep breath, tore the Coming Soon sign off the front window, and opened the door. At that moment, I felt as if I were standing on the street completely naked. I never felt so vulnerable before or since.

Then nothing happened.

What the f**k have I done? The silence was deafening—for about thirty minutes. Then the phone rang. Someone across the street wanted to inquire about a trip to Hawaii. I sighed in relief. What an incredible feeling!

Now the real work began. I was nervous about protecting my reputation and could not risk failure. I had a kid to feed, and my little house was on the line. I realized that this was way more than just selling travel—I had to create a functioning business from nothing. I had to build a team, and my only experience hiring was for babysitters. As entrepreneurs do, I put one brave foot in front of the other every morning. My mantra was "Feel the fear and do it anyway."

For my new employee, I wrote out why I started this company, including the values I held, where I came from, and why I did things the way I did them. I also documented our procedures, and we tested them together. How long would a client wait for us to call them back before we lost the sale? When was the best time to give clients their travel tickets? What should the office look like, smell like, feel like? What suppliers should we use? What customers were our best fit? Should we give a discount? How do we tactfully get rid of customers we don't want? What do customers want?

With all this data, I went to work building systems for my business. I put together money systems, selling systems, phone-answering systems, client-greeting systems, client-closing systems, ticket-delivery systems, coffee-making systems, dress code systems, and more.

That last one made me shake my head. One day, I looked around the office and couldn't believe the mismatches. Sue in her designer canary-yellow suit looked elegant but out of place. Elaine lived in housedresses but had forgotten her shoes that day, so she was wearing slippers. And Jodi, my young upstart, was wearing a fashionable super-short mini with bare legs. My next major purchase for the business was $8,000 worth of designer uniforms from Ella's.

Pretty soon, the business was running on autopilot. As the leader, I had set a vision of excellence. Each employee had authority and responsibility for their systems. I trained them well in the "Somerville way," so they always knew what to do, understood the value of why we did things our way, and felt empowered to do their work. Together, we created a $3-million-a-year money machine. We never discounted or advertised because our clients loved what we did for them and told their friends. I got to own my business and my life. During the seven years I ran Somerville Travel, I got married, had two more babies, and had the freedom to get involved in community projects. All without the internet!

I went from feeling terrified on opening day to selling the business at a time when a travel agency couldn't be given away. I experienced every low and high—what it feels like to have to cash your own paycheck on December 20 just so you can give your staff a Christmas bonus and what it feels like to cash a six-figure check.

After selling Somerville Travel, I worked with Michael Gerber, bestselling author of *The E-Myth Revisited, Why Most Small Businesses Don't Work and What to Do About It,* and founder of EMyth Worldwide. I was a program adviser; my job was to enroll people in the EMyth program. During my three years with Michael, I talked with over three thousand small business owners. However, most could not afford to pay their staff, let alone pay for help.

"If you could wave a magic wand right now and have one thing in your business, what would that be?" I asked everyone.

"Freedom," eight out of ten business owners replied. "I want my freedom back." They were trapped in debt and bogged down by more obligations than they could handle. They'd lost all ability to take time off, physically or mentally. They were spending their days, nights, and weekends just trying to stay in business. They never slept. *It's 3:00 a.m. How am I going to make payroll? Will I get that contract? Should I fire that employee? How am I going to get my orders out the door by noon? Is the bank going to pull my loan? When am I going to get a break? Why did I start this damn business in the first place?*

Their stories broke my heart. To this day, they're the driving force behind my personal mission of making life better for small business owners.

Is that you? Your business has been around for a few years. For now, you're in the thick of it. And I know—it's the worst. Any initial start-up capital you had is gone. Your energy is gone. Your enthusiasm is waning. And now you're just grinding away, face to face with the reality that running a business is way harder than anyone told you it would be. You've waited for that magical five-year mark to make a profit. Either that special day has come and gone, or you're approaching it, and you have no idea how you're going to dig your way out of the hole. In the meantime, you're giving up everything you have, starting with family time and ending with your soul.

Between years three and eight, everything goes to hell. Marriages break down, partnerships fail, and money stress debilitates you. You work twenty hours a day, often seven days a week. Like many small business owners, maybe you've mortgaged your home and gone into debt you don't expect to ever pay back. Profitability is so difficult to achieve. You know you need help, but you're too busy to search for advice and learn how to fix the big things that are broken. Even if you knew how to read an income statement, chances are the books aren't up to date, so the information isn't even accurate. If all that wasn't bad enough, small business owners often make hiring mistakes like bringing in their family members or, worse, their best friend. These mistakes cause further stress and tear relationships apart.

If you can get through those first years, you have a chance to make some real money and get the freedom you've dreamed of since day one. In spite of everything, you are resilient. Often, I am in awe of the herculean effort made to keep a small company going. Entrepreneurs like us have tenacity. No matter how hard we have it, we have this fantastic, incredible capacity for dreaming, staying on track, and pushing through when things get hard, which is most of the time. Small business owners struggle a lot and get little support past the start-up stage. There are few affordable resources to help you at this stage.

It took me eighteen months to get free from the day-to-day operations of my travel agency. I spent my time working strategically, building systems to get the business to run independent of me. The resulting freedom changed my life—I controlled my schedule, could drop off and pick up my son at school, take vacations when I wanted to, and volunteer in the community, all while knowing the business was running smoothly and making money without me.

After I sold that company, I knew what I would do next—share what I learned with people like Andrew.

And you.

There's Still Hope

When I chat with business owners, they beg me to tell them how to fix their businesses. So that's exactly what I've been doing for the last twelve years. When I met Andrew, he was successful in his own right, but he felt lost and frustrated. His confidence was gone. He was ready to run away from the whole thing. When I started asking questions about his systems and recording his responses on paper, things cleared up. He started to see that his challenges were missing or broken systems, not because he wasn't working hard enough.

"What are you taking away from this meeting?" I asked Andrew during one of our first Thursday calls.

"Hope," he said. "Hope that there's a plan so I can fix this. That it's just a systems issue. That this is not the end of the world."

All business owners have felt the enormous pressure that comes with the responsibilities of owning a company. This pressure often turns into feelings of anxiety, fear, and doubt that take their toll on the business owner's physical and emotional health. Nobody told you this would happen. You got into business for freedom, but you ended up in a trap. Yes, you own your own business, but now you're shackled to it, and chances are you're earning less money than you thought was possible. When you worked for someone else, you complained about the lack of freedom, but you always got to go home at the end of the night. You got your paycheck, so it didn't matter.

When you started your business, did you know how many things you'd have to figure out? You probably had no idea. I sure didn't. When I started my travel agency, I was overwhelmed by the sheer volume of what I needed to learn—leasehold improvements, rent negotiations, business insurance, source deductions, hiring, and bookkeeping. Bookkeeping—now that's a *big* one. Debits and credits and charts of accounts; shareholder loans; retained earnings; earnings before interest, tax, depreciation, and amortization (EBITDA); ratios; and margins. I hired, fired, and trained my team by the seat of my pants. I felt like the ball in a pinball machine, bouncing through the day from one crisis or big win to another, from up to down and side to side. It was exhilarating, exhausting, and ridiculously hard. And I loved every minute of it—until I didn't.

Even if a business is handed to you, you still have to figure it all out from there. One of my clients planned to take over a business from his dad someday. They had worked together for years and created highly sought-after glass products. When my client's father passed away suddenly in his early fifties, probate took everything. My client was left with only the core shell of a business he had no idea how to run. His dad had taught him how to bend glass, not how to run the business.

However you ended up with your business, it's now up to you to put systems in place—they're your ticket to freedom. When you do, tasks like bills and payroll take care of themselves. I don't pay bills. They just come out of my account automatically. I don't think about them. My payroll is delegated too. I figured out how to do payroll, I documented the steps, then I put someone in place who has the authority and responsibility to do it.

If you don't take the time to set up simple systems like this, you'll end up like Lori.

One morning, Lori got an angry call from one of her employees. Her paycheck had bounced. It'd been a rough week. Lori realized she needed to make time to go to the bank more often to deposit the daily cash, especially during the week of payroll. The problem was that by the time the day was over, her kids were hungry, and she needed to get one to soccer practice and the other to dance class. When the weekend rolled around, the cash was spent because it's a lot easier to dip into the money on hand than to make a trip to the bank. She's the boss, so who cares? To add to her frustration, her townhouse complex had just switched to community mailboxes, and it was a hassle to go across town to get the mail. This meant checks and bills went unopened, sometimes for weeks. She didn't file her taxes because she hadn't had time for that either. If there was time, she's not sure she could find all the receipts anyway. Money problems kept her awake at night, making her tired in the morning and late for company appointments with customers.

What Comes Before Systems

I believe in the power of systems to free you up to work on your business, not in your business. Setting up a system is like going to the doctor for your annual checkup. We know we should, but somehow, we never seem to get around to it. For small business owners, the choice to put off building that payroll system (for example) isn't the problem. It's the symptom. You see, while you were busy pushing to keep your business afloat, you lost something very important. You lost your leadership. It's not your fault, and you can get it back.

I was the first female Rotary Club president in our town. Every year, the international president picks a different theme. My theme was Lead the Way. As the leader of our businesses, we need to lead the way. If we don't, we abdicate our leadership. We let things happen the way other people want them to happen, and then it's no longer our business. We have systems, but they're not our systems, so the business drifts into chaos.

How you show up as a leader defines the kind of business you end up with—one that sets you free or one that enslaves every hour of your day. You started your business because you crave freedom. That deep-seated desire could not be met as long as you were an employee. So you went in search of it on your own. Yet if you're like 80 percent of small business owners, you didn't build freedom into your plan. You're frustrated and angry about being trapped in your company, not realizing you have a choice to step up and be the leader that your business, your family, and you need yourself to be.

As the leader of your business, it's your job to understand what drives you as a leader; to ensure that employees know what needs to be done to achieve your shared goals; to set no-compromise standards; to consistently fulfill your promises to customers; and to articulate, document, and share your vision. Do all this, and you will feel inspired to do your best every day.

- Take advantage of opportunities to grow your business
- Achieve meaningful goals regularly
- Have the confidence to make tough decisions
- Align your business practices with your values
- Stop managing people
- Build systems that free up your schedule (and your head space)
- Operate your business efficiently while generating more profit
- Pay yourself what you deserve

- Take care of yourself today and every day
- Spend quality time with your family
- Enjoy better health, less stress, and a company you are proud to call your own

Building an organized and profitable business that reaps rewards starts with you. Be the leader you wished you had as an employee, and you'll own the business you've always dreamed of.

CHAPTER 2
LEAD THE WAY

Leadership with a Purpose

You're at this point in your business as a result of the choices you have made, big and small. Choices you've made because of your beliefs, values, background, and experiences. Understanding what motivates you as the leader of your business is the key to unlocking your full potential. Your personal drivers support all your actions in business and in life.

What is driving you? What do you want from your business? When was the last time you stopped to consider why you're working so hard? Yes, there's a lot to do, and, yes, people are counting on you, and, yes, you have bills to pay. Yet somehow, this business must serve you on a much deeper level.

I was driven by wanting to take care of my son. I also wanted a better work environment and to provide even better service to my clients. Travel agencies were chaotic, stressful, and disorganized. I knew that if I were the boss, I could change that. At my travel agency, I had systems for everything, including buying lunch for my team every Friday. I banned gossip. If there was a problem, we talked everything out like adults, collaborating on ways to make things better. It was more peaceful, and I crave peace.

Owning a small business can be a wonderful way to live your life's purpose. I was not a travel agent for the love of travel. In fact, I hate flying and get sick on cruise ships. I was in the travel business to be of service to others.

I love to solve complex problems and was amazing at making other people's dreams come true. My way of making a difference in the world was to bring happiness, order, and peace to others' lives. As far back as I can remember, I have loved helping others. As a Girl Guide, I did volunteer work with seniors, which brought great joy to my world. Later, through owning my business, I reunited families and planned fragile older couples' perfect fiftieth- wedding-anniversary cruises. As a business coach, I continue to live my life's purpose of bringing happiness, order, and peace to others' lives.

When you figure out your personal motivation, you can leverage that passion to produce the best results in your business. For example, behind Walt Disney's desire to build a profitable theme park was his unwavering desire to play, create, and imagine. Aligning who you are with what you do every day has incredible potential for creating a positive impact on your life. Align your business purpose with your life's purpose, and you'll get the greatest rewards of all. I'm not talking about money or status. What I'm talking about is much bigger and much more profound. It's about who you are and how you show up in the world as the leader of your company.

That boy of mine grew up and started a business of his own. It wasn't an easy journey. After heading off to university to pursue a law degree and later quitting to try his luck with pharmacy, he came home discouraged. No degree, no dream. Only a job at a construction site. One day, I put my coach hat on and asked him to describe his perfect life.

He said to me, tongue in cheek, "I want to be at the BMX track from March to October and in the gym the rest of the year helping people get healthy."

"Great," I said, taking him seriously. "Now, how can I support you with turning that into a six-figure business?"

We didn't have an answer at the time, but we eventually found one. Today, my son is the proud owner of Iron Joe Athletics. He has trained with the Canadian BMX Olympic team and offers rider clinics all over the province. His passion for the sport that brought so much joy to his life as a kid now supports his young family. That's what entrepreneurship is all about.

If you're not happy in your business, you've got to make a change. If you're a downer because you have compromised on what makes you happy, the whole team goes down with you. If you're not passionate about your business, maybe it's time to put up a For Sale sign. And if you still have that spark, it's time to fan it until your passion shines brighter than it did on opening day.

Do some soul searching to rediscover your passion. Find a quiet, comfortable space with no distractions where you can focus. Then start asking yourself questions. Who are you, and what do you want from your life? What do you want people to notice about you now? What made your heart sing when you were a child? What contributions do you want to make to the world each day? Write down what best describes who you are. With this understanding in mind, think about what you could build into your company to keep you feeling inspired.

If having a good laugh while enjoying your work motivates you, your personal purpose statement might read, *I am funny. I need to laugh, to play, to have fun every day. I need to build into my business a fun culture, relaxed environment, casual clothes, and time to stop to play.* If you're a good-natured person who cares about giving back, your statement could read, *I am generous. I need to make a difference in the world, do some pro bono work, schedule company charity projects, and keep all communication positive.*

Going to work every day knowing that what you do is in alignment with who you are and what you need in your life will ensure you have the sustained energy to reach your desired business goals.

Goals That Mean Something

My client Dan is an electrical contractor. His company retrofits old factories with newer, more efficient technology. He sells his clients on the service, then hires subcontractors to do the work. At the start of a weekly coaching session, I asked Dan a question.

"What do you want to take from today's meeting?"

"I need to simplify things so I can achieve my goals," Dan said. "Everything basically boils down to my bigger goal. And it's less tangible than you think."

"Try me."

"Well, my *real* goal is I don't want to feel as much stress. On a scale of zero to ten, I want to be at two or three most of the time instead of eight or nine."

Like most entrepreneurs, he was stuck in a state of fight or flight and exhausted from the stress.

"What specifically would reduce your stress level?" I asked.

"Greater consistency in my business. Consistency means money in the bank. Consistency in sales to keep the financial pressure down. Consistency in knowing my team is on track, that they all know what they're doing so I don't have to worry. I can come and go, and it won't matter."

Dan paused for a moment. When he spoke again, he sounded hopeful. "Now that I think about it, I can see how consistency starts with me. I want to feel less stressed about everything, from having enough money in the bank to trusting my team. That means putting time into the operations and the systems."

"How much do you want in the bank? This is where a tangible goal enters."

Dan was quiet again.

"Right now, how much money in the bank would make you feel comfortable, safe, and able to sleep at night?" I said, "I always recommend at least three months of operating costs in the bank."

"I have over a year's worth."

"You still sound worried. Why?" I asked.

"It's still not enough to make me feel relaxed and confident. I only have twelve thousand dollars in recurring revenue each month. The rest of my revenue is so unpredictable. It's been like this for years."

"Why did it stop at twelve? What do you need to do to get that to fifteen or twenty thousand? Whatever that is, accomplishing it may give you the consistency you desire."

There is a lesson here for every entrepreneur. You can set a goal, but just writing it down doesn't make it mean something. That goal has to mean something to you personally. It goes deeper than just "I want to have a hundred grand in the bank." Why do you want a hundred grand? "Because then I can sleep at night." *That's* the real meaning of your goal. The outcome of the goal means something to you—it directly affects your life.

A goal is a target. What do you need to have in place to hit it? Most entrepreneurs just want to be happy. They just want to make enough money to take the issue of money off the table, whatever that means to them. And they want the personal freedom to come and go as they please. They also want respect—they don't want to look bad in front of customers, friends, or family.

Business goals can include sales targets, profit margins, increasing the size of your team, products you want to develop, marketing strategies, equipment upgrades, and training. They can also include leadership and personal growth goals to achieve greater balance in your personal life.

To achieve goals, you need a system. Any good project manager will tell you that. Having a defined system to follow, even if it's not perfect to start, is easier and less stressful than not having one. You're going to get busy, so you'll forget your goals if no system is in place. Start by breaking down your big goals, like increasing revenue, into smaller, more manageable goals. Think about all the actions you'll need to take to achieve the results—for example, joining the local chamber of commerce, socializing on Facebook, learning how to send tweets on Twitter, and updating your LinkedIn profile by highlighting your skills and experiences. Include the steps required to achieve these goals. Once you have this list of actions, assign them to a part of the year in order of their importance to you. Divide your calendar year into four quarters (often abbreviated Q1, Q2, Q3, and Q4). This will give you specific goals to work on during each quarter. Integrate this new structured form of goal achievement into your daily business activities. If you don't, it won't happen. Small business owners are often too busy even to think about goals.

As the chief goal setter of your business, you can only climb as high as your loftiest goal. Maybe instead of being a $2-million-a-year company, you could aim for $20 million a year. Two different printing businesses I work with are exactly sixteen kilometers from me in different directions and in different towns. My client Al is thrilled when he hits $30,000 a month in sales. Yet my client Andrea freaks out if her business doesn't do $200,000 a month in sales. If Andrea doesn't have at least $80,000 in the bank, it's a problem. Al is just trying to stay out of the hole—he's happy when he's got $2,000 in the bank. Yet these businesses offer the same service. They even share clients!

Our business results rise to meet the limitations we put on ourselves—we go no further, so neither will our business. For example, Dan's business brings in $12,000 a month in recurring revenue. It has stayed right around the same amount for six years.

"Let's go back to that question. Why has your revenue stayed the same?" I asked Dan during our next coaching session. "It looks like you've stopped where you're comfortable. If you thought about it, would you still want this to be where you max out? And if not, what do you need to do differently in your leadership to double your recurring revenue? And then double it again?"

"Hmm . . ." Dan scratched his beard. "You're right, I am comfortable. And I'd be even more comfortable if my profits doubled. I could probably delegate more of my day-to-day work and free up some time to pursue more clients. Hell, I could train my assistant to do sales consults too. He's always looking for more to do."

"Now you're thinking."

Dan laughed. "Yeah, I guess I am. So, where do we start?"

No-Compromise Values

Your core values dictate everything you do—in operations, finance, team building, leadership—and how your company shows up in the market. So what exactly are values? They are deeply held, rarely changing preferences about what is important, meaningful, and appropriate to you. The very decision to accept the responsibility of starting, building, and running a company is closely tied to your personal values. Values are not *what* your company sells, or even *how* you go about it; they are *why* you started the company in the first place. They reflect your sense of right and wrong. Use your core values to build an organization you love, and you'll have a company you're proud to own.

Generosity is a common core value—one that many business owners take too far, which can result in the demise of their financial stability. This can be prevented by building generosity into your plan so you can be generous and prosperous at the same time. Commit to your values and build your company around them, moving forward even in the midst of challenges.

In my travel agency, one of my highest core values was integrity. To me, integrity means being honest 100 percent of the time. Telling the truth, not only to one another but also to our clients, set us apart from other travel agencies. We made sure we responded to every inquiry immediately and with absolute accuracy. We never fudged or glossed over details to close a sale. We were an organized business in a chaotic industry.

Today, at my company Systems Business Coach, I still value integrity. Our other core values are respect, freedom, knowledge, and collaboration. To me, respect means we never judge a business owner, no matter what their situation. Freedom means our programs are designed to provide greater personal freedom for entrepreneurs. Knowledge means our program content contains proven, sound business practices (no fluff). Collaboration means we work together with clients to find the best possible outcome. And integrity still means telling the truth and guaranteeing our work. If a business task doesn't align with these values, we don't do it. The same applies to any relationship, opportunity, or deal.

Recently, I turned down a contract because the business owner was screwing over his family just to gain greater profits. Not a fit. Ask yourself, as the leader of your small business, whether you are out of alignment with your core values in any actions or relationships.

As you work through investigating how your core values show up in your organization, you may come across things you're currently doing that are out of alignment with those values. For example, valuing excellent customer service but being unable to return clients' calls on time points to a missing or broken system. You'll need to fix that system to get back in alignment with this company value.

Aligning the actions of all employees with your business's core values may prove challenging at first. Taking the time to identify your own core values is the first step. Understanding how these values affect how you currently operate and make business decisions is powerful. Sharing core company values with all stakeholders gives you a common language for alignment and helps others understand how you want your company to run.

For example, Dave, the owner of a scaffolding company, has had some heart problems for the past few years. One of his core values is health, but you'd never know it if you jumped into one of his company vehicles. The distinct stench of cigarettes left behind by a junior employee is over-powering. This employee lights up right beside Dave at safety meetings, and Dave hasn't said a word to him about it. Until recently.

After taking time to reflect on what was important to him and to his company's reputation, Dave shared his values with the team. Together, they made the decision to eliminate smoking from work trucks, job sites, and offices. The junior employee even quit smoking altogether, and the entire team appreciated the healthier working environment.

If you're out of alignment with your values, everything feels stressful. Sometimes, we compromise our values because we're just too nice. We never want to hurt anybody. Yet we often end up hurting ourselves (and the whole company) anyway. For example, I worked with a marketing company that refused to reduce staff hours or let anyone go when the world economy collapsed. In 2008, revenue stopped coming in. The owner stopped paying bills, including employee tax source deductions to the government. She ended up owing the government over $50,000, which took five years to pay off. She screwed herself and put her company in jeopardy—just to be nice. Her employees had unemployment insurance, so a layoff wouldn't have been the end of the world. She didn't want a confrontation, though.

Another value compromise small business owners often make is allowing employees to do whatever they want—even if it doesn't meet the standards the owners have set for their business. Perhaps you experienced parental fighting as a small child, and you're desperate not to relive that kind of tension. You can't let others do what they want just because you don't like conflict. If you start compromising, before you know it, you're not even running your business anymore. You've got employees holding you for ransom. Your top employees take Fridays off. Everyone gives themselves a cushy job—except you. It's more common than you might think.

Several years ago, I stopped in at a client's video store—a client who'd told me she valued time with family.

"Hi, Beverlee!" I heard a voice call.

"Hello?" I replied. "Where are you?"

"Oh, just back here cleaning the bathroom," she said, poking her head out from the employees-only area.

"Why?" I walked back. "Why are *you* cleaning the bathroom?"

"Well." She lowered her voice. "Sometimes I guess it's just easier for me to do it than . . ."

"Than what?"

My client peeked at her employee, who was putting on her coat.

"Than to make people think I'm a prick."

Sad but true—my client valued being perceived as nice more than she valued her own freedom. She valued employees' time more than she valued her own. She compromised her core values by staying late cleaning the bathroom because she was afraid of not being liked. She didn't want to be perceived as being a boss—even though she *was* the boss.

If you value family but you're not spending any time with them because you're at work 24-7, either your business will fail, or you will lose your family. Compromise your core values, and you won't have the emotional energy to run your business. You have to build your business around your family. Period. Full stop.

If the video store owner had a system in place with assigned tasks and a checklist for who does what and how, then an employee, not the boss, would have done the work. A simple system would have given her the confidence to stand up for her values—and to her employees.

Identifying and sticking to your values can be as simple as having a checklist. That's one system that will save the day. When you're running your business out of alignment with your core values, it's almost always because of a missing or broken system. Once my client put a checklist in place to make sure things got done, then handed that work over to someone else, she finally honored her family.

Worried you'll come across as the bad guy defending your values? It's worth it. At my travel agency, I once had an agent I had to call out for not telling the truth. She'd been working with us for only a couple of days, and the second time she didn't tell the truth—stretching a story, exaggerating, embellishing—that was it. If you can't keep your story straight, you can't work here. If you're honest, then you have my trust. At least I'll know what I'm dealing with. Whether it's good or bad, as long as it's honest, I can handle it.

In my one-on-one work, I have clients go through a whole list of values. "Check off every value that resonates with you," I tell them. Some check off every one; some just check off a few. "Now, write down how each of those values shows up in your company." I painstakingly go through every one with them. Eventually, we can distill their list to four to six core values that communicate everything that's important to the owner.

Think of a time when you felt like you were losing integrity because of something happening in your company. What unwritten rules do you have about how people should behave at work? Think of one of your no-compromise values. How does it show up both at home and at work? Let your values lead the way. If you value respect, you and everyone on your team adhere to high ethical standards, doing the right thing each and every time. If you value innovation, you are continuously challenging the status quo for the benefit of others. Your product development and business practices are most effective when in alignment with your core values.

Look at any failure in your business. Can you see where you compromised on your values somewhere? Perhaps you're not paying yourself, or you spent company money to buy something unnecessary (something you'd never do at home). Some things are out of our control, like COVID-related struggles or the death of a partner. Still, most of our everyday struggles come from compromising on what should be nonnegotiable. Write down the rules, and then follow them. This is your game based on what's important to you. You are the author of your business. What kind of story do you want to tell?

A Promise You Keep

A promise upheld by your entire team underpins your reputation as an employer and as a player in your market. It shows up in how you operate, how well you do financially, and most importantly, who you are to your customers. Knowing your company's promise is foundational for creating systems that are in alignment with one common understanding.

When building a system, you can use your promise as a starting point for your standards. Your promise, once identified, can improve all areas of your company. For example, your promise defines your systems standards, protects your company reputation, and helps maintain quality control. From a financial perspective, your promise builds brand equity and gives you the confidence to charge what you're worth. To customers, your promise delivers a clear and consistent marketing message. For example, the Purple Promise of FedEx[3] starts with the company's promise and includes every way employees fulfill the promise every day:

I will make every FedEx experience outstanding.

Every great organization that has stood the test of time has a promise. So what's yours? Is your small business the one place where customers get a unique feature, benefit, advantage, or experience? What do your customers *feel* when they hear the name of your business? What's the biggest difference between you and your competition? What brings customers back again and again? Your answers to these questions can contribute to a single company promise. You know you have it when everyone on your team feels so good about it that they want to hang it on the wall.

A Shared Vision

Entrepreneurs are great visionaries. We see what is possible. Something bigger than us drives us. Our vision keeps us going, gives us energy to get through the rough patches, and provides validation when things go well. To achieve our vision, we need others to participate—our banker when we need money, our employees to do the work, our partner to stay supportive during eighty-hour workweeks, our kids when we can't make it to one of their events, and our parents when we need to put off paying back the money they loaned us.

---

3   "The Purple Promise," FedEx Corporation, accessed February 8, 2023, http://www.fedex.com/purplepromise/docs/en/fedex_pp_booklet_purplepower.pdf.

When I shared my vision with Mr. V., he wanted to be a part of it. As a dad, he related to my desire to build a better life for my son. He worked hard for his family, and he knew I would work hard for mine. This made me a good risk. As a frequent traveler, he appreciated my vision of service excellence so much that he literally bought into it.

Your vision, when written down and repeated over and over, will inspire, motivate, and lead others. Martin Luther King, Jr. inspired a nation and later an entire world with his vision of equality in his "I Have a Dream"[4] speech. He had a vision, and you have a vision. Because of your small business, the world will be better—better for your customers, your team, your community, and your family. It's time for you to share it.

A shared vision inspires people to work toward meaningful shared goals. Your employees can see where you want to go and understand how they can help you get there. A vision of huge wealth for yourself won't get you far, but a vision of creating wealth by helping solve others' problems through your product or service will have your team moving mountains for you. When people feel like they're making a difference in the world, they're motivated to work harder because the work has meaning. Vision always inspires action. Apple's cofounder Steve Jobs once said, "I want to put a ding in the universe."[5] His statement was inspirational, clear, and memorable—people could instantly understand and feel the magnitude of his vision.

Before I started my travel agency, I had a vision that our industry could be better. I imagined what it could be like if we all worked together so everyone—owner, staff, and customers—were happy. I was selling $875,000 of travel per year by myself and carrying my son around while I did it. *If I had the kind of world I wanted, I would help everyone who needed me and, in turn, sell more. Someone else would be processing paperwork, and I'd just be selling.* I had a vision of how I wanted my business to look, and I made that vision a reality. I decided to pay every agent a salary, not a commission. Any bonuses were paid based on everybody working together. I hated doing paperwork, so I hired someone else whose only job was the paperwork. And the agents and I just sold. This way, we were able to offer a better customer experience. I wanted a predictable environment where I could

---

4   Martin Luther King, 1991, "I Have a Dream," August 28, 1963, Lincoln Memorial, Washington DC, National Archives, https://www.archives.gov/nyc/exhibit/mlk.

5   Tyler Lewis, *Put a Ding in Your Universe: An Entrepreneur's Guide to the Wisdom of Steve Jobs* (Scotts Valley, CA: CreateSpace Independent Publishing Platform, 2017).

keep doing the work I'd been doing. I wanted peace, and I got it—and so did everyone else on my team.

At Systems Business Coach, my vision is of a world where all business owners have the skills, tools, and confidence to positively contribute to a healthy world economy, creating secure, meaningful employment while maintaining personal prosperity and freedom.

Both visions are about *we*, not just *me*. If you make your vision all about you, it won't be very inspiring. Maybe you haven't even had time to brainstorm your vision. Perhaps you've forgotten it in the hustle of keeping your business running just one more day. Think back to when you first thought about starting your business. How did you feel? Were you excited? Did you envision how it was going to look? Were you imagining the revenue you were going to make? Did you think about the happy customers you were going to serve?

To achieve any vision, you need an action plan—in business, we can call this plan our mission. People often confuse these two. The simplest way to understand the difference between them is the statement, "We're on a mission to achieve a vision." Your mission is what you do every day in your company to reach your vision.

For example, a junk removal and recycling business in Vancouver features its mission on its website: "Our mission is merging junk removal and our planet's health into a world-class business where residential and commercial consumers are confident that they have done their part by choosing [us]."[6] Every activity that business does every day helps fulfill its vision to have a significant positive impact on the environment and the communities it serves. And just as it does with its core values, that business uses its mission to lead.

Once you have your vision and know your mission, put them together with your core values and your promise and create a declaration called a vision statement. Your vision statement is a simple document that gives everyone a similar picture and commitment to bring your vision into reality.

For inspiration, here is the vision statement of Systems Business Coach:

---

6   "Why 505-Junk", 505-Junk, February, accessed April 21, 2021, https://505junk.com/why-505/.

OUR VISION

*A world where all business owners have the **skills**, **tools** and **confidence** to positively contribute to a healthy world economy creating secure meaningful employment while maintaining personal **prosperity** and **freedom***

OUR PROMISE

To listen, and together find a way

TO KEEP OUR PROMISE WE MUST:

- Be curious
- Appreciate what is working & support change where needed
- Be tenacious and never give up
- Seek to see, hear and understand
- Be honest and pragmatic

OUR MISSION

To provide confidential coaching, effective training and practical systems focused tools and strategies to support small business owners and the communities they serve

OUR VALUES

RESPECT

COMMUNITY

LEARNING

INTEGRITY

PEACE

When one of my small business owner clients finishes their vision statement, they feel like a new person. They see everything their business needs to be on one page. Finally, they can share exactly why they're doing what they're doing, where the business is heading, and how they're going to get there. They have a document to lead the way.

Without a vision statement, you won't know how to get your freedom back. When life and business are a jumbled mess, go back to your vision statement, to your *why*. You will be reminded of the type of leader you're meant to become—a leader who, together with your team, can make a shared vision come true.

Thanks to your vision statement, you can shift your entrepreneurial mindset from "What needs my attention right now?" to "How can I make the world a better place?" You're taking the focus off what you can do and putting it on what your business can do. This critical mindset shift also allows you to extract yourself from day-to-day operations by building systems your employees can manage. In fact, you have to remove yourself from the center of operations if you're ever going to lead your team.

Now, driven by your vision statement, we're going to build your systems.

CHAPTER 3

WHY SYSTEMS?

Take Back Control of Your Business

Are you creating a job for yourself instead of building a company? Are you spending too much time being your hardest-working employee instead of leading? Are you still blaming yourself or your staff when things go wrong?

Far too many entrepreneurs are trapped, underpaid employees working way too hard for little or no return. What was supposed to bring freedom and financial wealth ends up taking over your life and draining your resources. How does this happen? Simple—there is too much to do! Training employees, dealing with landlords, calculating taxes, learning social media, contacting suppliers, paying phone bills, drafting contracts, making change orders, replying to angry customers, catching shoplifters, networking, updating computers, setting prices, researching competitors . . . it's endless. Every day you get a little more behind on something that costs you money or more of your precious time.

If you, the business owner, are stuck working as an employee, you're doing tactical work. This is the work that makes or delivers your product. Tactical work has you pulled back and forth by urgent day-to-day demands. You're the go-to person when anyone needs one-off, short-term answers. And when you don't know something, you take it upon yourself to figure it out.

It's faster if I do it myself. It's easier if I do it myself. Nobody on the team knows how to do this anyway, so I'm just going to do it. Besides, no one can do it as well as I can.

Sound familiar? Meanwhile, you're also expected to be the boss and lead your team with a compelling vision, which is exactly what strategic work entails. Strategic work is thinking, planning, and documenting. You improve your company's processes long term and empower employees to find the right answers without having to ask you all the time.

In short, *tactical* business owners frantically bail water out of a sinking boat every day; *strategic* business owners stop, pull the boat out of the water and fix the holes in the boat. So which are you? How do you spend the majority of each working day? Are you putting off major strategic projects because you're too busy doing minimum wage tasks? What is the cost associated with not doing the strategic work? It's probably higher than you want to pay.

Every time you experience a problem in your company, put off an important project, or get stuck in the office until three in the morning, the culprit is a missing or broken system in your operations. I guarantee it. Don't think that a system has to be a complicated process designed by a third party. A system is simply the way something happens. Every action in your business is either planned or decided by you or your employees in the heat of the moment. Without formal systems, these are your current systems, like them or not. Happy with the results you're seeing from your business? Then you'll benefit from documenting those systems. Share these best practices with future team members, and you'll produce consistent results. Not happy with your current results? You can quickly transform outcomes by strategically developing (and then documenting) better systems. Systems thinking reframes every problem in your organization as an opportunity for improvement.

The late Dr. W. E. Deming,[7] one of the foremost experts of quality control in the United States, was invited to Japan by the Union of Japanese Scientists and Engineers to help the nation rebuild after the Second World War. Dr. Deming continually increased the percentage of problems attributable to a system instead of to an employee or manager. Obviously, that doesn't mean those problems are inevitable. It just means that the most effective way to improve these issues and avoid them in the future is to improve the system. It could be argued that Dr. Deming's systems approach rebuilt the Japanese economy after the Second World War. If systems can turn an entire nation around, imagine what they can do for your business!

---

7   Rafael Aguayo, *Dr. Deming: The American Who Taught the Japanese About Quality* (New York: Fireside, 1990).

Most businesses start small without any such form of documentation. In the beginning, the business owner is willing to do everything. They hold most of the operational knowledge, so they're the constant go-to person for answers. They end up doing the majority of the work because they're the only one who knows how to do it—and it's faster to do it themselves than it is to teach someone else. There comes a point when everything is too much for them. They can't control this thing they've created. They've lost their freedom.

If this sounds all too familiar, it's not too late. I promise you. Once you shift your entrepreneurial mind to think in systems, you will gain control over the results your company produces. We business owners want control. Systems give you that control. It feels like magic! Systems free you from the complexities of ongoing frustrations. Remember Andrew? Strategically evaluating and documenting his systems give him so much freedom from daily operations that he takes two months off every summer to spend time with his kids. Today, the business runs just fine without him needing to physically be there.

Freedom looks different for everyone. Whatever your ideal version of freedom is, systems can give it to you. A documented system is a blueprint for business success—and a completed policy and procedures manual is a valuable asset to own the day you decide to sell your company. (More on your policy and procedures manual later.) Systematization allows you to:

- Leverage what you know
- Free yourself from the confines of a job
- Enjoy more free time
- Structure things the way you want them to be
- Give your clients a reliable experience with your company
- Grow
- Make expectations and processes clear
- Give staff a tool to contribute to continuous improvement
- Reduce errors
- Improve customer satisfaction
- Create a company that you can sell
- Avoid fraud and theft

- Retain employees
- Reduce risk
- Create consistency and predictability
- Build trust
- Generate referrals
- Encourage profitability

Possibly the greatest advantage to a systematized business is that it provides a process to blame, rather than people, when things go wrong. When you shift from blaming employees to collaborating on developing world-class systems, you create a better place to work. You don't have a people problem; you have a missing or broken system. That means you have to stop relying on your employees. Why? Because what happens if they're late, they get sick, or they quit without notice? Your system needs to take care of your business, not your people. You need to be able to replace an awesome employee with a new hire and have everything run smoothly. Yes, keep your great team members, but even your superstar employee needs to be just another employee—so it's the systems running the business, not the people. The people run the systems, and the systems run the business. Otherwise, you don't have a business. You have a stressful job you can't quit.

One of my first clients was all gung ho to franchise her business. She'd just opened her third restaurant location and planned to open a fourth and fifth. I met her at a franchise show, and we sat beside each other. We were the only two women in the entire room. We felt an immediate connection.

A week later, I got a frantic call from her.

"Beverlee, I need your help. My entire front of house staff quit this morning! This is just devastating. Devastating! I don't know what to do."

"That *is* a problem," I said. "Try to breathe—it's bad. However, we've got this. Don't worry. Your customers love you, and they love your products. No problem there. You can keep the doors open with some extra help from the servers at your other locations. From what you told me, it sounds like you have a fabulous back of house staff. Did any of them quit?"

"No, thank goodness. I think all the drama was confined to the girls in the front."

"Good," I said. "Now, we need to get you new staff and make sure this doesn't happen again. Tell me about your hiring system."

"Hiring system?"

"Yes, what are the steps you take when you hire a new employee?"

"I don't have a hiring system," my client said. "I just put a sign on the front door and let the front of house manager do the hiring."

"How's that working for you?"

"Hmm . . . Looking at who left, it was all her friends."

"How much do you think that contributed to them all leaving?"

"OK, I get it. Where do we go from here?"

"If these young women could have had the best working conditions possible, what do you think that would look like to them?" I asked.

"Oh, they had it pretty good." My client paused. "When I really think about it, there were a lot of little things that could have been better. I heard a rumor that they think I'm bossy, like I'm always trying to micro-manage them. I have no clue what that means. I *am* the boss." She paused again. "They don't like it when we run out of things or if they have to work alone. I'm not making that much money. Sometimes we need to send them to the store when we're really busy or send them home early when we are not busy."

"OK. Could you change the schedule so that there are always two servers working together?"

"Yes, I kept meaning to do that anyway—I just hadn't gotten around to it. There's also an issue with keys. I'm a little . . . I don't know . . . I guess I'm paranoid about keys. It feels like people are always driving back and forth to the different locations to get keys from me for things. I did hear that one of them had to wait outside in the dark in the cold for me to drive across town with a key. Another thing—I haven't conquered the challenge of making consistent schedules. My staff would often show up same day to see what hours they were working. Then they'd take a break whenever we were slow, and I'd have three of them on their phones."

"You need a key system and a scheduling system," I said. "Have your employees help you document your existing systems in your business, like your opening routine and your closing duties. And I'll help you create the systems you don't have yet. That will clear up a lot of ambiguity so people know how they're being measured and what's expected of them. You can't run your company in chaos. People need structure. They need to know when they're going to work, what they're getting paid, and when their breaks are."

Together, we put those basic systems in place. The next round of hires stayed and loved the job. Problem solved; business owner freed.

How to Prioritize Systems

When small business owners want to fix their companies, the first place they often start is with marketing. What happens when you grow a chaotic environment? You get more chaos, more mistakes, and less profit. So marketing systems come last. Begin with your essential operations systems.

What do I mean by *essential*? If a broken (or missing) system is hurting your reputation or costing your business money, start there. When I opened my travel agency, the biggest frustrations people had with agencies were the stupid little mistakes they made.

"You didn't book our seats on the airplane. Now my family doesn't get to sit together."

"You forgot my frequent flier number. I missed my damn points!"

"You mailed me the wrong tickets."

"Nobody told me my flight was delayed. I had to wait eight hours at the departure gate!"

I built systems to solve these problems. Our agents were required to ask every client if they were OK going to the airport without their seat assigned, or if they wanted us to book them on a different flight that allowed us to pick their seats in advance. That one question (a system) reduced so much stress.

We kept clients' frequent flier numbers in our system. If they didn't have a frequent flier number, we asked if they wanted one. It took less than a minute to get one. Once we had it, we put it in the computer.

Before the internet, if your flight was delayed, the only way to know was to call the airline. It was almost impossible to find the airline's phone number, though. To give clients peace of mind, we included every client's itinerary with airline contact information in the envelope with the tickets.

The travel agent who booked the ticket wasn't the one to seal the envelope. I had a second travel agent check all the documents first. This simple system eliminated 90 percent of ticket screwups. Once that second agent confirmed the itinerary and tickets were correct, she sealed the envelope with a gold Commitment to Excellence sticker.

How did I know to start with these systems? By that point, I'd been in the industry for twelve years. Every place I'd worked was chaotic because the work was paper intensive and labor intensive. No systems, no checklists, no double checks to prevent stupid mistakes. Ease and accuracy mattered to me since I'd never experienced them in this industry before. So my first systems aligned with how I wanted my business to run all day every day no matter what. All I did was work with what I had available to me to streamline operations and create a consistent experience.

My systems-building adventure didn't end with my own industry insights. At a national travel agency conference, I learned a head-shaking statistic from the keynote speaker—87 percent of people change travel agencies because the first agency they dialed never called back. So I came back and tested it. How long do we have before a prospect goes somewhere else? We found that at ninety minutes, 10 percent of people went somewhere else. At two hours, 40 percent. If we waited until the next day, nearly nine out of every ten prospects chose another travel agency.

A system solved the problem. If someone left a message, we had ninety minutes to call them back—even if the callback was as simple as telling them we got their message and would call them back with all the information they had requested.

We also came up with a new service system to handle walk-ins. We called it the they're-not-here-to-buy-men's-underwear system. Catchy, isn't it? If someone walks into a department store to buy men's underwear, what are they thinking? *I'm here to buy men's underwear. If I don't get it here, I'll get it somewhere else.* If someone walks into a travel agency, what are they thinking? *I'm here to buy a trip. If I don't get it here, I'll get it somewhere else.* If they're ready to buy, what does that mean? Our walk-in prospects likely have time off. They probably have enough money to buy. They probably know or have a good idea where they want to go. What do they want? *To be sold.* That's it. Yet the industry average close rate on people walking into a travel agency was only 23 percent.

Why so low? At most agencies, a person walks in and sees several agents on the phone, all with their heads down and hands scribbling. The person stands there. And waits. And waits some more. Twenty minutes pass. If they're lucky, someone looks up and acknowledges them.

"We want to go to Jamaica for our honeymoon," the person says.

The agent is frazzled. She has so much to do.

"Jamaica brochures aren't in yet," she says, scribbling another note from the last call. "Check back in a couple of weeks. Have a nice day."

I decided pretty much from day one that we would be different. I rarely build systems without getting the input of the people who will be using them, so as a team, we talked about the challenges of being so busy and at the same time needing to deal with customers who wanted our attention. We agreed as our standard operating system we would make eye contact and take turns on a schedule to ditch the phone to take care of anyone coming in the door. We also started a future travelers list that we monitored daily, ensuring that everyone who had asked us to do something would eventually get served. These systems got our walk-in close rate up to 92 percent.

See how simple systems building is? An easy way to get started documenting a system is to take your laptop or a pen and paper and write down each step to performing a task as you do the task yourself. Ask yourself a lot of questions. *How's this working? What happens next? And what happens next? Then what happens?* Then hand the instructions to someone else and watch as they follow them to ensure you haven't missed anything.

What about missing systems? To design a system from scratch, break it down into five key steps:

1. Identify the gap. What specifically is not working or could be working better? What impact is this having on you? What will be the outcome/benefit of having this frustration resolved?

2. Give the system a name that implies the problem is already solved— "How to . . ."

3. Identify and involve the person who usually takes responsibility for completing this task.

4. Ask the responsible person to help you create the system, document it, and test it.

5. Using a standard template, write down everything important about the way this system needs to happen.

Once you've designed your system, start using it—apply it immediately so you can see if it closes the gap.

I had the opportunity to interview Brian Scudamore, the founder of 1-800-GOT-JUNK? Early on, he had a problem with employees denting the roof of every single brand-new shiny truck. It turned out that to properly secure the vehicle to haul away a truckload of junk, employees had to climb onto the roof of the cab. The owner tested this for himself. Sure enough, no matter where he stood, he dented the roof. He could take the trucks to a body shop and have the dents fixed, but they'd just be back next month. As a team, they spent months trying to come up with a system to prevent people from stepping on the cab roof. They created incentives; they added penalties. Nothing worked.

"What if we didn't have to climb on the roof?" an employee asked.

That one question led to a new system that solved the problem for good—a metal grate on top of the cab so no employee would ever damage a truck roof again. Brian has created an environment where employees are encouraged to and rewarded for fixing missing or broken systems. Solving this one challenge has saved the company hundreds of thousands of dollars on truck repairs. If Brian's employees hadn't felt confident in bringing up the problem or suggesting a solution, I bet you'd still see dents on those trucks today.

If you're ready to start documenting your systems—and do it right— you're going to need help. Introduce systems thinking to your entire team. Once you have them on board, work together task by task to fix and document the broken or missing systems that are causing the greatest frustrations. Getting input from your team on how tasks can best be done is empowering and builds a culture of collaboration and continuous improvement. The Japanese word *kaizen*,[8] a business term often used by manufacturing companies, means never-ending improvement by everyone in the organization. The first draft of an existing system is your start-

---

8   *Wikipedia, The Free Encyclopedia*, s.v. "Kaizen," (last modified January 21, 2023, https:// en.wikipedia.org/wiki/Kaizen.

ing point—and you can't measure improvement if you don't know where you started from.

Get real about what you should and should not do. What are the things you do now that you don't need to be doing? What can you train someone else to do while you monitor them? Spend money on the proper technologies so you can scale. If you think you can't afford it, chances are you can't *not* afford it. For example, if you spend five hours every weekend manually doing a task that $500 software could do, you're wasting twenty hours a month you could use designing and implementing a sales strategy to bring in $500, $5,000, even $50,000 or more in sales.

I walked into my hair salon one day and saw the owner sitting behind the counter with a grumpy look on her face.

"What are you doing?" I asked.

"Writing paychecks. I hate it."

There's a system for that, I thought.

Why do business owners do work that they shouldn't be doing when the cost to the business is so high? Her grumpy look turned me off. If I were a new customer, I probably wouldn't have gone back. With the average woman's hair color costing $100, the average woman getting at least six to eight root touch-ups a year, and the average salon serving several dozen customers a day, being grumpy writing paychecks could cost the salon owner thousands of dollars per year.

Did she need to get in the way of her own success? Do you? Anything you don't like doing, you aren't good at, and anything that doesn't add value to the business needs a system, and you need to delegate it.

Don't be afraid to check in with your peers you're not in direct competition with. For example, if you're in Vancouver, check in with someone in Seattle who's doing better than you are and ask, "Can we share best practices or join a mastermind group together?" It's satisfying to hear someone else say, "Yes, I had that problem too. Here's the system I put in place that fixed it."

You can even learn a lot from different industries. I've worked with a number of construction contractors. Like my travel agency, their world can be messy without tight systems. One job gone wrong can put them out of business. They bid on most jobs months if not years in advance.

Contractors need to secure materials at just the right time and price. However, changes to the scope of work are common, so they need to monitor any new requests closely. Leave all this to the workers on site who just want to get the job done, and a lack of systems soon manifests as a lack of profit. This industry needs a system for everything—to monitor labor, to maintain productivity, and to document all project changes. Every business owner can learn from a construction company that runs well, whether you sell airline tickets or widgets.

How to Create Your Policy and Procedures Manual

Everything that happens in your company *must* be written down in a consistent format so the next person who has to do that task understands exactly how to do it. The format I recommend is policies plus procedures. Policies are the guiding principles of your procedures. Think of your policies as the rules of your business. Procedures are the specific steps you strategically design and document to deliver value to your clients and to make work better for your team. One policy may have several how-tos, and one procedure may link to several policies. Together, policies and procedures are the systems by which your company operates.

For example, if your financial policy is that no cash is to be left on the premises on weekends, your procedures need to address how to cash out the till, how to create a bank deposit slip, and how to open the safe. If your communication policy is that information is to be easily shared, your procedures address how to sync company calendars and how to update the customer relationship management (CRM) system. If your technology policy is to own all data, a procedure could address how to set up automatic payments for the company domain name and website hosting.

Know your policies, build your procedures around them, and include them all in your policy and procedures manual. Do this and you'll have an advantage over bigger, less organized companies. Based on the leadership standards you've set, your manual will ensure that everything happening in your business is on purpose rather than by accident.

Some of my more artistic business owners have given me a lot of pushback on the idea of documenting and following systems.

"Won't we lose our creativity?" asked Jennifer, executive director of a global not-for-profit organization.

"Think of your business as an orchestra," I replied. "Your team are the musicians, and you are the conductor. The policy and procedures manual is the sheet music. How else are you going to get everyone playing the same song? Even Cirque du Soleil has robust systems. Without them, their performers would risk serious harm. When it's time to raise your right arm to catch another performer, you need to raise your right arm!" She got my point. You probably do too.

Systems are not just for franchises like McDonald's or Starbucks. They're for every small business, even the creatives. Cirque du Soleil is known for masterful choreography. Everything the professional acrobat troupe does to charm audiences is planned far in advance of the performance. Any well-choreographed performance looks like creativity unleashed. Take a Philharmonic orchestra. The musicians all need sheet music. The individual players bring their talent and skills to the show to create beautiful music. Your business is art too. You're creating a beautiful machine that runs just the way you always imagined. Your systems are your acrobatic choreography, your orchestra sheet music.

Even one-person, solopreneur businesses need systems for autopay, client acquisition, and social media posting so they don't have to google the information every time they want to post a blog on social media, for instance. They just check the policy and procedures manual, and the information is right there. System documentation saves you so much time. Soon, your systematization efforts will create consistency—that means consistent profitability. With that profitability comes renewed confidence, freedom to innovate your product or service, and time off to plan for the future.

Want to sell? Your business is a turnkey operation, so it will attract buyers. You don't even have to sell your business. I've been told by business brokers that a small business policy and procedures manual can sell for $40,000 to $50,000! Want to hand your business off to the next generation? You can. Want to just let your business keep running on autopilot so you can take two months off whenever? Systems give you permission to do so. Your business, your choice. And isn't that why you started yours in the first place?

CHAPTER 4

FINANCE: SHOW ME THE MONEY

"But if I stop offering discounts, I'll lose customers," the travel agency owner next to me said.

"If you *keep* offering discounts, you will be out of business," I said. I grabbed a leftover napkin from the in-flight meal and scribbled a few numbers. "The average airplane ticket to Montreal is two thousand dollars. With the airlines capping our commissions, we're not making ten percent on that ticket any more. We're only making fifty dollars."

"Money's not my thing, Beverlee. I have an accountant for all this."

"Do you have an accountant showing you these numbers?" I handed her my napkin. "Look, when you factor in the cost of the ticket less our new commission, your discounting policy is costing you one hundred dollars to make fifty. You're losing money."

The poor woman cried until we touched down in Vancouver. I left her my card, but I didn't see or hear from her again until a travel agency conference at the end of the year. She ended up shutting down her agency's corporate division—she couldn't compete without discounting. I guess she couldn't wrap her head around charging her customers a per-ticket fee.

I don't want to call this woman out as a failure. She's an example. Like her, most small business owners have issues with money. Almost every one of them I've met in the last twenty-five years has felt as though they have no control over their money. It doesn't have to be that way. You *can* take control of your money. After reading this chapter, you'll find small business finance is easy, practically speaking. Love it or hate it, small business finance is basic math. If you're going to own an organized and profitable business, embrace your inner mathematician and learn everything you can about your money.

Now, you probably have questions such as if money is so easy, why is it the top worry small business owners have? Why do so few know what their numbers are? Why do so many businesses fail because of cash flow? Why do owners pay themselves last and so little? And if they're investing everything back into the company, why don't they have a well-thought-out financial plan to get that money back?

For many small business owners, financial trouble is the effect; emotion is the cause. When it comes to money, we worry we'll be judged. A woman recently confided in me that if she charged what she was worth, others might perceive her as greedy. So while she worried about what others thought, her credit card debt kept growing, she stressed over the high interest rate, and her business failed because she couldn't make a profit.

Why do we have these money issues? Think about what you learned about money as a child. In a lot of households, kids grow up surrounded by money drama and shame. If your family had money, you got the latest electronic toy for Christmas. If they didn't, you got hand-me-down socks. Oh, and then you got made fun of at school every day. *I guess I don't deserve nice things*, you may have thought.

I don't care how business savvy you are. If your upbringing was anything like that, you're going to handle money in your small business the way you learned to handle money as a kid. When my client Aaron was four years old, his dad walked out on his mom, leaving the family with limited resources. As the eldest, he was the man of the house and was expected to take care of his mom and younger brother. For the next twelve years, Aaron took his responsibilities seriously. Starting at age seven, he earned money delivering newspapers, collecting recyclable bottles, and doing chores for neighbors.

He never kept anything for himself. He was poor and proud. Fast forward forty years, and Aaron is still working hard and keeping nothing for himself. He isn't comfortable paying himself. Every time his company starts to earn a profit, he sabotages it and goes back to his comfort zone of scarcity. Last year's profits were loaned to an employee with a gambling addiction disguised as a sob story. This year's profits are paying off credit cards Aaron maxed out to prevent his manager from using them.

Aaron justified these poor decisions with "common sense" ideas about profit. Most of us have fallen for these at some point in our careers. Have you ever heard that it takes five years to make a profit? I don't know why everyone's waiting five years. If you can't create a viable business model in eight to twelve months, you're headed in the wrong direction. Build a profitable business from day one and put that profit aside. Breaking even isn't good enough. We're in business to make money. Even if you run a nonprofit, you're making money for somebody else so they can make the world a better place.

What finally turned Aaron around was a conversation about keeping money in the business. We set funds aside so his employees would have secure employment, and their families would be safe. The stress of money didn't bother him—he was used to that. In fact, it was what drove him to work so hard. He never considered the impact it was having on others.

What's your money story? How are your beliefs affecting your ability to make and keep money? Consider what your family discussed around the kitchen table years ago. Are those conversations keeping you from business success? One of those conversations was probably about taxes. Maybe about how bad taxes are. Have you ever met someone who put all their personal expenses through their company so they wouldn't have to pay taxes on them? You wouldn't believe how many people write off their home toilet paper and cleaning supplies just to save money. Attempts to decrease the business taxes we owe can sabotage our financial future. What if you want to sell your small business someday? Let's say you made a modest profit of $10,000 a year for the last five years, then you wrote off $11,000 a year in expenses. You can justify most of those expenses, sort of. Your tax return shows you've lost money every year for five years instead of showing a $50,000 profit. Which company can you sell? And yes, you *can* sell small businesses even with small profit. The goal is profit. *Any* profit. I can't tell you how many times small business owners have told me that they're ready to retire, but they have to spend a couple of years making the books look good so someone might want to buy it. Up until then, they were writing off their mother's car, their brother-in-law's cell phone, and every other expense they thought they could get away with. Not smart.

You want your business profitable, and you want the owner (you) paid well. Both, not one or the other. My travel agency earned a profit every month, but looking back, I see that I didn't pay myself enough as the owner. What was I doing with the money I should have paid myself? I bought matching sweaters and purses for the agents. I wanted my travel agency to look like an expensive lawyer's office. I went to a local auction house and bought solid wooden desks and tables. I hung antique school maps on the wall. I collected vintage globes. We served fresh coffee and homemade cookies. I bought the staff birthday, Christmas, and work anniversary presents. I paid for more sick days than I should have. All those little things added up. I always put the needs of others ahead of my own.

Are you paying yourself the same or more than your employees doing similar work? If we can't pay ourselves a fair market wage for our work, we don't have a viable business. If you work as a hairdresser at your salon, you need to earn at least a hairdresser's wage. If you're the project manager of your construction company, you need to make a project manager's wage. Pay yourself, or you don't have a business—you have an expensive hobby. Owning a small business should be financially and personally rewarding.

Since starting his company nearly two years ago, Lewis has worked eighteen hours a day, six days a week. Finally, his business started to stabilize. There was money in the bank and a competent team in the office. Lewis could cut back to "normal" hours. You'd think he'd be happy. But when I met Lewis, he was seriously considering shutting the whole thing down.

"Why would you want to close your business now?" I asked him. "After all the hard work you've put in, it's finally paying off."

"I just don't think this whole owning a business thing is worth it. All the stress, the worry . . . And if that wasn't enough, whenever I *do* turn a profit, it all goes to taxes! And when I lose money, I have to borrow against my own house to fund the loss. Either way, there's nothing in it for me."

Sound familiar?

As I dug deeper with Lewis, I learned that all he wanted was some cash of his own and some time to enjoy it. The constant worrying about making sure rent was paid, payroll was funded, and money was left to feed his family made him feel guilty about spending any money on himself at all. The result was a no-win for him.

"In a perfect world, what would make you happy with owning this business?" I pressed him.

"If I had five hundred dollars more a month . . . I mean, above what I'm paying myself now." Lewis sighed. "Then this would all be worth it. I'd spend it on things that are important to me. I could buy my partner flowers. I could save up for a motorcycle. I've always wanted one, ever since I was a kid."

"If I can show you how to get that extra five hundred dollars a month, would you carry on with your business?"

"Absolutely. I'd have my energy back."

Remember Andrew? His company was making great revenue, but he wasn't happy, either, because he personally had no money. Notice a theme here? Working too hard for too little reward makes everyone burn out.

"Looking at your income statements over the past few months, I'd say you're making good money," I said to Andrew.

"I know, I know." Andrew nodded. "Business is doing so well. There should be more than enough. I don't know where it all goes. Whenever we're making a profit, something always comes up that we need to buy or fix. It's so hard to get ahead. I just want to save some cash so I can buy a house someday."

"Well, what if you committed to saving one hundred and twenty-five dollars a month and pretended it was an expense—just like the other things you have to pay for? Put it in a separate business account. Pay tax on it later when you take it out."

"That's nothing. I can save that much a week, easy. But save it for myself? That seems . . . irresponsible."

"Andrew, your top technician owns a condo and is driving a new car. Build your business to create at least some prosperity for yourself and your family. Don't you think you deserve it? It's your company."

He agreed to save money. He ended up saving more than $500 a week. After four and a half years, he used that lump sum as a down payment on a $1 million house, which he now owns. A decent accomplishment for an entrepreneur with a young family.

But Beverlee, you're probably thinking. *How the hell am I going to put cash away when I can barely make payroll? I can't even pay my suppliers.*

Even if you're thousands of dollars in debt, commit to putting fifty dollars away every month. You'll take comfort knowing you have some cash. *Your* cash. No one else can touch it. Paying yourself goes a long way, but a good money system is more than money in the bank. When I started my travel agency, my business banker told me, "Have at least twenty-five percent more cash on hand than you think you need. If you're going to borrow money, the time to do it is when you *have* money, not when you *need* it. No one is going to lend you money when you run out." Wise advice.

In small business finance, little things come up that you may not have thought about. One of my clients owns a small business that provides help for seniors. She charges customers twenty-five dollars an hour. Last year, she was so thrilled with her staff, she decided to give her three employees one-dollar-an-hour raises.

"Do you know what a one-dollar-an-hour raise is for three full-time people?" I asked her.

"No."

"Seven thousand five hundred dollars a year."

"Oh."

"Did you budget for that? Have you notified your clients that you're raising your prices?"

"No, not really. I mean, I wasn't planning on charging more."

As crazy as this may sound, most financial decisions are made this way. Business owners hand out one-dollar-an-hour raises because it feels good, they're due, or they're expected. All arbitrary reasons. Owners lose money and wonder why.

Recently, I worked with a first-aid company. The business was doing great, but the owner didn't have the capital she needed to buy products from suppliers to fulfill her orders. And she had a lot of orders. She had to wait a month to get paid from her clients, and she had less than a month to pay her suppliers. The result? Money went out faster than it came in. As she got further and further behind, her suppliers got tired of her late payments and issued cash-only invoices. She had orders of over $40,000, yet her bank account was $10,000 in the negative. She couldn't close the gap. Thriving business, no cash.

That's the worst place to be. You know that if you could just catch a break, you'd start turning a profit. So you make decisions that dig you even deeper into the hole. In the last few years, I've been called in to help three different business owners get out of big trouble because they borrowed money at insanely high interest rates. They were desperate, and their money problems caused them to make irrational decisions. One is paying an alternate bank 32 percent interest leveraged against his receivables. Another client calculated he'd paid nearly 80 percent interest on the money he borrowed from a loan shark after interest and late penalties. The third, sadly, lost his business because he borrowed black-market money. The stress nearly cost him his life.

How do you keep yourself out of these all-too-common scenarios? To achieve the freedom we all want as small business owners, we've got to stop living payroll to payroll. We need a financial system. And checking the bank balance a few times a month is *not* a financial system. We've got to start tracking everything that happens inside the business. I learned that lesson almost too late.

During my first year owning the travel agency, I got a notice from the IATA requesting a review engagement. I didn't act right away because I was busy. The next letter I received said I had three days to submit the required paperwork. *Three days? That's it? Something must be wrong.* I called my friend Darren, who worked for a major accounting firm. He agreed to meet me for coffee.

It was a Friday afternoon, and boring paperwork was the last thing I wanted to think about.

"Can you tell me what this means?" I slid the letter across the table.

"Oh crap." Darren looked up after the first paragraph. "This is bad, Beverlee. You have to get your stuff together. *Now.* If you don't hand these reports in on time, you'll have to close your doors."

"But I don't know what half these documents are!"

"I'll help you. I'll come back to your office. Let me call my assistant and move some things around."

Fortunately, Darren had the credentials and experience to help me make sense of my agency's financials. He camped out in my office that night, all day Saturday, and all day Sunday, working for pizza and cookies. An accounting firm would have required weeks if not months to prepare these documents.

I had until Monday at 5:00 p.m. to drive into Vancouver and hand everything in. I sat in traffic, sweating. Scary. Somehow, I managed to walk into the IATA office and hand over my documents at exactly 4:59. I spent the rest of the week building my financial reporting systems so I would never be in that position again.

Today, one of the most common penalties paid by small business own-ers is to government tax offices for late filing of reports. In Canada, if you pay your employee remittances late even a few times, the Canada Revenue Agency (CRA) can (and often will) freeze your bank account until they get their money. That's happened to several of my clients. Whatever you do, don't spend the tax money you collect. It's not yours. It'll cause you more trouble than it's worth if you don't have it on hand when it's due.

Is this a good time to ask you to think about creating your own tax management system? Consider opening a business savings account and transferring all tax money to this account as you receive it so that you have it when you need to report and pay taxes. For annual payments, put the money in a high-interest savings account and make money on it. Next, schedule recurring tax due date events on your calendar so that you never accidentally pay these late.

You can get help from qualified professionals like Darren, but at the end of the day, you have to set up the financial system in your business. *You*. So often small business owners get their family or friends to do their books so they don't have to mess with them. Abdicating your responsi-bility can be (and often is) catastrophic. I learned that the hard way too.

My very best girlfriend was always efficient and hardworking—when she worked for someone else. After Darren helped me get my finances in order, she needed a job, so I hired her to manage my books. Once she was on my team, our relationship changed. She didn't like the fact that I didn't spend a lot of time in the office (or with her once I got married). My business ran well without me there, and she got jealous. She told stories to the rest of the team that I'd spent all the company money on my wedding and wouldn't be able to make payroll. Not true. The day I'd planned to promote her to outside sales, one of my staff took me aside and filled me in. I had to let her go. It turned out she was struggling with a lot of prob-lems of her own. Side note: don't ever hire your best friend. It's way too high a price to pay when things go sideways. After that event, I hired an experienced bookkeeper to run my financial system. That way I had the information I needed when I needed it, with all key payments scheduled.

Who's doing your books? How's that working for you? If you're one of the few who has your business finances under control, I say a heartfelt, "Congratulations!" For those still working toward greater financial clarity and reward, keep reading.

A Simple System to Track Everything, Pay Yourself Plenty, and Stay (or Become) Profitable

You know as well as I do that if you can't pay yourself enough to live comfortably, there's little point in working for yourself. Success starts with knowing where your money is going and where it's coming from. You have to know what each product you sell costs and how much you make on it. It helps to set reasonable goals to predict future sales so you can plan for growth and profit. Getting enough sales and charging your customers the right amount can be tricky. You have to charge enough to cover all your costs, pay yourself a meaningful wage, and plan for future growth—yet you don't want to charge so much that you attract no customers.

When you're finished with this chapter, you'll finally know your numbers. You'll understand what your financial statements are really saying. You'll be able to earn a higher wage for yourself. You'll figure out which products earn you the highest profit. And you'll start making decisions that lead to profitability, stability, and growth.

Over the last twenty-five years, I've developed a simple system to know your numbers (and know what to do with them). The Three Rs: record, report, and review.

Come on, I keep records. I have everything in QuickBooks. I've heard some version of this statement many times. Regardless of which bookkeeping program my clients are using, I usually find income at the top and expenses at the bottom, each lumped together in random order. Most often, I don't see a detailed breakdown of sales and corresponding cost of goods sold (COGS). You can't tell which products are viable or which products make the highest profit. You see numbers, but they don't tell you anything.

"What's your gross revenue?" I once asked a new client.

"About a million," she said.

"Are you profitable?"

"According to my accountant I am, but I have no idea what she is talking about because I have no money. I still have to pay a lot of taxes this year, and I don't know where I'm going to get that money from. I spent what little cash I had left paying down the company's credit cards. I still have to get a loan to buy a new piece of equipment that we desperately need to stay competitive."

That's how you can mismanage yourself right out of business. Yet when you accurately *record* everything, you can *report* your numbers so you know the financial health of your company. Then *review* this information to make the right decision about everything going forward.

The First R: Record Everything

All too often, busy entrepreneurs leave the bookkeeping for last and wonder why, at the end of the year, they have a money problem they didn't expect. It could be a big tax bill they didn't save for, a realization they weren't charging enough, or a service they'd long stopped using but forgot to cancel.

Financial records, when up to date, are your road map to profitability. Data collected empower you to control costs, increase profits, and build and protect cash reserves. So what can your bookkeeping records tell you? Quite a bit if you dig deep enough:

- How much you sold to your customers (revenue)
- The type and amount of payment
- The date of the transaction
- The party who paid the money
- The work performed or the goods provided
- How much it costs you to provide those goods and services (COGS)
- How you paid for that expense (credit card, cash, check number)
- The date of the transaction
- The party to whom the money was paid
- The particular type of expense involved (e.g., office supplies, equipment, rent, utilities)
- The total cost of operating your company
- How much you have in the bank
- How much your customers owe you
- What your vendors are charging (bank fees, gas, interest on loans, etc.)
- Which products or services are most popular
- Sales growth
- Anything that might be leaking money

- Net profit (all the money left over after you've completed all trans-actions)

Becca owns a successful talent management agency with a fantastic reputation for excellence. In fact, her company is so successful that she and her team literally work around the clock coordinating principal and background actors for Toronto's busy movie industry. We met recently for coffee.

"I don't know if this is all worth it. I have so much work, yet I suspect I'm doing all this for nothing."

"Can I see your financials?"

She looked away. "I haven't done them. I've been too busy."

There are many reasons why bookkeeping is done last or not at all. None of them are good. To figure out if your business is viable, you need to record your numbers. Becca's numbers were sitting in years-old piles of folders in her office. She hadn't recorded this financial data anywhere else. This meant she didn't know if her efforts were paying off, and she wasn't able to file her personal income tax returns. That, in turn, meant she lost family tax credits and could not apply for a mortgage. Not doing the books is the dark, dirty secret that small business owners keep and suffer from until they get help. If this is you, please make getting and keeping your books up to date a top priority. You will thank me.

Save all receipts, invoices, canceled checks, and contracts requiring pay-ments by you (e.g., leases). Keep records of your business's assets as well, such as any equipment you own (e.g., computers, vehicles, property). As with your revenue and expenses, you're required by law to keep accurate records of your assets, including

- The date of acquisition
- The total amount paid for the item (plus taxes, delivery charges, fees)
- The sale price and date of any assets sold
- Whether you personally use the assets
- How much time the asset is employed for personal use

What do you do with all these numbers? The first step of my system is to keep detailed records of everything. The easiest, fastest way to get all these numbers in front of you is by using a software program. Quick-

Books is popular. Wave is free. No excuses—you need *something*. Your records are way too valuable. It's no longer enough to throw receipts into a shoe box or type everything into a spreadsheet. (Although I do want you to keep those receipts; more on that in a later chapter.) Most programs today connect directly to your business bank accounts and generate the reports you need.

To summarize this system: decide which bookkeeping program to use, decide who is going to be accountable to enter the data into the program, decide where to physically keep the paperwork, and decide what reports you need to see and when. Got all that? Great. You can move on to step two.

The Second R: Report Everything

Every small business has (or should have) four basic financial reports: **income statement, balance sheet, statement of cash flow**, and **cash flow forecast**. You'll learn everything you need to know about the financial health of your business from these four reports. If you take the time now to get comfortable with them, you'll make confident, sound business decisions based on facts, and you will protect yourself from failure. If you wait and review your income statement and balance sheet with your accountant only once a year or neglect to create a cash flow forecast, you lose the opportunity to improve your financial position. And if you don't have these four reports up to date, you may not be able to get a line of credit, a business loan, or a business credit card.

Let's say your four reports are up to date, and you secure a business loan. Your income statement records the interest expense on that loan. Your balance sheet records the amount of the loan and what is still owed. Your statement of cash flow shows the funds moving in and out of the company. And your cash flow forecast tells you the actual cash amount you are going to need to pay the principal and interest on that loan.

Now let's dive into the four financial reports, one at a time.

Income Statement

Your income statement is a financial report that captures your sales, cost of sales, gross profit margins, and overhead expenses. The confusion for small business owners often starts with the name. Your income statement can also be known as your statement of earnings or your profit and loss (P&L) statement. Accounting professionals are notorious for having multiple names for one thing and the same name for multiple things. I am not surprised that most small business owners tune out when I start talking about financial reports.

Whatever you call your income statement, this report shows the net profit or loss incurred over a specific period. It's a summary of how your business earned and spent its money. I like to think of an income statement as a report card because it reflects the daily decisions the small business owner makes.

Set up right, your income statement tells you how much you sold, what the costs associated with those sales were, what the cost of running the company was, and how much profit you made. Setting it up right means working with your accountant or bookkeeper to ensure you have all the details broken down the way you need to see them. This can be done by adjusting your chart of accounts.

OK, don't roll your eyes—this is important. Your chart of accounts is simply the account numbers associated with each of the items on all your reports. The only challenge is that out-of-the-box charts of accounts were set up to make life easier for an accountant. More often than not, they're missing the details a small business owner needs to run a profitable company.

For example, let's say your company sells two products: bananas and apples. If, on your chart of accounts, you have one account showing your total fruit sales and one showing your total cost of buying and delivering that fruit, you will know what your gross profit is for selling fruit. Fair enough. What if you want to know whether it's more profitable to sell apples or bananas? You need to create a separate account for each revenue category—one category for the costs associated with apples and one for the costs associated with bananas. Each account needs to include the costs of purchasing the fruit, any costs associated with shipping the fruit to your company, and the direct labor costs to get that fruit to your customer. Having this additional information can be an eye-opener.

Let's start at the top of a typical income statement and work our way down. Grab yours and follow along. If you have questions, put a big circle around the numbers that don't make sense and get help. There is no shame in asking your bookkeeper, accountant, or coach about anything on your financial documents. There could be shame, however, if you don't learn these numbers and have to close your doors because you missed something important.

Sales (Revenue)

Revenue is money your business earns from the sale of goods and services to customers. These are your sales. They count as revenue whether you've collected payment yet or not. This might be a good time to bring up the issue of under-the-table revenue—you know, those jobs you do for cash, for friends, or for customers to save them the tax. Seems harmless enough, right? The only loser in not recording all revenue is you. Keeping money out of the company may have felt like a good idea at the time, but when you go to sell your company, it either won't be worth as much or will be worthless, and you won't be able to attract a buyer. In the meantime, you're reducing your growth options, killing your cash flow, and putting your business at serious risk of failure. Worse, you don't think about it until it's too late—when you try to get a mortgage or loan. You need that cash on your income statement so that the bank can see you have a healthy business, you are making money, and some of that money is going into your personal account. This is one of those touchy subjects business owners defend or don't consider a problem until it's too late.

Now let's look at the different types of revenue. *Gross* revenue (sales) is the total brought in from the sale of products or services with no adjustments made for discounts, returns, or taxes. *Net* revenue (sales) is calculated by taking your gross sales and subtracting returns, sales allowances, discounts, taxes, and damaged goods.

Look at your income statement. Is your revenue lumped into one line item, or is it broken down by the different product categories you sell? Check to see if you are happy with the way your product sales or service sales are listed. If you sell only one straightforward product, you will have all your sales listed on one line. If you sell multiple products or services, you need to decide how to categorize them to give yourself the information you need to build a profitable business model. For my travel agency, I had corporate and individual sales listed separately. Later, I added a revenue line called service fees. A hair salon owner would want to list services separate from the products they sell. A mortgage broker may want to categorize their sales by vendor or by agent.

Cost of Sales

COGS is sometimes referred to as *cost of sales*, which may be a more descriptive title. Think of it this way—if you didn't have to make or deliver the product or service the sale, you wouldn't have this expense. COGS shows all the expenses you incurred to get, create, and deliver the product or provide the service. COGS includes inventory, direct labor, shipping, and everything else directly related to producing and delivering your products or services to your customers. For a service business, your COGS is your time. For a bakery, your COGS is the ingredients, the cost of heating the oven, the wages you pay your baker, and all costs associated with physically making and delivering that food item to your customer. If you had no customers during a particular period, your COGS would be zero. I often find the COGS section missing from income statements because of poor chart of accounts setup. Check yours now.

When you organize your COGS to the corresponding revenue item, you will be able to run reports on which products are the most profitable. You will also know if you are charging enough, if your cost of supplies is going up, and if a product line is even worth the effort of keeping.

Let's put the top half of this report to the test. Say you own a bakery and sell fresh bread that you make yourself. You purchased a display of kitchen gadgets from a supplier to keep by the register as impulse buys to raise your sales. The bread you sell costs you $1.00 a loaf to make ($0.25 for the ingredients and $0.75 for the labor), and you sell it for $3.00. The gadgets cost you $1.50 each to buy, and you sell them for $3.00. Let's say you sold $300.00 worth of bread and $300.00 worth of gadgets one day. Which is more profitable?

The report of your income statement might look something like this:

Revenue:

Bread—$300.00 (one hundred loaves)

Gadgets—$300.00 (one hundred gadgets)

Total Revenue—$600.00

COGS:

Bread ingredients—$ 25.00 ($0.25 × 100 loaves)

Bread baker's time—$ 75.00 (5 hours @ $15.00 an hour)

Gadgets inventory—$150.00 ($1.50 × 100 gadgets)

Total COGS—$250.00

While it may appear that bread is more profitable, there are other variables you could have included in your COGS. The cost of utilities for running the ovens, the cost for the sales clerk selling the gadgets and bread, waste because you never make exactly what you sell each day and bread doesn't keep, and shrinkage (merchandise lost by shoplifting) weren't accounted for. Your business has its unique recipe for financial success. Set up your financial reporting systems based on what you need to know. Do it based on facts and careful strategic considerations of what information will help you make decisions. Again, you will need a customized chart of accounts that includes all the costs associated with sales.

Gross Profit (and Gross Profit Margin)

When I first started my business, I felt like my accountant was speaking a foreign language. My eyes glazed over when he discussed the required ratios and profit margins for success. Just like learning a new language, the more you use financial tools, the faster you become comfortable. With languages, two words often sound similar but have completely different meanings. The same holds true for learning your financials. When it comes to profit, a few sections of the income statement have the word *profit* in them—gross profit, gross profit margin, net profit, and net profit margin.

Gross profit is calculated by subtracting the COGS from the net revenue. For example, I sold $300 worth of bread. It cost me $150 to make the bread. I subtract $150 from $300. My gross profit is $150.

Gross profit margin is expressed as a percentage. Take the same net revenue minus the COGS. Divide the difference by the net revenue. Then multiply your answer by 100 to get a percentage. For example, $300 in bread sales minus COGS of $150 is still $150. Now divide the $150 by $300, the revenue, and you get 0.5. Multiply 0.5 by 100 to get the percentage, which in this case is a gross profit margin of 50 percent.

Gross profit totals should be a consistent percentage of your revenue from month to month. You can increase your gross profit margin by increasing your prices, lowering your COGS, or both.

Net profit, your bottom line, is calculated by subtracting operating expenses from gross profits. More on that after we look at operating expenses, which are next on the income statement.

If you hate math, your eyes might be glazing over at this point. Hang in there. There won't be a final exam to check your memorization. You can always come back to this section to look up what each term means. I'll continue to provide simple examples to break the heavy thinking into more manageable bites. Read this section a few times if you find it confusing, and you'll be rattling off these terms before you know it.

Operating Expenses

Ever get your VISA statement and go into shock when you see how much you spent? Same thing happens when I review operating expenses with a small business owner. Your operating expenses are what you pay to keep your company running. These are expenses you would have whether you ever made a sale or not. Think rent, vehicle lease, your cell phone bill, and marketing expenses.

Operating expenses are generally organized by expense type. Administration, marketing, and facility expenses along with salaries and employee benefits make up the majority of operating expenses.

Examples of operating expense include:

- Office supplies
- Rent, utilities, and phones
- Legal and professional costs
- Insurance
- Marketing
- Administration and management payroll
- Employee taxes and benefits
- Training

Net Profit

Your net profit is shown at the very bottom of your income statement. It is calculated by subtracting your COGS and operating expenses from your net revenue. This number ideally is a positive one. If it has brackets around it, then it means you spent more in that period than you brought in.

Profit in business is the goal. Why are you working so hard if not to earn a profit?

How much profit should you make? If you wait until the end of the year to see how you do, you are gambling. What is reasonable for your industry? Do you know? According to Greg Crabtree, author of *Simple Numbers, Straight Talk, Big Profits!* your business is on life support if your profit is at or below 5 percent of revenue. He goes on to suggest that 10 percent of pretax profit means you have a good business, and 15 percent or more of pretax profit means you have a great business. What is your net profit number telling you?

Feeling overwhelmed by all the numbers? After spending an hour going over his income statement, Marvin, owner of a successful promotional company, said to me, "Congratulations, you made me feel stupid." Not what a coach wants to hear. Marvin told me he felt embarrassed that he couldn't explain to me what many of the line items were. For example, half his COGS were in the operating expenses section, so he couldn't tell me which product lines were doing the best or why he had over $70,000 listed as amortization of tangible assets in expenses. He didn't know what that meant or where that huge number came from. Then there was $5,000 more in bank service charges that year than there had been the previous year. It took a lot of digging to determine if he was charging customers enough for delivery because there was no line item showing what he collected for delivery. There were expenses not in the COGS section but in the operating expenses section. The kicker was a $12,000 deposit on a new rental space that didn't even belong in this fiscal year. He'd never adjusted it out.

You know the saying "Garbage in, garbage out." Know your income statement inside out and backward so you can create a strong, profitable business. Don't know it, and you'll do the opposite.

Balance Sheet

Looking at your balance sheet can be comforting or terrifying. The balance sheet shows the financial position of your business. It tracks your assets, liabilities, and equity. In plain language, it shows what you own, what

9   Greg Crabtree, *Simple Numbers, Straight Talk, Big Profits!: 4 Keys to Unlock Your Business Potential* (Austin, TX: Greenleaf Book Group Press, 2011).

you owe, and how much money you've invested into the company. It's the first report your banker looks at when you apply for a loan. All those nasty credit card balances along with any unsellable or bloated inventory value plus the money you borrowed from the company . . . They're all right there for everyone to see.

The balance sheet is divided into two sides. On one side you will find all the company assets, and on the other are the company liabilities and owner's (shareholder's) equity.

$$\text{Assets} = \text{Liabilities} + \text{Owner's Equity}$$

As the name indicates, your balance sheet must balance. If it doesn't, you have an error to fix. Your balance sheet contains your assets, which must equal your liabilities plus equity.

On your balance sheet, you will find your bank account balances, amounts owed on your credit cards, and loan balances. If you've given credit to your customers, their balances due to you are on this report. If you purchased equipment, the value of these items is shown here. Your owner's equity on your balance sheet increases when profit shows up on the income statement. If you put your own money in to start the company, the balance sheet tracks those funds. If you paid yourself a dividend instead of a wage, this is where you will find those details.

Repeat after me: "I am not a bank." Do your best not to give credit to your customers. If you must, keep the terms as short as possible and invoice immediately. Net 30 sounds cool, but it can end up being at least two months before you get paid, even by your best customers. Have a robust credit application process in place before you fill your first order. If applicable, ask for a deposit up front to cover materials, labor, or other out-of-pocket expenses. If your customers owe you money, it's your responsibility to ask for it. Stop feeling bad for asking for something you've earned. Review your accounts receivable weekly. Be that squeaky wheel who keeps chirping at clients with overdue payments. Think you might lose them if you nag? If they can't pay their bills on terms you've both agreed to, maybe they're not such great customers after all.

When a business shows a profit on their income statement but they have no cash, we can find out what happened to the money by looking at the balance sheet. Let's break it down.

Assets

An asset is something of value owned by the company. Assets have different classes depending on how soon you could cash them in if you needed to. Cash and accounts receivable are current (short-term) assets, which you can withdraw almost immediately, whereas the building you own is a fixed (long-term) asset, which you have to sell first. If you purchase a $10,000 server you are going to use for many years, that would be a fixed asset. Long-term assets have value lasting longer than one year and include land, buildings, and copyrights.

How well do you know your current cash position? What you think you have at a glance may not, in fact, be correct. Cash in the bank doesn't mean you have cash available to spend or that you are profitable.

Liabilities

Liabilities are financial obligations your company needs to pay at some point in the future. Liabilities include accounts payable, bank account overdrafts, and short-term loans, including credit card balances, taxes due, and mortgages. If you own rental properties, the damage deposits would be a liability because you need to pay that money back to tenants when they move out. Like assets, liabilities fall into one of two categories. Current liabilities are due within one year, whereas long-term liabilities can be due at any time beyond one year.

Owner's (Shareholder's) Equity

You want positive equity. Equity refers to ownership. It's the value of your business once all business debts and liabilities are paid. Owner's equity is like home equity, which is the amount you'd keep if you sold your home, paid off the mortgage, paid back your mother-in-law for the down payment she loaned you, and paid off the line of credit you took out against the home. If you closed down your business today, your owner's equity would be the amount left over after you sold everything of value (your assets) and paid off all your debts (your liabilities).

$$\text{Owner's Equity} = \text{Total Assets} + \text{Total Liabilities}$$

Think of owner's equity as the accumulation of all your profits with adjustments for dividends paid and additional funds invested.

Retained Earnings

Your business profits are listed under retained earnings on your balance sheet until they are paid out to you as a dividend. Dividends are taxed differently than a salary and are something you need to discuss with your accountant. When you take out more profit than you earned, you end up with negative retained earnings.

Cash Flow Reports: Statement of Cash Flow and Cash Flow Forecast

Demystifying your cash flow reports starts with identifying the purpose of the tools you can use to get information about the cash flowing into and out of your business. Understanding how cash moves in and out of your business strengthens your ability to make good business decisions. How you spend or save your cash affects your company's financial health as well as your ability to market, develop your products and team, and take time away from work. Unfortunately, it's not unusual for business owners to struggle with cash flow.

While it is important to look back at your cash flow history, it is more important to be able to look ahead. Your **cash flow forecast** shows you what is going to happen. Your **statement of cash flow** shows what happened.

Statement of Cash Flow: Your Cash History

The statement of cash flow included with your annual financial statements (provided to you by your accountant) is a historical look back at cash and cash equivalents movement during that specific year. The cash comes and goes from three different sources: **operating**, **investing**, and **financing** activities.

This report shows your company's ability to operate, based on cash flowing into and out of the business. Looking at where you spent money last year gives you valuable information to consider moving forward. You can look back and see that all those cupcakes you sold consistently brought in a wheelbarrow of cash, enough to pay all your bills with some left over every month. That's great. You know to keep selling cupcakes. That would be considered an **operating** cash activity. On the other hand, if you sold a piece of equipment owned by the company, that cash would be an **investing** activity. If you personally put your own cash into the company as a short-term loan, that would be considered a **financing** activity.

How is this different from your income statement? Let's say you made a sale in June, but the client didn't pay you until July. On the income statement, you would see the value of that sale in June. On the statement of cash flow, the cash from that sale would not show up until July.

Bankers and potential investors love to see a positive historical cash story on your statement of cash flow.

Cash Flow Forecast: Your Cash Planning

Cash planning is how you build your cash flow forecast. This important planning tool is what some accountants call a receipts and disbursements projection or cash flow projection. There goes that frustrating name game again. Regardless of what you call your cash flow forecast, it's typically a look ahead anywhere from thirteen weeks to a full year. When COVID hit, we shared a six-month emergency cash flow forecast report, which is still available on our website.[10]

Cash planning will help you navigate your cash horizon so you can prepare for emergencies, lean times, and growth. In a business, cash is oxygen—if you don't have enough when you need it, your business will die. You can have a million-dollar sale and celebrate the numbers on your income statement, but you'll ultimately go broke if the customer doesn't pay you in time to cover your expenses (and you don't have that cash in the bank or a credit available).

Take Becky, who was fortunate enough to have been gifted her business when the previous owner retired. It wasn't a hugely profitable business in the past, but she felt confident the company would soar under her leadership.

When Becky took over, she didn't plan for ups and downs in cash flow. Forty thousand dollars in orders sat on her desk—orders she couldn't process because she had no cash to buy inventory. Customers got angry. Delays cost her the best accounts. Meanwhile, she had to use the money from sales for normal operating expenses like employee wages and business taxes. She was spending more than she was making. Add this to

---

10   Beverlee Rasmussen, "Why Cash Flow Reports Are Important to Your Small Business Success," Systems Business Coach, October 4, 2022, https://www.systemsbusiness-coach.com/.

customers paying later than their agreed terms, and eighteen months later, the business closed forever.

The scenario is all too common. The good news is that it's avoidable. Knowing when and how you generate the most cash can help you plan for leaner months.

With a cash flow forecast, whether you adopt the popular thirteen-week look ahead or do a full year of cash planning, you will know when and how much actual cash is physically coming in and how much you need to pay.

Why is this important? If you don't manage your cash flow, as previously mentioned, you could find yourself out of business.

As you create your cash flow forecast, ask yourself:

- When is cash being generated and how much?
- When do I need cash and how much?
- What business activities have the most impact on my cash?
- Which customers are affecting my cash?
- How are my vendor relationships affecting my cash?

Monthly or even weekly cash flow monitoring and planning is essential for all companies, especially when you don't get paid right away. Contractors, for example, often don't get paid until months after they finish a job. Let's say a contractor wins a million-dollar job and nets 20 percent profit. If they don't have plans in place to pay for employee wages and building materials, they could go bust before they ever see their profit.

Each business has specific reporting metrics that will allow the owner to confidently make financial decisions based on facts. What are yours?

The Third R: Review Everything

My client Raj runs two companies that share a head office. We worked hard to get his older company profitable. Then a few months ago, he shared with me that he hadn't been watching his younger company's financials, and they'd lost half a million dollars! How could that happen?

Like most business owners, Raj did not have a system for review. If he had, he would have realized that his "top" sales guy was not producing.

His annual salary at $150,000 was way more than he deserved for his contributions. Over the slow winter months, he was literally doing nothing, and no one noticed until it was too late. Everyone, in fact, was overpaid based on their performance. Had Raj looked at his financials, he would have been able to make changes sooner and hold his team accountable. A review system tracks labor costs, missed invoices, uncollected accounts receivable, and all other profit-draining mistakes.

The point of knowing your numbers isn't to become an accountant in your spare time. Small business finance is a means to an end, not an end in itself. For you, that end is freedom. Accurate information gives you control over your business. Finally, you can make informed decisions to increase profit and take home more cash. Let me give you an example of how knowledge becomes power.

When Andrew and I started working together, he had been generating $500,000 in revenue every year for the previous three years. Looking at the income statement, I noticed that he had spent zero dollars on marketing, and at the time, we couldn't measure which of his many products were having the greatest success in the market. With the goal of increasing growth, he focused on the four main revenue factors—sales, marketing, service, and innovation.

To bolster sales, we first looked at adding new innovative products and expanding his geographic market area. Then we took a closer look at the service he was already providing. Without a system to calculate client data usage, he'd been giving away tens of thousands of dollars in free services! With my help, he developed a system to track every second so he would get paid accordingly.

Andrew also settled on one core offer with a higher price point. He stopped trading services for free lunches and used that time to design new customer service systems that everyone on the team could follow.

To improve his marketing, Andrew hired a web marketing company to build a vibrant, responsive website; publish weekly blog articles; and email monthly newsletters. Knowing that he was great at closing sales but not as great at getting the leads, he hired a lead generation company to feed him opportunities.

Over the next two years, Andrew's revenue quadrupled, his company's reputation soared, and he took the lead in IT services in his region. That's how your business can turn around once you've reviewed your numbers.

Let's go back to the beginning of this chapter. To make reviewing reports meaningful, you need to have accurate data. Put a system in place that ensures you have your books fully up to date, with bank and credit cards reconciled within two weeks of the end of each month. Your bookkeeper will cringe, but insist on it anyway. You can't run a company looking too far back. You need current data so you can make changes if needed.

At least once per month, print out your income statement and review every item on that report. How are your sales? Any strange amounts showing in expenses? Do you understand and can you defend every item on this report? Do you need to check in with your suppliers to ensure you're still getting their best rates? Are you profitable?

Beware of out-of-control monthly subscriptions and credit card debt. Take action immediately. Even if you are busy. Even if you don't know exactly how to fix it. Call your banker. Hire a business coach. Talk to your industry peers. There is no shame in talking about money. Be the one to start the conversation—your banker, coach, and colleagues will thank you. Review your monthly costs for everything from telephones to video hosting to project management apps to rent.

I was at a rotary club meeting when one of the guests approached me to talk about her business. We arranged to meet at a local coffeehouse the next day. She shared with me that she was scared she was going to lose her home and business. Since starting her well-established national brand, she had self-funded, using a line of credit against her house. Now that she was maxed out at nearly $500,000 into her line of credit, she was not sleeping. She'd been waiting for that magical five-year mark for her business to be profitable. It wasn't. It took one look at her income statement to see the problem.

"Why are you paying ten thousand dollars a month in rent? Either move out or negotiate this down."

She was surprised to hear that she could possibly renegotiate her lease. The next day, she got it reduced by half. Her landlord would rather have her pay $5,000 than risk an empty building.

We went through each line item on her income statement, and I challenged her. "Is this a nice-to-have expense or a need-to-have expense? There is a big difference."

Based on this question, she decided that an office in Toronto was a nice-to-have expense. She didn't need it. With a better administration system, she could conduct all company business from her Vancouver office, saving her thousands of dollars each month.

Business is math—you need to bring in more money than you are spending. In just six weeks, my client was profitable for the first time in the history of her company. She made $4,500 her first month, then $10,000 her next month. She's now a profitable international distributor in Canada. Her home is secure, and her stress level is lower than it was before she started the company.

Every few months, review your biggest expenses, such as employee wages versus productivity. Is everyone doing their job? How do you know? Are people taking holidays during your busiest season, forcing you to pay overtime to others? Look at your reports and keep asking questions and making changes until you have a profitable business model.

I worked with a roofer who loved his vendors. He bragged that he'd been loyal to one such vendor for over twenty years. One day we audited everything they charged him for and compared their prices to six other companies in town. Turns out he was paying 30 percent more than what other vendors charged! He'd never thought to question this expense because he thought he was getting the best deal in town. Cutting that expense was the difference between not being profitable and being profitable.

Now What?

I'll be honest—this is a lot to remember! The fastest way to put the three Rs in place so you don't forget anything is to put it all on your calendar. For example, schedule your accounts receivable, accounts payable, and sales reports. Then schedule your taxes so you pay them on time.

Whether you're budgeting for taxes, cutting costs, or paying yourself, you have a responsibility to be fearless about money. If you don't like doing the books—fine, no problem. Hire a bookkeeper. Work closely with an accountant. No matter what, you will set up a money system. You will record, report, and review.

I get it—everything in this chapter is tedious, boring, and not fun at all. And it may just save your business.

CHAPTER 5

HIRING:

BUILDING A TEAM YOU CAN TRUST

"I *have* to wear all the hats because it's easier to just do it myself."

Nine in ten small business entrepreneurs do this: filling three or more roles in their company. Nearly half of us do the jobs of five or more employees simultaneously. You're the owner who started this thing. And if you are anything like the other owners I've coached, you also call the shots as CEO, file documents as the administrative assistant, run the numbers as chief financial officer, reply to customer inquiries as the tech support specialist, and make hiring decisions as the human resources vice president.

So many hats, so much work, so little time left to search for help. That's why, in my experience, that last responsibility—hiring—frightens small business owners the most. When you're doing most of the work yourself, you feel like you hardly have the bandwidth to fully review everything that needs to get done in your business. As a result, you do most of it yourself. I get it. Finding, training, and paying employees can be frightening and risky. Your business is your baby; you can only trust the right person to care for it while you're doing what you need to be doing as the parent.

So what happens in most small businesses? So often, owners abandon systems thinking when it comes to hiring a team. They end up working double or triple duty to fill gaps in the roster of employees they already have. When or if they get around to it at 2:00 a.m. On Sunday morning, they thumb through the pile of resumes collecting dust on their desk. *Anybody here who can help? Anybody at all? I just need somebody . . . anybody.*

Why wait till the last minute like this? Small business entrepreneurs usually don't know if they can really afford the help they need. Maybe you're confident you can cover a new employee's salary for two to three months. Beyond that? It might not be sustainable. It's a huge dilemma. Without the right systems in place, business owners pay today's bills with tomorrow's money. Will that new hire earn their keep? The last thing anyone wants to do is disappoint a family who counted on you for a paycheck to pay their rent. When you start hiring staff (or hiring more), you really are dealing with people's livelihoods. You want to create secure, meaningful employment. That means you don't want to bring people in to rescue you; you want to hire people strategically.

That's what this chapter is all about. You're going to discover the same hiring techniques used by thousands of small business entrepreneurs before you to mitigate hiring risks, build a dream team, and fully realize your personal and business goals. Protecting what you have worked so hard to build and leveraging your strengths through others to earn more income lead to personal freedom. When combined with the systems for training, communicating with employees, and solving top personnel problems, you will be empowered to organize, lead, and inspire your people. You'll develop a company culture that attracts new talent and retains a productive, loyal team of employees who are more than willing to clean the bathroom so you don't have to.

First things first. How do you hire the right people? Often, small business entrepreneurs can think of a half dozen or more hats they want someone else to wear. Who are the right people to hire? Which positions should you fill first?

Filter that decision through the money. What if you hired Jack to take on Brian's busywork, and Brian is the salesperson generating the most revenue right now? That's a big return on hiring—you're investing in Brian's productivity and, therefore, profitability for your company by simply hiring Jack. If you're to get organized, profitable, and free, you have to keep top of mind that money is what brings freedom. To identify your biggest return on hiring—that is, answer that all-important question "Who should I hire?"—you need an organization chart, which most small business entrepreneurs don't have. Yet.

The Organization Chart: Map Your Way to Freedom

Most people get into business for greater prosperity and freedom; many end up simply creating a job for themselves. Very few realize how much work and how many different jobs they will be doing. Before they know it, they're a business owner with the equivalent of three full-time jobs, no money, and no freedom. Let's have a reality check.

Before you hire anyone to help you grow this thing, you need to know exactly what it is that they're going to be doing. Enter the organization chart. The organization chart is a graphical representation of all your current company roles. It organizes the work on your and your current employees' plates by position. An owner who wears multiple hats like accounting, customer service, and operations manager has three roles on the organization chart besides owner—accountant, customer service rep, and operations manager. Your small business may employ only five people, including yourself, to fill twenty-one different positions on your organization chart. If so, you would put each of those positions on the chart, along with the name of the person responsible for the tasks associated with that position. Even small and micro business owners with as few as one key person on the team benefit from creating an organization chart.

Creating your organization chart is the first practical step toward real freedom. Yes, adopting the systems mindset will get you organized. Becoming the leader your company needs will improve your stability. And knowing your numbers will empower you to become profitable. Yet true freedom comes when you have a trustworthy, efficient, productive team who will ensure your business runs and grows without you there. After all, it's not really freedom if you can't leave! If you take every job that you personally are currently doing and name each one as a position, you give yourself the opportunity to delegate those roles. To keep the "jobs" you love and hire out the ones you don't. To work to find people who can do those tasks better or for less money than you can. To see where your time is most valuable.

Your organization chart also gives you control. It's expensive to hire new people. And it's scary. Even the most confident entrepreneur in the world breaks down the night before they have to fire someone. To tell someone they no longer have a way to provide for themselves and their family, whether it's fully justified or not, is a brutal feeling. That's why many small business owners hang on to the wrong people too long. It's just easier. Figuring out who you need to hire and why before you add someone new to the payroll means needing to let go of a lot fewer people.

Organization Charting 101

So how do you start building an organization chart for your small business?

First, **list literally every position** on your team: the bookkeeper, customer service agents, photographer, server, janitor, salesperson, trainer, et cetera. Include your lawyer, accountant, coach, and anyone else who supports your company. Also consider must-have people that you haven't been able to find or hire yet, for whatever reason. Include contractors you'd like to hire (more on these in a bit) and any other specialist roles you need to fill.

Then think about **your personal position.** As the owner who works *in* the business and *on* the business, you have two distinctly different jobs: identify your workload by making a list.

Now **organize that list of team members, owner responsibilities, and must-fill open positions** in an order that makes sense to you. Let's say you have an in-house accountant named Priya. You may also need a part-time bookkeeper. You are the owner, and you also do sales calls. So Priya's name goes under the accountant position, the bookkeeper position is blank, and your name goes on the organization chart for owner, sales director, and any other functions you perform.

The resulting structure is your organizational hierarchy. How should yours look? If your business employs more than one person (you), think about:

- Who's ultimately in charge of each department or team?
- Who's in charge of money?
- Who's in charge of the people?
- Who's in charge of operations?
- Who's in charge of marketing and sales?

No two organization charts will be the same. That said, for most small businesses, it makes sense to group positions into departments based on how your company operates to produce, sell, and deliver products or services. You could organize your chart by product line if, for example, you own a software-as-a-service (SaaS) company with multiple software solutions. The development team would be headed by one individual whose direct reports each work on a different SaaS product. Some businesses are better organized by strict traditional functions with production, marketing, finance, and human resources departments that all report to a president. Does your business serve multiple customer types such as consumers, SMBs, enterprises, and government? Map out your chart according to these groups. If your business is an international operation, your chart could be structured according to geography. Midwest, Southeast, and Central territories, for example, might each have their own "sub-chart" within the overall organization chart. And if your business's operations are process driven like construction, manufacturing, commercial transportation, or landscaping, your organizational model can reflect that. One general manager might oversee the site prep crew, the mowing and mulching team, and the exterior designer and her graphic design intern.

If your name is on each position of your organization chart, that's OK for now. Step by strategic step, you can promote yourself out of each role so you are only doing work you enjoy.

Then, below or alongside each position in your organization chart, **list the key duties or tasks associated with them**. This step applies even if nobody has filled that role yet. You will then repurpose these position-based duties and tasks lists to create a position agreement for everyone on your team today and in the future.

Before we draft those position agreements, however, we need to confirm that your organization chart has avoided what I call the general manager trap. The general manager trap claims many small business entrepreneurs' dreams. It's the "I'm exhausted" version of hiring.

I need a manager to take over for me. . . . I don't need systems, more like I need a babysitter to keep everyone and everything on track. . . . If I only had a general manager in here to run this place that would fix everything. I'm done.

Right . . . and all you end up doing is moving the chaos from your head to somebody else's. Take Carol the nail salon owner as an example. Online reviews report that she's the best nail technician in town. Her salon has grown so much so fast that she is now managing twelve other nail techs. Carol simply can't do it all anymore. So what does she do to alleviate pressure? She hires her best technician, Sandra, to be her general manager. Sandra reminds Carol a lot of herself. Now Carol can go back to doing nails full time. It's happily ever after!

Except.

No.

It's not.

Now Sandra is just like Carol—she hates her management job! Hiring a GM didn't solve any of Carol's problems; it just passed them on to someone else who is far less knowledgeable and equipped to handle them. The downstream consequences are (at best) operations mistakes, dissatisfied customers, and lower revenue. By the time Carol looks up from her nail table to notice, the damage is done.

I tell Carol's story not to imply that you should remain stuck as the owner-manager forever. In fact, I applaud small business owners who are able to step away and take their management hat off. The trap is what you hire a manager to do. A general manager who enters a disorganized workplace expected to pick up where you left off has little chance of success.

On the other hand, if you were to hire a GM to follow a precise position agreement that included the responsibility of job-shadowing you and key team members to create that policy and procedures manual from Chapter 3, it *would* lead to your happily ever after.

About half my small business owner clients have told me they want a general manager during our very first meeting. I introduce them to the GM trap, and they realize they don't need a generalist to manage their business; they need to empower their people by giving them authority and responsibility for their jobs. How? Write each of your employees a position agreement, also known as an employment contract. These act as thorough to-do lists for all current and future employees. I'll teach you how to write a position agreement/employee contract in the next section. Together with your policy and procedures manual, these agreements clearly outline guidelines for performance, put people in charge of their positions, and make everyone happier.

That's the short of it. The long of it is that putting your expectations in writing will prevent the situation that unfolded when I sold my travel agency in 1999. At the time, I had no general management, and I liked it that way. I would hire someone to work Tuesday to Saturday, and that was their shift. If they needed the weekend off, they would talk to the other girls to switch shifts and figure it out themselves. In fact, I told them, "I'm not making your schedule. You're hired for this position, and you have the authority and responsibility to do the job along these guidelines." My employees were adults, and I respected them enough to give them the freedom to work out the details. They did, and the business just ran.

Then, after I sold the agency to a major national chain, the new owner's first order of business was hiring a general manager. He offered my top salesperson (who was selling $1 million in travel per year) a $1,000-a-month raise to take the position. She was put in charge of all the staff. Up until this point, they had all been coworkers. So of course, the new manager puffed up her chest. She set a strict schedule, micromanaged other employees' work, and let her own sales drop—by half. Two longtime employees quit right away because they didn't want to be told what to do. People don't like to be managed. They want to own their jobs and contribute positively to making the business better. They also want their ideas heard.

This didn't have to happen. My policy and procedures manual was only twenty-seven pages. It wasn't difficult to read. All the new owner had to do was stay out of daily operations and let everyone do their job—at least until he had a solid handle of how the company operated. I had already trained everyone to use my systems. (See Chapter 6 for more on how I did this).

A few days before closing the deal, I mailed a newsletter to the 1,700 customers of Somerville Travel promising that we would never have a voice mail. I had always paid for twenty-four-hour phone service. If a close relative who lived far away had unexpectedly passed away, and our client needed to book a flight to the funeral immediately, they could call us at 2:00 a.m., and we'd take care of it. This was a valuable promise that only cost us $150 a month. One month to the day after my letter went out, the new owner installed a voice mail system.

The decision to hire a general manager coupled with broken promises dropped sales in half within eighteen months. My former top competitor in the Canadian travel agency business told me years later that selling my business was the best thing that ever happened to them.

Lesson: there are no hiring shortcuts. A general manager can only help you grow your company if they follow your systems. An organization chart, a policy and procedures manual and position agreements must already be in place—unless you are hiring a general manager specifically to help you create these through shadowing you and other employees. When it comes to hiring a generalist, your gut is going to let you down. *Hire this person. They're just like you!* it tells you. The last hire you need is someone just like you to do what you're doing. You need someone who's going to help you in areas you're not skilled in or to take care of the things you don't want to do. What are all the things you want your new hire to do? Clean the bathrooms? Yes, you can get employees to clean the bathrooms. In order to allow candidates to see how they can help you, you need to have a precise position agreement that lays out all the ways you need help.

If you don't already have a position agreement for everyone who's currently on your team, a great time to create them is when hiring someone new. Like a job description, these agreements spell out the exact terms of employment to ensure you're investing in the right person with the skills to do the exact required work. By getting clear on what you need, you have a better chance of attracting candidates with the skills, attributes, and experience you're hoping for.

Position Agreements: Set People Up to Succeed

People in your company deserve to know what is expected of them and how they are being measured. Conflict happens in employer/employee relationships when there are different expectations of what and how things need to be done. You can significantly reduce this tension by creating a clearly defined position agreement for everyone on the team, including yourself.

Position agreements **clearly outline the authorities and responsibilities of each employee.** Similar to a job description, the agreement lists the expected tasks and states the purpose of the job. Yes, that task list can include things that you as the owner simply don't want to do! One of my girlfriends owns a retail store here in BC. I caught her one night cleaning the store bathrooms. (Can you tell owners wasting time cleaning bathrooms is a pet peeve of mine?) When I asked why she was doing that, she said, "No one else does it, and it needs to be done." Had this task been on someone else's position agreement from day one, my friend would have given herself that valuable time back to do important, strategic work.

A strong position agreement also **lists company-wide standards and any legal requirements** including confidentiality, assignment of rights, and noncompetition. The no-compromise standards list ensures everyone who works for you knows the rules and is expected to play by them. A restaurant owner, for example, may include the dress code in their agreement. A roofing company could include standards governing appropriate language on job sites. Maybe a condition for working at your company is adherence to universal values like integrity. You might expound upon that with employees directly so there is no miscommunication. For example, if an employee tells you their project will be done by the end of April, and they realize they can't finish by April 30, they are expected to be straight with you and let you know early enough that you can be flexible and find someone else to help.

As you start to think about what standards should go in your position agreements, you may realize that a few (or many) current employees fall short of them every day. It's easy to let rule breaking slide once you've done it before—especially if these rules aren't in writing. Is it worth it to avoid conflict? No. Not emotionally. And definitely not financially.

Here's what happened when one of my clients got to the company standards section. Jim owns a tree-cutting service and has a contract with the utility companies on Vancouver Island to keep the roads and highways clear.

Jim was having problems with his crew members. They were great tree cutters. It's just that they showed up late every day, swore and used vulgar language on the job, did drugs, drank, and sometimes had no vehicle to get to work. Jim had basically hired warm bodies who had "tree cutter" on their resume, never considering that their values were out of alignment with his own.

I helped Jim redefine his company standards—and therefore his position agreements—to align with his core values. Remember those from Chapter 1? To discover those standards, Jim thought about what he expected from the people he employed. That's when he realized he was surrounded by a bunch of guys he had nothing in common with and didn't want anywhere near his kids because of their truancy, vulgar language, and substance abuse.

So Jim did the right thing—he fired three of his four employees. It was a painful, terrible, soul-searching process to find replacements who could live up to the new standards. Jim did realize that his core values would not only help him find like-minded people, but they would also differentiate his business from the competition.

After rewriting his position agreements and publishing job postings that included his values-driven company standards, Jim found volunteer firefighters and paramedics who genuinely liked his company and proved themselves trustworthy.

Jim hired his new team members based on values. He can teach tree cutting; that's no problem. Most business owners can teach the work they do. They can't teach attitude, integrity, or values. Because those cannot be learned.

One of the values Jim wrote down was "responsible." Just recently, one of his new hires ran over an extendable chainsaw worth $1,500. Ex-employees had lied about job site accidents like this and hidden the evidence in a cabinet somewhere. This new employee, like Jim, shares the value of being responsible for his actions and reported the accident and took full responsibility.

Not all company standards have to be so serious. Jim also values having fun. If you're not having fun on the job, you might as well quit, go home, and look for a different one. Jim aims to be someone his clients enjoy having around, and he now expects the same from employees. Owning a business is so much easier and more rewarding when everyone's values are aligned, and position agreements help ensure that.

As a result of the company-wide standards, Jim was able to turn his whole company around. The previous year, he made $1 million in revenue with zero profit to show for it. By figuring out his acceptable standards, Jim and his new employees generated a $30,000 profit.

After the job tasks, job purpose, and company standards sections of your position agreement come those **essential legal sections** I mentioned earlier. The **assignment of rights** is very simple. All position agreements should say that anything an employee builds, makes, initiates, or creates while they're at your company, whether they're a graphic designer, a photographer, or a plumber, is yours. You own it, thank you very much.

Your position agreements also need **noncompete** and **confidentiality clauses**. If you don't have these in place, you're vulnerable—they can walk out the door at any minute with all your stuff. Consider this unfortunate true story. A brother and stepsister both worked for their dad's company for ten years. The stepsister got mad and decided to start her own company. She took client contacts, intellectual property, and the company website URL. With no written position agreement in place, there was little the company could do to stop this breach. Make sure that every position agreement has these simple yet essential sections.

A common concern over position agreements that I hear from small business entrepreneurs is that by putting a job in writing, they are setting it in stone. What about growth potential? How can you give employees an opening to accept greater responsibility beyond the position you've hired them for? Say you hired someone for ten hours a week, and you find they are able to take on more duties and responsibilities. To address this, you can put right in the agreement that duties and responsibilities are **subject to change**. And you may not necessarily be the one to change them. As new employees grow into their roles, they can effectively self-promote. For example, my team member Jennifer joined Systems Business Coach in her third year in college. She started as a part-time bookkeeper and has now taken on a leadership role as my technology project manager. The plan is to promote her to full-time developer when she graduates. We've recreated her position agreement a few times—together.

As you write or edit your position agreements based on the organization chart and initial tasks list you develop, you might realize that by reorganizing tasks, you don't even need to hire someone. Instead, you can readjust the team and tasks that you have, saving you money and gaining efficiency. For example, I have a client with three salespeople whom he believed needed a project manager. Because of the COVID-19 outbreak, new customer acquisition slowed to a near stop. One of his salespeople was a single mother, and her commissions-based income had taken a hit. Unlike my agency's buyer, who took a top performer out of her genius zone to boss around coworkers, this lady's management promotion had her doing more of what she was already good at. She was meticulous and friendly and had already bonded with the team. My client didn't want to lay anyone off. It hadn't occurred to him that he could train a current employee to take on a new role, which he could—and did. Here he had been spending all this money on job-posting ads when the right fit was already there.

Sometimes the best hiring decision you can make is none at all. To see if promoting within your small business is right for you, get curious about your people's skills. You may be surprised by the latent talent you have in front of you. Going back to your organization chart, is there someone else on your team who can do the job you want to delegate? You've obviously got to know your people, and that's often as simple as speaking plainly with your employees. During the next staff meeting, bring it up.

Say, "We have some responsibilities that need to get taken care of over here in this department. Before I considered hiring someone new, I wanted to see if anyone here was interested in taking on additional responsibilities. If these tasks seem up your alley or you would like to get trained to do this work, please speak with me one-to-one."

Whether you pass off unwanted hats to current employees or recruit new ones, you must get clear on one more key element of your position agreements: **compensation**.

Small business entrepreneurs are among the most generous people I've met in my entire life. That's why I'm so saddened when I meet one who is "winging it" when it comes to paying their team. Fair compensation means fair compensation for all parties. Too little for employees, and they feel demotivated; too little for you, and this whole entrepreneurial thing is hardly worth it.

So what is a fair day's compensation for a fair day's work? To know that, we need to define compensation and the different forms it can take. According to its dictionary definition, compensation is a form of monetary value used to recruit and retain qualified employees. It can be an incentive to increase morale and is often linked to job satisfaction, low turnover, and company loyalty. Money as a reward can encourage performance. However, compensation does not have to always be cash. Employee pay can take the form of:

- Hourly wages, salary, base pay, and commissions
- Overtime, holiday pay
- Bonuses, gifts
- Profit sharing, stock options
- Travel, meal and housing allowances
- Extended benefits, including dental, life, and medical insurance; vacation pay (on top of mandatory source deductions); leave; retirement and pension plans

Every small business has a limit on what it can afford to pay and still stay in business. You need to know yours.

Fortunately, there's a system to measure every dollar you spend on wages, and I'm going to teach it to you. It's pretty simple. You take your total paid to all employees (including you) in wages, benefits, and other perks;

add your total sales; and divide total wages by total sales to get your percentage of sales. For example:

- Monthly sales are $120,000.
- Monthly wages are $30,000.
- Therefore, wages cost 25 percent of sales.

What does your number need to be? Small business compensation costs are typically measured as a percentage of sales, averaging between 20 to 35 percent. This does vary by industry. Service industries tend to be higher with 50 percent or more. Check with the industry associations you're a member of to learn how much you can expect to spend and adjust your budget accordingly. All it takes is to be a few percentages over in your employees' wages, and your profit is gone. Not planning for profit or paying yourself less than a market wage creates a false economy in your business. Unless you had planned to be a volunteer in this organization, calculate the value of the work you personally do and include that in your budget. If you add in your wages and the business is not profitable, then you may not have a viable business model. Somewhere, adjustments need to be made in the business system so that you can be compensated for your hard work. Otherwise, why bother?

You may find that you're overpaying your employees. This is terribly common. For example, my client Alex owns a framing company. His crew works for him because he makes it easy. He used to pick them up in the morning and drive them to the job sites. Many of his employees didn't own vehicles or have valid driver's licenses. Alex figured that was OK because they were hard workers, right?

Meanwhile, Alex was losing money and didn't know why. Looking closer, I noticed that he was paying his crew for their one-hour lunch break. Why? He felt guilty that he often kept them longer than eight hours a day and hadn't paid any overtime. Paying for lunch was apparently keeping them from complaining. On slower days, Alex's workers would be done before their boss, and because the boss was driving, everyone was paid until they got in the van to go home.

It's the little things that can take you out as a small business owner when it comes to compensating employees. If Alex had simply stopped paying for the one-hour lunch break and instead paid the occasional overtime, he would have been $30,000 a year more profitable. He also could have hired a driver to drive the employees home when they were finished.

When it comes to fair compensation for everyone, you also need to be mindful of the rules. Employment standards exist to protect employers and employees. If the law says employees must be paid overtime after eight hours of work, then you pay overtime. Even if you're "getting away with it," you're hurting yourself the most.

Most countries, states, provinces, and cities have rules you need be aware of, including:

- Minimum wage
- Tax withholding
- Vacation pay rates
- Time off
- When to pay
- Information employees get about their pay
- Documentation of hours worked, days off, and sick time
- Hiring contractors versus employees
- Probation periods
- Raises

Unless the law requires it, an annual raise may not be a wise investment in your personnel budget. Remember when we ran your numbers? If you give an employee a $1-an- hour raise in Canada with taxes and burdens, that's over $2,500 a year out of your pocket. Learn to give raises and discounts out very strategically.

At the same time, trying to get a "deal" on labor will come back and bite you. If an experienced project manager goes for $100,000 a year, and you cheap out and try to get one for $70,000, that $30,000 you save is not going to be worth it. You'll end up spending more time and money correcting the mistakes of subpar work from an unqualified or inexperienced employee.

Recently, I asked a client what the single greatest achievement of her past six months had been. She said she had spent more than she had expected to pay for a great sales manager . . . with outstanding results. I get it. Everybody wants to save money. However, considering the long term, you're looking for a fair price for the talent you need. Sometimes that means spending more to make more.

Gut Check: Are You *Really* Ready to Hire?

Hiring can be one of the most stressful processes owners take on. Am I *really* ready to commit to bringing another person into this? What if I hire the wrong person, pay too much money for poor results, or just make more work for myself?

Here are a few questions I've asked clients that help them reach a 100 percent "Yes, we're doing this" or a 100 percent "No, now is not the time." There is no right or wrong answer. There is only what will grow your business and help you achieve more freedom and prosperity . . . and what will not.

- Why exactly do I want or need to hire someone?

- How will hiring this next person affect the others on my team?

- Through training or restructuring, are there ways to get this work done using the team that I already have?

- What fears, concerns, or challenges do I need to face to be able to move forward with this next hire?

- What did I learn from my last hire that I will or will not do again?

Job Postings: Attract the Best Talent Your Business Can Afford

You have your organization chart. You know who is doing what today and who needs to be doing what tomorrow. Your position agreements reflect this. Now what?

It's time to publish your help-wanted ad! This element of your world-class hiring system is surprisingly easy. Simply use the information from your position agreement to create the job posting. In my experience coaching small business owners through the candidate filtering, interviewing, and hiring process, the job posting step is more difficult emotionally than practically.

Think about any additional info your job ad needs. You've gotten the tasks, duties, responsibilities, purpose, and company standards from your position agreement. Now add a brief summary of the job, a little background on your company, any relevant details on working conditions (e.g., if manual labor is involved), and the expected attributes and qualifications of the ideal candidate.

I'll stop here and clarify *ideal*. The best candidates don't always meet an employer's qualifications. The right person may not have the years of experience you expect, for example. They may not have held the same job you're hiring for or worked in the same department. That's OK. A prima donna who checks all your boxes is rare. Instead, hire for attitude and attributes. Credentials matter; however, somebody you can train to do the work is the better choice over the candidate who is perfect on paper yet unteachable.

Don't be fooled by older, wiser people or those who have more letters after their name. If they're a great fit and they have the credentials you need, great! Just remember the credentials don't automatically mean they'll be a great employee. Look at everything else they bring to the table, too, including personality. Even small companies of one to five employees would do well to do personality testing like the Myers-Briggs Type Indicator, the DiSC Behavior Inventory or CliftonStrengths (formerly StrengthsFinder) to see if there's a fit. I'm not a testing expert in any way. However, I can tell you it's worth it to ask candidates to take a personality assessment.

The Search: Filtering, Interviewing, and Hiring Like a Boss

Your recruiting process, like other systems in your business, is about creating consistent, predictable results. Whether you're a two-person business or a company with 300-plus employees, a smart search system takes the guesswork out of hiring. Here are the ten steps I recommend to help you filter, interview, and hire the right person for the job:

1. Publish your job posting.

2. Search for candidates.

3. Sort and make a shortlist.

4. Send short-listed candidates three to five preinterview questions via email.

5. Prepare for interviews by creating a more in-depth set of questions.

6. Conduct the first round of interviews, keeping each at thirty to sixty minutes maximum.

7. Check and double-check candidates' work history and references.

8. Conduct a second round of interviews.

9. Select the top two candidates. (Save one for later.)

10. Use your position agreement and an invitation letter to make an offer in writing.

Welcome, onboarding, and orientation come next, which we'll cover in Chapter 6. For now, these hiring steps alone are a lot to take in. Don't worry—we'll explore everything you need to know. Just as the general management trap is to be avoided as you design your organization chart, there are big traps to avoid before you start (or continue) hiring.

The Five Don'ts of Your Candidate Search

Don't Concede Your Power

Owners also worry about losing the "perfect" candidate. *I want Johnny. Johnny's the best in the industry. I'm going to do anything I can to get Johnny. Pay more. Outbid everyone.* This mindset allows Johnny to hold a business owner for ransom. Johnny has all the power; not you. In this whole process, hold on to your power. *You* are the boss. Yes, you're judging other people. It's difficult. And you have to do it. Fortunately, this hiring process takes emotion out of it. That's a key advantage of having a system in any part of your business—a system generally takes emotion out of your decisions.

So hold on to your power. This is the time when you, as a small business owner, have all the power, and you don't want to give it away. If at any point you feel like you're giving in, that's a red flag.

If you feel you haven't been in control of hiring in the past, take your power back now. Double-check candidates' resumes. Ask for more references. Do another interview. Bring in another group of candidates. It's a pain, I know. Approach anyone you're bringing into your company the same way as dating. When you get married, you're financially responsible for the other person. Treat anyone you hire as if they're going to be running your company.

Don't Hire Family, Friends, or Neighbors

Hiring is not a time to cut corners and just hire the first person who is available, though we've all done it. Remember my bookkeeper? When I owned my agency, I hired—then had to fire—my best friend. It cost me that important friendship. I was in a hurry to find a new bookkeeper and didn't imagine what lay ahead when I hired her. It was a disaster. She shared confidential information with my staff and told lies that made everyone worry needlessly. Of course, I learned later she was struggling with some pretty serious personal issues. As her boss, I had to fire her. I wish I could have been there for her as a friend. I could not. The risk of hiring family and friends most often outweighs the benefit. Sometimes it works out; most of the time it doesn't.

Don't Compromise

Does this sound like you? The candidate "sorta fits, but not really." You "prefer not to hire Mom, but she's the only one who applied." Or your new hire wants way more than you're comfortable paying. Don't compromise on hiring. It's guaranteed to cause you both emotional and financial pain when it doesn't work out. I see this as the biggest hiring mistake: compromising or trying to take a shortcut in the process. Start early so you don't feel backed into a corner hiring someone you may regret. Wrong employees are expensive. Take the time to find a great fit.

Don't Treat Hiring Like a Transaction

My son Jeff once worked for a company whose owner walked him around the plant, did all the talking, and hired him on the spot. "You can start Monday" were his exact words. It turned out to be a horrible, unsafe place to work. The owner was completely disorganized. Within a week, Jeff was already looking for a new job. Fortunately for Jeff, his brother was working for a great company in the same industry and put in a good word for him. Whereas the disorganized owner made a hiring decision within an hour of meeting Jeff, the other owner took three months. He does his due diligence before hiring anyone; that's the system.

Three interviews and a personality test enabled them to determine if Jeff was the right fit, which he was. During the final interview round, the hiring manager asked Jeff what his favorite job had been so far. "Public speaking!" he said. This took them aback. Here was this nineteen-year-old who had started his own foundation and online community for kids with ADHD. He gave a seven-minute speech to teachers, doctors, and parents and got paid $500. The owner appreciated this part of Jeff's world. It was a relationship-building process. They made Jeff wait, and it was worth it. I think Jeff is on track to tell me that now *this* is the best job he's ever had. Treating people like people goes a long way.

Don't Skip the Vetting

The biggest filtering mistake small business entrepreneurs make is not doing it. They don't expect candidates to adhere to the resume submission guidelines in the job posting, they don't ask preinterview questions, and they don't check references. "Hey, I like you. You're hired" is about as sophisticated as their filtering gets.

With today's technology and fast-paced world, it's easy to slip a little lie through on a resume or in an interview. I worked with a client whose CEO lied about having a Harvard MBA. The company didn't check—which almost cost them the company. Pick up the phone and check with previous employers, high school teachers, and service groups they are in. Fact-check to find out if what they are saying is true. Better to take a little extra time now than to lose a lot of money on a bad hire over the next several years.

Tips for Filtering Candidates

Now that you are aware of the five big mistakes many small business entrepreneurs make throughout the hiring process, you're set up to succeed. Finding good, smart people at this point is as simple as following the steps I've outlined. So let's pick back up with your job posting.

Your job posting is your first filter. For example, say you want a PDF copy of every candidate's resume emailed to you. If you receive an MS Word copy from someone, you may not want to read it. This person obviously doesn't listen. Having two resume piles—a "no" and a "maybe"—streamlines the filtering process. Check for spelling. Check for answers to questions you wrote in the job posting. Do they include everything you asked for? Try not looking at the names on resumes so you don't make assumptions about anyone's background.

This simple step weeds out 50 to 60 percent of candidates. From there, the ones in the "maybe" pile receive an email back from you. Thank them for their resume and ask them to answer five questions. These questions amount to a preinterview. I work with small business owners to figure out what questions they need to ask, whether they're specific to their industry or the values they want in a new hire.

For example, a construction company with an accounting position open had these preinterview questions:

- If there was a cash flow crunch, and you had five suppliers to pay now, how would you handle that?

- If you were responsible for monitoring a projects budget and protect the company profit margins, what strategies, tools, or systems would you use?

- What was your most important contribution to a recent employer?

- Describe your reputation as an employee.

- Why should our company hire you over the other finalists?

The preinterview email back-and-forth is super important. Did they answer quickly? Did they take their time and answer? Did they not answer? If they answer within the hour, it could mean they're extremely interested. Or it could mean they spend too much time on their phone. If they take a little while, keep in mind they might have a job and a family. Still, a response that takes much longer than a few days might not be worth reviewing.

Tips for Interviewing Candidates

One of the most important things to do during an interview is listen. After all, how can you learn about a prospect if you're the one doing all the talking? If you're doing more listening than talking, you'll hear what you need to know. After the initial hello and banter to make them feel welcome, keep the ratio to 20 percent you talking and 80 percent them talking. This helps you keep yourself from "feature dumping" your company. This is not the time for that. Remember, you want to keep the balance of power. What you have to offer is important to them; otherwise they wouldn't be there. Asking questions and carefully listening are the best strategies for keeping calm and staying in control of the interview process. If you get nervous, take a breath and ask another question. Being prepared with your interview questions in advance will help keep you on track.

As you listen, you will spot green lights like "I just really want to work for this company," "I love to show up and contribute," and "What you do here is just the coolest." Genuine statements like these are tells for a giver. Hire givers, not takers. You will also catch red flags. For example, a family friend has bounced jobs her entire life because she is all about what's in it for her. "I want this. I want that." I know this attitude comes across in interviews, yet businesses hire her anyway. They must not be listening. Employees like her are a drain on your resources—they are takers, not givers.

If you really want to see what a candidate is like, walk with them back to their car when the interview is over. If you're looking for someone meticulously clean, and this person's car looks like the garbage bin behind McDonald's, don't give them the job.

What about someone who checks all the boxes, yet the prospect of making an offer just doesn't sit right with you? First of all, never hire on the spot. Never, ever. You're too enamored. You've just been gobsmacked by someone who is potentially able to make your life a lot easier. You need a moment to stop and think. Check your notes. Compare them to other candidates. You're the boss. Put distance between you and your candidates. Even if you really, really want to hire that unicorn of a candidate, say, "Thank you. I'll get back to you in a couple of days." Always put your offers in writing. Second of all, if your gut tells you it's a bad hire, then chances are you're right. Better to keep looking than to make a bad hire.

As much as I know these hiring steps will help you find someone perfect for your company, they won't make your hiring process foolproof 100 percent of the time. No system is entirely perfect. That's why it's better to know what to do if a hire doesn't work out than just to hope and pray it always does. If you do need to terminate an employee, fire as fast as possible.

I caught an employee at the travel agency lying to a customer during a phone call.

"Why did you tell them that those hotel rooms were soundproof? We know they're not," I said.

"I dunno," she said.

"Well, we tell the truth here," I said. "So tell the truth."

The next day, she did it again. So I fired her.

No Full-Time Work? No Problem!

Hiring Part-Time Employees 101

What if you need help, but not forty hours a week worth of help?

Back in 2007, the economy was booming. It seemed like everybody was working. Small business entrepreneurs couldn't find workers. So owners had to get creative.

A printing company owner I worked with had a delivery guy who was going on a four-month leave for a surgery and the subsequent recovery and physical therapy. Who would take that job? My client only needed someone to run deliveries two hours a day Monday through Friday at thirteen dollars an hour.

"There's a job for everyone," I told her. "Some people will actually accept money to clean people's teeth. You couldn't pay me a million dollars an hour to do that. Somebody is thrilled to get their very first job, and it's working four hours a week at McDonald's. When I was a kid, I had friends who got paid to catch chickens on the neighbors' farm late at night."

Sure enough, when the print shop owner published a help-wanted ad— delivery worker needed for two-hour shifts during the work week for four months—she heard right back.

"This is a perfect gig for me," a retiree said via email. My client hired him right away, and everything worked out.

Getting creative worked for another client. She hired moms who were otherwise unable to find a job that fit into their available time. Their shift would start at 9:30 in the morning once the kids were on the bus and end right at 2:30 p.m., with just enough time to spare to pick up the kids from school. There's a job for everyone.

If you need someone for ten hours a week, put them on the organization chart. When you hire, it's about finding a good fit. Someone needs a job; someone has a job. There's a job for everyone, and there's a person for every job. No matter what.

Hiring Contractors 101

A huge opportunity for busy business owners is the current ability to easily outsource work projects to contractors anywhere in the world. Outsourcing is simply the process of paying for tasks or services to be completed by someone other than an employee. Consider how beneficial it could be to hire someone great to support you with administrative assistance, website development, market research, graphic design, data entry, video production, or any other of the many tasks business owners need to get done in a day.

Planning in advance for this type of hire will set the stage for a successful business relationship beneficial to both the contractor and the employer. Consider creating specific contractor systems for hiring, communicating, monitoring, and delivery.

In today's fast-moving technical business environment, it helps to be able to outsource tasks and projects to others who have the skills, knowledge, and time to make things happen quickly. There are many places online to find great people to work for you. Upwork (www.upwork.com) is a popular choice and a great example of a system to find the right candidate for the job. It has a built-in communication system, so you know what work is being done and your cost in real time.

Everything You Need to Know about Project Descriptions

Just because you're hiring a professional doesn't mean they're automatically better than others on your team. Keep the systems the same for employees and contractors—position agreements for everyone.

In order to find and hire the best contractor to work on your project, it's important to present a detailed, organized, and thoughtful project description. Here's a template you can use from the website Upwork.

Project Name:

Project Overview:

1. What is the challenge you need solved?
2. How does this project tie into your business goals?
3. What is your timeline?

Logistics:

1. What is the project deadline?
2. How much do you want to spend on this project? Remember, the highest-caliber freelancers usually have higher rates, so take this into account. You get what you pay for!
3. Would you like to pay hourly? Or pay a fixed price?

4. Do you want freelancers to answer a question or two when creating a proposal for this job? (This is highly recommended to help you identify the highest- quality freelancers.)

Project Description:

1. What will be the contractor's responsibilities?
2. What qualifications are you looking for?
3. What does the finished product look like? What is the ultimate goal?

Skills:

1. What specific skills are needed for the project?
2. Is there a specific development language the freelancer needs to know?
3. Is there existing documentation for the project already in a certain format (.pdf, .ai, .eps, etc.) or program (Photoshop, Illustrator, etc.)?
4. Not sure? This might be an opportunity to hire an expert with experience in this type of project.
5. Are there any artifacts from your company you could attach to give freelancers a better understanding of your project?
6. Are there external examples that are inspiration for your project?[11]

After you write and post your project description on a hiring site such as Upwork, you'll start getting proposals from contractors and freelancers. You can review these in a similar way to how you would an employee candidate. If you don't get any proposals, go back to the budget you listed in the description. Research what other professionals are charging to complete projects like yours. Chances are you're being too cheap.

Business Partnerships 101

Not going it alone? When you bring in or start a business with a partner, you're also hiring. Trust is required. So take any potential partners through a similar filtering process. If you have thirty years of experience, and a partner has $10 million, that's great. What's your position going to be? What's theirs? Interview them so you avoid getting scammed into doing most of the work and earning little to no profit.

---

11 "Find Talent", Upwork Global, accessed March 29, 2023, https://support.upwork.com/hc/en-us/categories/360001184214.

Position agreements are especially valuable for partnerships in business. Strive to get clarity on who is going to do which tasks early on in your partnership. Even if one partner is just bringing in funding, get that in writing so that no one forgets that you will be doing all the work. Make sure it's an agreement you can live with long term. Like a marriage, business partnerships can get messy and be difficult to get out of.

Here's what position information to include in your partnership agreement:

- Your company vision, values, and promise
- Who is going to do what jobs in the business
- How you will make decisions
- How much money each of you will earn as employees of the business
- What personal/business expenses will be allowed
- Effort and hours per day of work expected from each other
- Expected vacation and personal time allowed
- An exit plan should one partner want out
- A dispute resolution agreement
- How and when to share profit
- What will happen if the business partners are married and divorce or one passes away

While your spouse is a convenient option for a business partner, you should make darn sure he or she really wants to own and work in this business. It may be better in the short term for one partner to have an income outside the business. Also, consider testing working together for a period to see how this affects your relationship. Create ground rules for working together. Write a family charter with rules of engagement related to the business. This could include no discussing business at the dinner table and an agreement to close down or sell should the business start causing damage to the family.

Most importantly, see a lawyer early in the process and get all agreements legally documented. This includes all partners having an up-to-date will that explicitly defines the terms of your agreements. Oh, and use the same hiring process when choosing a lawyer. Remember, they are working for you, not the other way around.

Hiring Interns and Students 101

It's been so much fun to watch my intern Jennifer grow. The Canadian government provided a grant for me to hire her in the first place. I have already seen her talents emerging. I've been able to see where she fits in the business beyond the tasks I've assigned her during the internship. It goes back to my organization chart. What responsibilities did I need to delegate? What projects would produce my biggest return on investment of time in onboarding her? A lot of business owners who hire students or interns don't have a clue what they're going to do with them. If you have a position agreement for every intern, it will be a productive, rewarding experience for everyone.

One Final Note: Don't Wait Too Long to Hire

A new client of mine recently wrote this on their onboarding form:

Working for a small business is often a stepping stone, so it seems to be a constant cycle of recruiting amazing people, helping them learn their potential, facilitating their growth, then seeing them blossom and move on.

I can relate. One of my own employees gave me her notice after she was headhunted by a big company. Working for me was part of her personal growth plan, and I expected it. Even if you follow the best system in the world, some of your employees are going to leave you. All you can do is be prepared.

If you have plans to hire in the near future, give yourself at least a couple of months to find someone. Go back to the return on investment. Yes, it might be a little hard for a couple of weeks or months, depending on your sales cycle. If you plan your hires in advance by creating the organization chart, position agreements, and detailed job descriptions, you won't have to lay anyone off later because it turns out you couldn't afford them.

Keep in mind that great candidates looking to work for you will want to give notice to their current employer. Assume that once hired, they won't be able to start for two weeks. Give yourself enough time to do a thorough search for the right hire and time to check references. As a part of your hiring system, consider creating an ongoing way to accept resumes, keeping your future options open. If you don't have options, you don't have freedom.

CHAPTER 6

TRAINING:
DO IT YOUR WAY

In between selling Somerville Travel and starting up Systems Business Coach, I worked in sales at several companies. When a Florida-based business brought me on as sales representative, they flew me down to their headquarters for training. My flight was on a Sunday, and I arrived at their office Monday morning bright and early. Because nobody had created an account for me to log into their computer system, I just sat there. All day Monday, all day Tuesday, and most of Wednesday. I wasn't even able to start my orientation until Wednesday afternoon. They weren't at all prepared to onboard and train me.

We ended up wasting my first week. I had hoped to start selling the company's services within three days. I had a four-year-old and a six-year-old back home in BC, so I just wanted to get onboarded properly and get back home. Instead, it took me three weeks to figure out everything on my own so I could get on with the job.

As you might know, it's expensive to train employees. It's even more expensive when you don't have a training system in place. As a sales representative, I could have been making sales and earning my keep in three days or less. Instead, my training cost the company precious time and money through no fault of mine.

Small business entrepreneurs are often hesitant to hire new people because they don't have time to onboard and train them. The promise of finally having help comes with the fear of taking on this huge responsibility to teach. If you can offload some of the work you're currently doing, you can look forward to getting more done. *If.* Employee onboarding can be an overwhelming task when there's no system in place to welcome, train, and develop a highly skilled workforce. You may end up both paying new hires and doing their work yourself. *But it's just faster if I do it*, many small business owners think. This is *so* not true.

I've dedicated an entire chapter to onboarding and training new employees. Not only are there costs to not training employees—there are also countless advantages to having the training system that every small business owner deserves. For example, properly training your team empowers them, eliminates errors, and provides an optimal working environment. Empowered employees make better decisions in the moment, which goes a long way toward ensuring you keep promises to customers. Training also provides an opportunity to continuously test and improve your systems as you learn from watching new people follow them. If you've struggled to document your processes in the past, you can ask new employees to document what they're learning and add it to your procedures manual.

Getting organized to train employees not only enables you to quickly onboard new people and set them up for success, but it also allows you to scale your company. For example, I helped a local retailer document her processes, build her policy and procedures manual, and train her employees. Getting everyone on the same page allowed her the time to upgrade her online retail shop. When COVID-19 forced her storefront location to close indefinitely, her sales doubled, and her staff kept their jobs simply because of her Shopify site and the systems behind it.

Before you glanced at the table of contents or saw the title of this chapter, you may not have thought about welcome processes or employee manuals. I get it. You don't have time. By now, you've probably realized you need to make time for these training essentials. Whether or not you eventually work your way out of daily operations depends on it.

So when it comes to training, where do you start? Is it as simple as having all new hires memorize their position agreement and read your policy and procedures manual cover to cover? If only. Training needs to include process *and* purpose. Training is about **doing**, **thinking**, and **being** part of your team. **Doing** is following the policy and procedures manual. This shows your team what you need done and includes why your company believes this is the best way to do it. **Thinking** is taking the opportunity for innovation, improvement, and feedback. Be open to questions and suggestions on better ways of doing things. **Being** is personally aligning with your company values. Ideally, you want everyone on your team working toward a shared desired result with organizational accountability. Here's where the training process begins—at the beginning.

Orientation: Welcoming New Hires

Think about someone coming into your home for the first time. Would you let your guest just stand awkwardly at the front door while everyone else went about their business? Of course not. You would greet them, introduce them to your family, show them around, and make them feel welcome. It's no different in business. Lay out the welcome mat for your new hires. Meet with them one-on-one on their first day and introduce them to their new team.

Share your vision statement, your company promise, and your core values in person, in addition to giving them a copy for reference. Explain how these show up in your organization. You can't just pay these lip service. They must actually live in your organization, and that should be obvious to all new hires. The girls I hired at the travel agency all understood what we did and why we did it from day one. "You're a part of this organization now," I'd say. It's very important that employees see what they do as more than just a job.

Just as you make house guests feel welcome by getting them talking, allow new hires to freely share about themselves on their first day. No, this isn't a waste of time. Taking an extra five to fifteen minutes to get to know your new employee is a worthwhile investment. People need to be seen, heard, and understood in order to trust you and your company. And building trust right from the beginning is critical.

At my son Jeff's company, the owner has a policy that on an employee's first day, their boss or another top leader takes them out to lunch. Compare that to his previous employer, who hadn't even bothered to tell him that he got a thirty-minute lunch break every day. At the travel agency, I would ask new hires something about their childhood and about an accomplishment they were most proud of. When anyone starts a new job, they wonder why they're there, what their potential fit is, and whether others will accept them. People need some kind of answer to these questions. For new hires, those answers come in the form of *your* questions. Create an environment where you know something about your employees beyond their work history.

The Employee Policy Manual: Showing the Way

Once your employment offer is accepted and both parties have signed the position agreement, all new hires need to have access to your employee policy manual.

Don't have an employee policy manual yet? This is a separate document from your company's procedures manual. This next section will help you create your employee policy manual. In short, your employee policy manual establishes the company rules, and the procedures manual states the way you want things done. At the travel agency, I had what I called "the Somerville way," which is what I titled my procedures manual.

Build Your Employee Policy Manual

When I help small business owners draft the first version of their manual, we go over the ten essential sections.

1. Introduction
2. Joining the Organization
3. Remuneration and Benefits
4. Travel Policy
5. Vehicle Policy
6. Performance Development
7. Code of Conduct
8. Disciplinary Procedure
9. Employment-Related Policies
10. Leaving Procedure

The **Introduction** is basically orientation in print. It opens with a welcome letter from you and your leadership team; provides background on your organization; and lays out your mission, core values, and organizational chart.

Joining the Organization is your go-to for what happens as soon as someone gets hired. What forms do they have to complete? What are their working hours? How do they access the building? What's the parking situation? Is there a dress code? Who do they report to? Does their schedule change each week? If so, when and how do they find out what their hours are? How do they clock in? Where do they work, and where do they have lunch? Where is the bathroom? Answer all these basic questions here in the second essential manual section.

Remuneration and Benefits is exactly that. Describe salary and wage payments, the salary review process, deductions, and anything else employees need to know about compensation and benefits.

Travel Policy is self-explanatory. If or when employees travel, how do they book flights, hotels, and rental vehicles or public transportation? What are the parameters for using company credit cards? Lay out the expense reimbursement policy here.

Vehicle Policy has to do with use of company cars or employees' own vehicles. For example, how are traveling salespeople reimbursed? Put it in here.

A **Performance Development** system is so important it gets its own chapter (the next one). In this section, you'll describe your quarterly performance review, expected employee competencies, and any additional training and development support employees may need beyond the policy and procedures manual, such as how to access procedure training videos.

The **Code of Conduct** comprises your house rules. Just as your position agreements include noncompetition, confidentiality and copyright protection clauses, so should this manual section. Often-overlooked policies include rules for dealing with the media, giving interviews, and handling customer and employee information.

Your **Disciplinary Procedure** is a tough one. It's awkward, uncomfortable, and just plain hard. It's also one of the most important procedures in your entire business. What happens when someone breaks the rules? Put it in writing so everyone knows, and there are never surprises.

Employment-Related Policies include an equal employment opportunity policy and your company's discrimination and harassment policy, both of which should follow the letter of the law in your jurisdiction. Other policies you can put in this section include:

- Health and safety
- Leaves of absence
- Community services leave
- Jury service leave
- Alcohol and drugs use
- Internet, email, and phone
- Misuse of internet, email, and mobile phones
- Security
- Software purchases
- Abandonment of employment

The tenth essential employee manual section is your **Leaving Procedure**. When an employee quits, is terminated, or gets laid off, what happens? For employees who leave voluntarily, often requiring two weeks (or longer) notice and an exit interview and providing a written employee reference makes sense. Regardless of circumstances, however, you do need a policy covering return of company property. You don't want somebody walking out of there with your stuff with no way to get it back!

Include these ten sections in your employee manual, and you will avoid so much guesswork and so many headaches down the line.

Make sure you or someone on your team schedules time to address all these fundamentals on your new hire's first day. Because every hour you pay an employee to wait for you is an hour wasted. It's good business sense to put what matters in writing. If the biggest reason you're the best mortgage broker in town is that you call people back within fifteen minutes, then that must become a company policy. Put it in your manual so that as you build your team, your new brokers all live up to your standard.

If new hires don't know the rules, they'll make up their own. They'll make assumptions based on what they've done in the past or what they observe others doing. "Well, at my last company I got to smoke in the office." Or "Well, I saw Pam ignore a customer who walked in." The younger generation is used to having a lot more freedom. If your expectations aren't clear, your generation Y and Z employees are going to do whatever they're used to doing. Their version of "done" may not be yours.

Essentially, your employee policy manual puts you in the position of a firm parent. It articulates your great values so you can model them. It explains what it means to be part of this family. It sounds strange to compare employees to children. This analogy works because employees, like children, are our mirrors. Their attitude, behavior, and results on the job reflect our leadership. If you create an environment of high expectations right from the beginning and are not afraid of how your kids might feel about the rules, you enable those children to thrive as they grow up. Same with employees. Sometimes small business owners are afraid of their employees, and they tiptoe around their feelings. Parents who do this end up with brats.

You're the parent. This is your company. You're putting your money into it. It's your investment, your risk. So your people need to know where the line is right from day one. Even if your employee manual is still in progress, your expectations must be clear. If an employee is ten minutes late, it might not seem like a big deal to you, but you still need to have a conversation about it. Your rules are meant to be followed. Rule enforcement affects everyone else on the team. Are you a leader your people can trust to do the right thing, even when it's uncomfortable?

Up to now, we've talked about the policy manual with some mention of procedures. Your procedures are your systems, and your policies are the guiding principles that underpin those actions. Policies can be thought of as the rules or laws of your organization, Procedures are the specific action steps that you strategically design and document to deliver value to your clients and to make work better for your team. Ideally, you would document both. One policy may have several how-tos, and one procedure may link to several policies.

Your policy manual states your company rules; your procedures manual states how specifically to follow the rules.

Once you've built your employee policy manual, have other employees read through it for feedback if possible. They may find something unclear, remember something you forgot, or learn something new themselves. They'll also appreciate that you value their feedback.

As you can see, your policy and procedures manual puts your expectations in writing and prepares new team members to succeed from day one. The policy manual together with your procedures manual are the two essentials every new hire needs. They form the basis of every new hire's training. So what does this training look like? Some business owners think they have to spend eight hours a day with a new hire for weeks on end. Others tell me they don't have even five minutes to deal with this. Once orientation is over, and the employee receives their handbook and policy and procedures manual, it's goodbye. The question of your involvement in the overall training process brings us to a super important point.

Delegate, Don't Abdicate

Even though your new hire has everything they need to know in their policy handbook and procedures manual, make sure to schedule time to address all the fundamentals in person (or via video chat for remote positions) on your new hire's first day. Embrace this opportunity to meet with your new hire. This is the moment you have been waiting for—more freedom for you moving forward. Your new hire will remember their time with you; they will remember how you made them feel. Take this time to learn who they are as a person and why this job is important to them now. Don't underestimate the importance of this first "date."

If you have other employees, it's tempting to throw the new hire at someone else and expect them to bring them up to speed. *Oh my God, I finally got somebody in here. I can have a lunch break now! First time in five years.* However, small business owners need to delegate training rather than abdicating it. Abdicating is washing your hands of the responsibility, whereas delegating is training an employee to run new hires through your well-thought-out training process.

When we do small business assessments at Systems Business Coach, one of the first questions we ask is how new employees are trained. Everyone replies with a version of "Oh, someone else shows them the ropes." Few of them personally train their employees. Too busy. No time. What happens when another employee "shows the ropes" to new hires without having your policy and procedures manuals? They water down your standards. They lower the bar on the quality you expect. They can misinterpret company policy. They forget important information the new person needs to be able to do their job. I'm not implying that this is done deliberately. It happens because your senior employees are also busy. They have their own jobs to do, and now they're assigned a training role on top of their already heavy workload, most likely without any additional compensation. *Gee, thanks.* And if the employee you picked is not a trainer by nature, you've invited unnecessary tension into your company.

This is not to say that you yourself must take employees by the hand and run their training personally. The greater point is that your onboarding system—the policy and procedures manuals—guide all training. If you want to delegate the training of new hires, make sure the employee you choose is up to the task. Don't tell them at 8:45 a.m., "Hey, a new hire is coming in at nine; do you mind showing them the ropes?" Have a conversation with them well ahead of time about becoming an official company trainer. Take other projects off their plate, give them more hours, or offer them additional compensation to take on this new role. Then make sure they've thoroughly read and understood your employee policy manual and your company procedures manual. That's how you delegate this vital task.

Here's an example of how the two documents work together. A restaurant client of mine found that having both eliminated the hassle of onboarding. Thanks to the employee policy manual, all new hires knew what to wear and when to start—and not to wear perfume. And the procedures manual had clearly laid out detailed instructions for every task. This is how to plate the dessert, this is how to pour coffee, et cetera. When everyone is trained the same way, there is consistent, excellent customer service. And everyone knows what to do. Everyone is on the same team and the same page.

Update Your Manuals as Needed

Be mindful of what new hires need to know about the way you do things. Employee manuals are evolving documents. In a recent conversation with one of my own hires, the employee said, "I'm starting at ten today." Before COVID-19 sent everyone home to work out of their closets, this employee had started at 8:30 a.m. every day. I realized I had not made my expectations clear. Just because you're working remotely now doesn't mean a 10:00 a.m. start is authorized. No one authorized that. Guess what I did? I opened up an editable version of my employee policy manual and added a new section about working from home.

I smiled when I heard this story from a girlfriend who worked for a manufacturing company as their payroll administrator. She noticed there were an awful lot of employees attending funerals on Fridays. I knew where this story was going because I had heard it before from clients. In Canada, employees are entitled to paid bereavement leave. One engineer on the team had gone to three Friday funerals in the same year. It just so happened that these were all-day events. My friend brought this up to the owner, and he updated his employee policy manual's company bereavement policy. The new rule said that employees could attend whatever funeral they wanted as federal law allows. Employees' relationship with the dearly departed didn't matter. No problem. They just had to provide a copy of the obituary. The following year, there were apparently 70 percent fewer deaths.

Employee Training: Follow the Procedures Manual

Training begins the moment a new hire shows up for orientation. You've created a warm environment where they feel welcome. You've given them the two primary tools they need to find their way around your business and do the job you hired them to do. Now what?

On an employee's first day of training, give them an idea of what to expect, including when they'll be taking a break and when they'll be dismissed. Tell them how you'd like them to handle questions—ask as they arise, make notes for later, ask other employees, et cetera. Throughout their training, check in to see if they're "getting it." If a new hire tells you, "I understand," say, "OK, feed it back to me so I know that you've got this." Then if they do well, you say, "OK, you've got it. Good!" This is important because some people have arrogance around learning new things.

In addition to basing employee training on the procedures manual, I strongly recommend you supplement with video training. The biggest cost where training new hires is concerned is the time you, a manager, or another employee dedicates to training them. Video helps solve this problem. Once it's done, you can use it over and over, partially replacing costly face-to-face training with a digital alternative. Document your product tutorials, the processes from your procedures manual that cover their day-to-day tasks, and anything else that can be taught through an audiovisual medium.

One of my retail clients noticed how much time this saved her. Rather than personally train every new sales associate on everything they needed to know to sell a new product line, she spent a Saturday recording product training videos. She handed these videos over to her store manager to use for training. Now her salespeople can get right to upselling customers on new products in a few days rather than weeks or months. And she gets the day off at the beach!

If you sell products, your employees need to understand and memorize their descriptions thoroughly in order to excel. You've worked hard to develop or purchase these products, and you need to transfer your knowledge out of your head into your employees' heads and then into the customers'. Small business owners are usually the best people to sell their stuff. They are the consummate salespeople. So how does the employee know what the features, advantages, and benefits of each product are? Grab that mobile phone and hit record.

Some small business entrepreneurs get discouraged when I suggest video training because they don't know where to start. Their procedures manual is only partially assembled, and their employee policy manual is even further behind. They worry about giving the new hire a bunch of stuff to do without enough direction.

Here's how to resolve these concerns. Get your new hire to help you write the sections of the procedures manual where their responsibilities are concerned. Just because you haven't written it down doesn't mean you can't hire for it. And ultimately, you review anything a new hire documents about their job before making it official.

The question is, what should new hires document? If you or your employees do X task on a regular basis, X task goes in your procedures manual. For retail businesses, that could include how to open the store, how to close, how to greet customers, how to restock a shelf, where to put products in the back, how to manage inventory, how to pack and ship, and so on. A well-trained new hire can read the procedures manual, complete their training, and perform their duties at or above the standards you set right away because everything was explained to them step-by-step with no step skipped.

Going forward, every employee who helps document their role for your procedures manual or "the way we do things" is an ideal trainer for anyone else you hire to work alongside them. You may have heard that people retain 10 percent of what you tell them and 90 percent of what they teach. Welcome to Adult Learning 101! The fastest way to train employees effectively is to ask them to document what they do as part of their job. This puts them in the mindset of a trainer, needing to meticulously record anything and everything about their job so the next person can do it at the same standard you expect. As a result, that employee reaches a new level of proficiency they otherwise would not have.

If you have someone else training new employees, you and your trainer have to stay in communication. Dialogue about what they're noticing. What's working well? What are they concerned about? Overall, be involved enough to see if this individual is going to work out or not. If not, consider letting them go sooner than later. During a new hire's first ninety days, look for their strengths and also for any red flags that made it through the hiring process unseen. You already know the cost of keeping someone you know won't work out.

A Learning Organization: Acknowledge New Employee Ideas

Keep your training strict while you, the owner, and therefore the business itself are constantly learning. As the saying goes, the only thing that doesn't change is change. Just because you say today that we're all wearing blue ties doesn't mean that tomorrow we're going to wear blue ties. We're all learning, changing, and improving together. Keep in mind that new employees have ideas too.

"I noticed you're using version 2.1. Did you know there's a version 4.0?" a new hire says. "I can download and configure the update for you."

"Great," you say. "I appreciate you bringing that up. I'll put you in charge of leading that project and getting everyone else on the team trained to use the new version. While you are at it, can you update the section of the procedures manual related to that software?"

That's continuous improvement. We want to get better. We want to improve. We want the business to grow. We want you to grow here. We want your responsibilities and your compensation to increase. Training is a two-way street. You're training employees to be responsible for their roles. You're teaching them your current measure of success. "Meet this standard day in and day out, and you get to promote yourself." A well-trained employee is essentially in control of their future. They're always looking for ways to promote themselves by suggesting ways to do the job smarter, faster, and cheaper. Put this in your procedures manual. Go back to your position agreements and make sure they say that if employees have suggestions or ideas, the company welcomes them.

This is what it means to be a learning organization. There is "the way you do things around here," and part of that way is finding new ways to do them better. In a learning organization, even a strict, fine-tuned process is open to improvement. Ingrain this into your employees so they understand the purpose of their work, the point of getting it done, and any way it could be done better. Employees who accept your vision and share your values will bring these ideas to you.

In a learning organization, the systems everyone is expected to follow actually permit incredible creativity. For example, a restaurateur client hired a new employee who suggested moving a section of tables because she and other servers kept bumping into them. Many small business owners onboarding tech-savvy employees would be wise to welcome suggestions on new software that the employee used somewhere else to save time and money.

Still, when you bring employees on, you need to be firm in your onboarding. Stick with the system; let employees try it your way first. Again, that doesn't mean processes will always be that rigid. Your employees simply need a starting point. They need to learn the basics before they can jump in, see what's wrong, and change it. Mastery, then improvement.

You can acknowledge an employee's idea without agreeing to it. For example, a small business coach my organization certified came to me with an idea for a new intake form. She didn't know I had already tried that, and it didn't work. I didn't shut her down, though. Continuous improvement means being open and curious, even to ideas you don't like at first. So I told her, "Let's try it this way first."

She did. It worked. That's what happens when you have operations systems documented, and employees follow them. And when your new hire onboarding and training system is in place, you ensure that your team does things the way you want them done—right.

CHAPTER 7
TEAM:
SOLVING PEOPLE PROBLEMS

Let me tell you about a small business owner named Vincent. Vincent has always been driven and is now very wealthy. Because of a great economy, a little luck, and some sound business decisions, his company has grown beyond his wildest dream. With over 150 employees, it's hard for him to remember what it was like back when he was just starting out. With all this success, you may assume that Vincent must be a great leader. The exact opposite is true.

Vincent is a bully. He yells when he's mad. His staff is afraid of him and rarely confides in him. Because he's so busy, he's developed the habit of walking down the office hallway once a week reminding each worker of their transgressions, making them feel bad if they didn't do exactly what was requested (even if they had good reason). Rarely does this walk include any positive feedback.

Like Scrooge, Vincent never willingly gives out raises or praise and expects his team to give 150 percent all the time, no matter what. If they don't ask for help, he doesn't give it. And if they do ask, he provides only the bare minimum to save money. Only when a key employee gives their resignation does he open his eyes, and by then, the damage to these relationships has already been done. Many of Vincent's employees are struggling. Vincent doesn't see the damage he's caused the people who work for him or the opportunities he's lost because of his negativity.

People problems go both ways. If you came to this chapter hoping I'd show you how to "fix" your employees, then *you* might be the problem. When you berate an employee like Vincent does, it's a death sentence for that relationship.

I once worked for a "Vincent" at an automobile insurance company. I was a top-ten salesperson in the province for several years in a row. My boss was a mean and inconsiderate person. I had recently separated from my spouse at the time and was living on a friend's couch. My manager never asked how I was doing or if I needed anything. She couldn't be bothered to notice.

It was a difficult time, so I often got to work three to five minutes after 9:00. Not every day. Maybe one or two times a week. To (over)compensate, I stayed until 7:00 or 8:00 p.m. every night.

My performance review that year said nothing about all the sales I'd made that filled the organization's pockets with profit. In fact, it mentioned nothing that I had done right. It was all about what I was doing wrong. My manager had page after page about my handwriting, my messy desk, and my tardiness. I was forced to defend my job to her boss, the area manager. The next day, I walked into the office at 9:03 to find the top boss sitting at my desk.

"We're going to have a talk," he said. A copy of my performance review lay open in front of him. "About your punishment." Several other employees were in earshot. They turned and stared at me.

Punishment. You take a top-ten producer who works ten- and eleven-hour days, and you punish her? This punishment, he decided, was moving me out of my local office to a location a thirty-five-minute drive from my home across a busy toll bridge. How was that going to help me get to work on time? No one ever asked me what I had going on in my life that caused me to show up a few minutes late. No one gave me warning that my hours worked would have consequences. And no one ever complimented me on the job I was doing.

After that meeting with the owner, I took a sick leave and left. That event traumatized me for years. No one there understood the importance of continuous improvement. They brought in all this horsepower and used it to their detriment. The boss didn't care to listen.

Fast forward thirty-five years, and that insurance company still has the same culture. I know because my cousin worked there after I did. The (same) management has employees do all these "rah-rah" activities to "build culture." Everyone has to stop for twenty minutes three times a week for some mandatory activity. At the same time, they don't give people the resources they need to do their job. Never once did anyone express appreciation for the skills my cousin brought to the table. She found ways to save the company time and money, yet nobody cared to take her advice. Once she caught a bookkeeping mistake that had resulted in senior management being *very* overpaid. She brought it up to her manager.

He didn't care because the senior managers were his friends. In the same meeting during which she pointed out the mistake and how much it was costing the organization's bottom line, the manager found time to scold her for being behind on her work. She felt crushed and quit.

Why am I sharing how this business made us feel? Because poorly performing management devastates the employees unfortunate enough to work for them as well as the business itself. The good, smart people simply leave.

So What's the Real Problem Here?

As the leader of your small business, you will face many problems that you need to solve on a daily basis. Dealing with these challenges is stressful, time-consuming, frustrating, and demotivating. Especially since you didn't sign up to be the chief problem solver of everyone's life.

What separates great leaders from horrible bosses is not the number of problems they face. It's how they respond. The insurance company couldn't be bothered to consider the cause of my lateness. No questions, no offers to help, no suggestions for improvement. Just condemnation. Remember, a true leader inspires people to do their best; the insurance company did the opposite, to the point that my cousin and I both left. We moved on to help different companies make and save more money. Their loss.

The fact is that "problem employees" like Five-Minutes-Late-Beverlee are not the real issue in organizations. Most of the time, the people aren't the problem —it's the business they're brought into. You can change the people, but if you haven't fixed the system, the same thing will likely happen again with the next employee. What system are these people working within that's causing the problems? Maybe employees aren't getting reports done on time, for example. You want something from your people, and you're not getting it. What else is going on? Make assumptions about the employee, and you may soon find yourself looking for a new one.

If you're dealing with more people problems than you'd like, I recommend keeping your employees, clearing up your expectations, finding and removing any ambiguity, improving your systems, changing offices, buying essential software, upgrading your equipment, and whatever else sets your employees and your business up for success.

Perhaps the work environment is the problem. Are employees expected to produce optimal results in subpar conditions? For example, I worked with the owner of a horticulture gift company who complained about her workers taking too long and making too many errors while making their products. Upon observation, I noticed not only how far they needed to walk to reach each element of the product, but also that they had to bend down two or three times to complete the process. The problem wasn't employee productivity; it was a workflow issue. Simply moving those parts to within employees' reach solved the issues.

Deming[12] famously remarked, "Eighty-five percent of the reasons for failure are deficiencies in the systems and process rather than the employee. The role of management is to change the process rather than badgering individuals to do better." Later in his life, he updated his own quote to "The system that people work in and the interaction with people may account for ninety or ninety-five percent of performance."

I see exactly this play out in organizations of all sizes in all industries. The owner is convinced there's a people problem when, in reality, it's their systems.

A good friend of mine works for a "Vincent" who thinks he has a people problem. My friend has worked there for over ten years. She's added several million dollars' worth of value to the company. She's a top performer, loves the work, and is highly respected in the industry, yet she's considered a problem. Why? In this case, her boss has one set of expectations, and she (based on her own values) has another. Even though the work is getting done on time and on budget, the way the work is being performed is causing friction and frustration for her boss. When her boss told her to "focus," my friend asked me, "Focus on what?" She later learned that it was better to do less detailed work, even though she knew it would save the company money, rather than risk facing the anger of her boss.

While onboarding a new client, I interviewed one of his key employees. She described my new client as a "Vincent" as well. She calls her company's weekly meetings the penalty box, and every Monday, they all take a beating. At these check-in meetings with the boss, all the boss cares about is what they're doing wrong. Never once has he asked, "What are you proud of this week? What are your ideas? How can we improve?" Questions like these would go a long way toward gaining more support from his team. Then he could bring up the issues that need addressing. "So I noticed that this re-

---

12   Paul Jocelyn (@PaulJocelyn), "'Eighty-five percent of the reasons for failure are deficiencies in the systems and process rather than the employee. The role of management is to change the process rather than badgering individuals to do better.' W. Edwards Deming," Twitter post, February 10, 2022, https://twitter.com/PaulJocelyn/status/1491678879932686343.

port's not done. What support do you need to get it finished? What barriers are getting in the way?" This type of discussion would have gotten my client some solid, decent, reasonable facts from her employees.

The employee I interviewed also mentioned that when her mom was dying and eventually passed away the previous year, no one in the company even acknowledged it. She's worked for this company for seventeen years, and no one sent a card. No one showed up at the funeral. At least no one tried to stop her from taking bereavement leave, which is her right under Canadian law. Less than a week after the funeral, her boss gave her a new major project to manage after someone quit. She shared with me that since then, she hasn't cared about the company as much as she used to.

Beware the Inner Circle Effect

You want your employees to feel like they're part of a team. So how does a good-hearted founder like you turn into a Vincent? This most often happens when there's no performance management system in the organization. Instead, there is only "founder's syndrome."[13] This appears when the owner has a disproportionate amount of power and influence on how things are done. Everything—every decision, every raise, every detail of every job—is reviewed and managed by you, the founder. It is exhausting, it will prevent your company from growing, and it causes people problems.

Have you noticed how some owners tend to hire only family or friends? They have an authoritative command-and-control perspective of their business, giving privilege only to senior management. I get it. When you only have a few employees, you can all be buddies. It's what makes working in a small business great. Until it doesn't.

At some point in your company's growth, you need to bring in some structure to help you with your people. You need human resources systems in place to ensure that all people feel valued. You may no longer be able to have the entire company show up in your backyard for a swim or take everyone with you on vacation. At the same time, it becomes painfully obvious to everyone whom you include and whom you leave out. You have created a people problem.

---

13   Stephen Block and Steven Rosenberg, "Toward an Understanding of Founder's Syndrome: An Assessment of Power and Privilege Among Founders of NonProfit Organizations," *Nonprofit Management and Leadership 12, no. 4* (June 2002): 353–368, https://www.researchgate.net/publication/227952324_Toward_an_Understanding_of_Founder%27s_Syndrome_An_Assessment_of_Power_and_Privilege_Among_Founders_of_NonProfit_Organizations.

It's only natural for a small business to grow. As you do, prune and get rid of what doesn't work for everyone's benefit. My florist client bought expensive, high-quality company apparel for her daughters who had started the business with her. As the business grew and the owner hired more staff, she gave them cheap jackets while continuing to give family members something better. This sent the message "There's an inner circle here, and you're not in it."

Owners must be careful about an inner circle and its perceptions. It's common for tight-knit relationships to form around a business owner and the core team, intentionally or unintentionally. As other employees come along, they are, by default, *not* in the inner circle. It feels right that only the people you can count on should have access to you. After all, these are the ones you rely on the most. The ones you like. However, if you want buy-in from your whole team, you have to make sure everyone feels like part of the inner circle. Everyone needs to feel valued. Think about the burger flippers at McDonald's. They might not be perceived as an important part of the team. But if those burgers aren't grilled correctly, nothing else happening in the organization matters. Whether the top manager or the janitor, we must all be included. We're all part of making this business work, together. Everybody's important. Anyone you leave out of your inner circle may become a source of problems.

All employees want to contribute to the success of the organization. Chaos gets in the way. Edgar Schein[14] asks, "What are you systemically paying attention to?" I like to ask my owners the same question. The systems and structure of the business are important. So are your relationships with your employees. It's things like how you handle praise, how you play favorites, how you fight with your partner or manager, and how you hand out raises that cause the most challenges in an organization.

Maybe your most productive employee is an ass. You need him because he makes you a lot of money. Let his detrimental behavior slide, and you're showing your other employees that you value productivity more than people. How does that contribute to your people problems? Nobody wants to work with the ass. Put a calm, cool, collected guy to work with the favorite employee, and he'll throw the nice guy under the bus the first chance he gets.

If there are people problems in your organization, and if people are not behaving properly (or leaving), there could be something else going on. Let's say you have six women working together, and two of them are

---

14   Edgar Schein, *Organizational Culture and Leadership* 4th ed. (San Francisco: Jossey-Bass, 2010), 237.

going out for secret smoke breaks. While the two smokers are out smoking, the other four are picking up the slack. These same smoking women never take their turns emptying the break room dishwasher. If you don't deal with these two problem employees, the good ones are going to quit.

On par with missing or broken systems, abdication of leadership is the cause of most people problems. When I first started working with the owner of a manufacturing company, I learned that he had been so fed up with the people problems, he had hired a general manager named Adam. He abdicated his responsibilities to the new GM, and worse, he didn't tell his employees about him until Adam's first day. Adam had promised him the world and came in and did nothing. He ate pizza at his desk all day, leaving the dirty boxes stacked up behind him, and started cutting the budget without asking any questions. Not only did he create instant chaos; he also destroyed the already damaged morale of everyone in the company.

When you have a really small business, you can keep an eye on everybody. But when it starts to get bigger, you don't always know what people are doing. You start getting worried, so you rely on your inner circle even more, which ends up alienating others because they feel you don't trust them. Maybe you even enforce rules more strictly with them while letting your inner circle slide. Then what?

What If There Is a Problem?

At some point, even your besties are going to do something wrong. A big one is employees who start showing up late.

This is a tricky one to write about. On the one hand, I quit my own job after being punished for being late. On the other hand, it's the most common people problem I hear about from clients. Barring a one-off personal crisis, recurring disrespect for start times needs to be dealt with. It's often a result of the owner not setting clear expectations or not being clear on what will happen if their expectations aren't met. If the employee gets away with being late Monday, Tuesday, and Wednesday and nothing happens, why would they ever bother to show up on time?

Having policies and procedures in place before there's a problem is important, as is working with the individual to create a flexible work schedule that they can commit to. So decide right now. Is lateness a problem or not? If it's a problem, then a system needs to be established and agreed upon between you and your employees. If it's not a problem, then a different system needs to be established. For example, maybe employees can work seven hours, four hours, thirteen hours, or any hours they want, as long as they produce the top sales you're looking for. Decide what's important and clearly communicate it to your entire staff.

Other common problems include poor employee training, unwashed dishes in the sink, and dress code violations. Is your dress code clear? Maybe the policy manual says white shirt and black pants, but nowhere do you state that shirts must be tucked in with no underwear visible. I had a restaurateur client whose female employees were wearing thong underwear sticking out of the back of their pants. Sure, it was trendy but not professional. The employees thought it was acceptable because it wasn't specifically prohibited in the dress code.

What about when someone doesn't meet a sales quota? If multiple employees have to share an assistant, maybe expectations aren't shared about what needs to happen. Often, a competition for resources can cause problems, as can inconsistency between employees in the way things are done. In her book *Thinking in Systems*,[15] Donella Meadows describes this as a systems trap. "Systems structured in ways that produce truly problematic behavior; they cause us great trouble." When there is a limited shared resource (like an overworked assistant) leading to systems failure, she refers to it as "the tragedy of the commons."

One of my clients owns an apparel shop that's been around for twenty-five years. Their favorite employee, the office manager, still does everything by hand. I understand they're trying to accommodate her. Yet when they say yes to her, they're saying no to all the other employees who can't do their jobs properly because the office manager isn't in this century.

Gossips and Debbie Downers are also a problem. Unpleasant attitudes that don't technically break any rules are still no fun to have around. This ties back to your hiring process. Let a problem employee rule your roost, and the damage is done before you realize it. Often small business owners let troubling behavior like this slide when the offending employee is making them a lot of money. Or when the offender is their mother-in-law. That employee essentially holds their business ransom. Are you willing to pay that price? It would be great if you could change their behavior. Can you? Not really. If someone gossips, the only way to stop them is through other employees who can keep them in check. You can have a team meet-

---

15   Donella Meadows, *Thinking in Systems*, ed. Diana Wright (White River Junction, VT: Chelsea Green Publishing, 2008), 111.

ing to address the issue without pointing fingers so everyone knows what the standard is. You can even ask the team, "What are we going to do about gossip? How can we handle it?" Or "How does gossiping align with our company values?" This is effective leadership in action. A too-busy owner would not hold a meeting to address the gossip or would make the offending employee feel confronted.

Bottom line: remember that most people are generally good. If showing up for work ten minutes before a shift in uniform is essential, that needs to be clearly communicated. Right from day one. Then decide what will happen if those expectations aren't met. Do you have a "three strikes" policy? A written or verbal warning? Docking of pay? Will the offender be suspended or fired? Make clear decisions and communicate them to your employees. Include these rules and the consequences of breaking them in your employee policy manual.

Is the Problem Worth Fixing?

Is correcting a problem employee worth it? This question must also be asked. We live in the real world where a thousand and one things come at you every minute. The last thing you need is to take two hours out of your day to plan and hold a meeting about Becky's underwear. Ideally, you would resolve every people problem as soon as it arises; however, we must be practical.

To decide whether or not to invest time, effort, and even money into correcting a people problem, ask yourself a simple question: What's the impact? If a hot-tempered manager is causing turnover, hurting your reputation, and costing you money, that must be dealt with. If your night-shift janitor cusses every other word, smells like cigarettes, and never interacts with customers, you might want to make the decision to let it slide. Or not. I don't know. Only you do. Whatever your decision, *you* must make it. Don't abdicate.

Even when you have clear expectations and enforced consequences, it doesn't mean you won't get bad eggs. Don't be afraid to fire. When you really do have a problem, make sure you document it. Laws in every state, province, and country make it clear what justification you need to let an employee go. Take this seriously by writing down the transgression and getting the offender to sign the document. Then figure out how and why it happened. What can you do to make sure it doesn't happen again?

As a leader, you're trying to get things done. You feel like people might be letting you down, but you don't really know without a performance management system. So here's how to build one.

Designing Your Performance Management System

Dr. W. Edwards Deming understood the performance management process way back in the 1950s.

The merit rating [also called performance management] nourishes short-term performance, annihilates long-term planning, builds fear, demolishes teamwork, [and] nourishes rivalry and politics. It leaves people bitter, crushed, bruised, battered, desolate, despondent, dejected, feeling inferior, some even depressed, unfit for work for weeks after receipt of rating, unable to comprehend why they are inferior. It is unfair, as it ascribes to the people in a group differences that may be caused totally by the system that they work in.

The idea of a merit rating is alluring. The sound of the words captivates the imagination: pay for what you get; get what you pay for; motivate people to do their best, for their own good.

The effect is exactly the opposite of what the words promise. Everyone propels himself forward, or tries to, for his own good, on his own life preserver. The organization is the loser. The merit rating rewards people that conform to the system. It does not reward attempts to improve the system.[16]

At Systems Business Coach, I currently have a team of four. They're all working from home, and I always know what three of them are doing. But the fourth one, a summer student, wasn't following my system of documenting what she was working on every day. I have a grant for hiring her, so I told her, "This system is part of the grant. I absolutely need this documentation." Was her not following my system my fault rather than hers? Yes. She wasn't meeting my performance expectations because I only thought I had set them—in reality, she needed more clarity. A successful performance management system isn't just me telling her what to do. It's two-way open communication.

The last thing you want is a good employee getting into trouble because nobody told them the right way to do things. A Gallup poll shows

16   William Edwards Deming, *Out of the Crisis* (Cambridge, MA: MIT Press, 1982), 102.

that only about half of employees strongly agree that they know what is expected of them. Most people do their best when they know what's expected. Small business owners with a clear vision, values, and company promise are in the best position to set those expectations.

Like your employee policy and procedures manuals, your performance management system puts everyone on the same page. Performance management is all about keeping an open line of communication and making sure your employees are getting what they need to succeed. It is the part of any system called a "feedback loop" that both employer and employee can count on to gather data to move forward together. What are their goals? What are your goals for them? Create a system to communicate those expectations. Employers tend to do this once a year, which is not often enough. A lot of organizations have quarterly goals for their employees. What do the next three months look like? Who's going to check in with your employees to see if they're on track?

Performance management is a two-way conversation. What would make it easier for you to do your job? How else could you contribute to the company? Do you need a bigger office, a smaller office, or a home office setup? Do you need additional training? Who on the team could you pair up with to better reach your goals?

Whether it's once a quarter, once a month, once a week, or every day, let's look at what a performance management system could look like for your organization.

Measuring Performance Fairly

A performance management system isn't just about promotions and raises. How you compensate people is one thing. How they perform every day is different from a once-a-year meeting to see if they checked a bunch of boxes and are going to get an automatic raise. The process of employee performance management needs to be integrated into the culture of your company.

Create opportunities for feedback to and from your team members. Model appreciative dialogue in which you share what's going well and ask what could be better. Focus on a shared vision of what can be accomplished by working together. Listen first. Learn about employee frustrations and take action on anything getting in the way of their performance. People don't like performance reviews any more than they liked report cards in school. Considering how humans are wired, these reviews are counterproductive unless the individual is only getting praise. Performance reviews cause anxiety and fear in the person being reviewed. There are more effective ways to measure performance. What works better is a yearly written performance plan with which you sit down together and collaboratively establish personal goals that support the company's objectives.

The most effective way to measure the past and plan for the future is to involve your employees in the process. Try asking any of the following questions:

- How has the last year been for you working here and why?

- What do you consider your most important achievements?

- What are the things you like most about working for this organization?

- What elements of your job do you find the most challenging?

- What elements of your job interest you the most? What bores you?

- What would make your job better?

- What do you consider your most important goals and tasks in the next year/next three months?

- What actions could be taken to improve your performance in your current position by you and your boss?

- What kind of work or job would you like to be doing in one/two/ five years' time?

- What sort of training/experience would benefit you in the next year? (Name any specific training programs you would be willing to let them take.)

- In light of your current capabilities and your future growth and/or job aspirations, what activities and tasks would you like to focus on during the next year?

Communicate expectations clearly and work together to set performance goals. As the leader of the business, create a similar plan for yourself and review it with someone on your team. From that plan, you'll be able to create performance goals that inspire both the employee and the boss. This delegates the responsibility of good performance to the employee, getting it off your shoulders. If you don't delegate any authority, you're going to be stuck doing everything. Remind employees of their responsibility—and that they have the authority to meet it. When you do this, you ensure that everyone feels like part of the team.

CHAPTER 8

APPRECIATIVE INQUIRY:
MAKE MEETINGS MATTER

Most small businesses don't have regular staff meetings. Why? Because they just don't want to. Considering what happens in most meetings, I can understand why. Little problems often come up in both team and company-wide meetings when you're really there to talk about the bigger picture. Little complaints make the meeting drag on. Before you know it, you're an hour into a thirty-minute meeting, and you still haven't gotten to your meeting agenda because everyone wants to talk about their problems. They get caught in the traps of blaming, shaming, and lording their grievances over others. It's no wonder most business owners see these meetings as an absolute frustration.

Usually, meetings are only held when there's a problem. When my cousin got called to a meeting at the insurance company, her supervisor would just tell her what the problem was and ask her what she was going to do about it. That was it. Unfortunately, that's a very common meeting model.

Marilee Adams, in her brilliant *Change Your Questions, Change Your Life*, describes this model as "Results of Judger Questions."[17] With this model, you end up:

- With a mood of pessimism, stress, and limitation
- With a mindset that's judgmental, reactive, inflexible
- Relating with attack or defensive behaviors

These meetings are like going to court to be judged. It doesn't have to be that way. Soon, you'll learn about the superior alternative to judg-

---

17   Marilee Adams, *Change Your Questions, Change Your Life: 10 Powerful Tools for Life and Work*, 2nd ed. (San Francisco: Berrett-Koehler Publishers, 2009), https://experiencelife. lifetime.life/wp-content/uploads/2021/06/CM_InquiryInstitute_2011.pdf.

ment—appreciative inquiry (AI). AI encourages curiosity into what is working. The results, to paraphrase Adams, are:

- A mood of optimism, hope, and possibilities
- A mindset that's thoughtful, understanding, flexible
- Relating that is connected and collaborative

Appreciative inquiry asks you to stop focusing on what is wrong and start working together to build toward what you, the owner, and your team want. When you're only focused on the problem, you're angry, upset, and frustrated. *Hey, we need to have a meeting.* It's a light-in-the-face interrogation. It's awkward because we don't like having to sit in front of someone. As the business owner, we feel like we have to tell our employees what they're doing wrong. That's uncomfortable. Think about all the meetings you had with your kids when something was going wrong. You sat them down and told them they *will* have a curfew, and they *will* obey you or else. This attitude doesn't have a place in our workforce.

A public staff meeting is no place for humiliation. Remember the meeting that made me resign from the automobile insurance company? What was the purpose of that meeting? Did the manager want to get rid of me, to humiliate me, to discipline me? His purpose should have been to see what was going on and how he could support me in having a better outcome next month. That should have been a closed-doors conversation. He could even have offered me a couple of sessions with a coach to help get me back on track. The cost of losing a top salesperson is huge for any organization.

Often, business owners get caught on the receiving end of grievances. People bring who they are into their work. If someone had a difficult childhood, they may always play the victim. For example, your employee Luke might say, "I can't get this project done because Josie never listens to me. She does the spreadsheets; she never answers the phone. I never get the information from the supervisors I need." Blame, blame, blame. As the owner, you feel like you need to have all the answers. Yet you don't know who to believe or whose side to take. So you talk to Josie, who blames Luke and his sour attitude. Then you're right back where you started. Round and round the blame circle spins.

When meetings aren't stirring up negative emotions, they're often just wasting time. Many meetings I've attended at various companies and not-for-profit boards were just boring lectures. The chairperson was checking the meeting off their list to make it look like they were in charge and getting things done. Nothing got done because the leaders who called the meetings were either not prepared or not really interested in others' contributions.

This takes me back to that insurance company I worked for. I was hearing through the grapevine that the managers were talking about my senior day trip project for months at their weekly meetings. One day, my supervisor called me into a meeting and told me to cancel all my future bookings on this project, which had been a great way for me to find new customers. I was just told to stop immediately. No explanation. I knew what was coming, so I went into this meeting prepared with numbers.

"We're a five-division company now," I told him. "I've been putting three hundred and twenty local seniors on these day tours per season. I'm only charging twenty bucks a person, which just covers our cost. We're consistently selling out. Yes, it is taking me out of the office once a month, but out of those seniors, one hundred and fifty have purchased other full revenue trips from me. More than half are new auto insurance clients. And over seventy bought home insurance. So my sixty-four-hundred-dollar senior trip project is worth one-point-two million dollars to the company." Not only did my supervisor look uninformed while listening with a blank stare, but he also kept his position, and the trips were canceled.

There are two main takeaways from this story:

1. Don't have meetings if you're not interested in hearing contributions from people you're meeting with.

2. Have all stakeholders included in your meetings so you're discussing facts, not fiction.

Let's do the math on how much money pointless meetings can waste. Say we have a weekly one-hour staff meeting scheduled. We go over that time, as meetings usually do, and end up with a two-hour meeting. The eleven people there are paid an average of $25 an hour. A one-hour meeting that should have cost $275 now costs $500. Do that every week for a year, and we've wasted $14,300. That number is even higher if staff meetings are held after hours when overtime pay is required. Is this an effective investment? No, especially not if the owner spends those two hours venting to employees, or employees spend them complaining. Do you want a motivating meeting with a positive outcome or a confrontational meeting that stirs up negative feelings?

If we view these meetings through the lens of systems, what do we realize? Those awkward, costly meetings indicate a missing or broken system. It's not your fault, and it's not your employees' fault. Even if it feels like the people are the problem, the system is the real problem. For example, I have a client who ends up talking during his whole meeting. It's awkward. She barely pauses for air. There's no engagement, even though people are dying to have input. If she had a way to plan her meetings so that everyone who attends can contribute positively to the organization, productivity would improve.

Fortunately, there is such a system, and it's proven to be an empowering framework to get everyone on the same page, motivate employees to take ownership of their work, and make those meetings count. It's called appreciative inquiry.

Appreciative Inquiry: A System to Make Meetings Matter

Appreciative inquiry is an affirmative approach to solving problems and generating positive change. AI is based on the premise that you can't solve problems by focusing your attention on them. Instead, look only at what is good about what you have and what it is possible to create in your future. Every organization does *something* right—those things that give it life when it's most effective, successful, and connected in healthy ways to its team members, stakeholders, and communities. AI eliminates blaming, shaming, and ruminating over details of past problems.

Appreciative inquiry enables you to leverage your leadership to bring positive solutions to even the most complex challenges—without all the negative drama. When we stop spending our time looking at problems and blaming our team for what's wrong (or allowing them to pin the fault on each other), we can create positive change. Appreciative inquiry stops the fighting. It stops the blaming. It stops the arguing. It stops people from feeling left out. There is no "us against them"; it's "us against the world." AI positively changes attitudes, behaviors, and practices through appreciative conversations and relationships. How? By asking positive strength-based questions about what is good, what is working well, and what else is possible. These conversations will help you and your team members create the best possible future.

Appreciative inquiry is useful in every interaction you'll ever have in your personal and professional life. In your small business, you can use AI to engage your team, create systems, solve problems, create new products, and take your company to a whole new level of growth.

The model of appreciative inquiry I teach small business owners fits perfectly into meetings, transforming them from angst-ridden time wasters into relationship-building experiences that move everyone toward greater prosperity. Instead of scheduling meetings only when you "need to talk" or skipping them altogether, you can use AI to make meetings an asset for your culture.

The Four Stages of Better Meetings

Appreciative inquiry is a four-step process of setting a purposeful agenda for any meeting. Every meeting agenda includes what you're trying to accomplish, who's the best person or people to get it done, and who's going to walk out of the meeting with the authority and responsibility to make it happen. Appreciative meetings ensure everyone knows what happens next.

Appreciative inquiry begins before you start your meeting. What's the purpose of the meeting? The human brain can only look in one direction at a time, negative or positive. Which direction do you want your employees looking?

If you've scheduled a meeting every week with your staff and you're not prepared, you don't have a purpose for that meeting. Either find a purpose for the meeting or cancel it. Don't meet for the sake of meeting. Don't have people sitting there just for the sake of sitting there.

If you're going to have a meeting with a purpose, people need to know what that purpose is and when the meeting is ahead of time, and they need to show up. I got one of my corporate clients to create a new reporting system with scheduled meetings with his divisions, but then he'd let people not show up. He neglected to share why these meetings were important and how these meetings were going to positively affect those expected to attend.

Ultimately, you want a positive outcome from your time spent. Do you need to meet about that issue that's bothering you? Maybe, maybe not. Perhaps your staff simply requires the knowledge to have their reports to you every Friday by five, another essential system we'll get into shortly. If there's an issue with only one employee, schedule a one-on-one conversation. At that meeting, be open to receiving feedback. If you as the boss are angry and always looking at what's wrong, no one will want to be honest with you. It's not about focusing on the problem; it's about solving the problem together. Figure out what system is missing or broken and discuss ways to delegate responsibility and authority to build or fix that system.

So, you know the purpose of your meeting and what outcome you want from it. Everyone knows when the meeting is and shows up to it. It's go time. Now what?

Appreciative Inquiry Stage One: Discovery

The very beginning of your meeting is the discovery stage. Set the tone for the meeting by appreciating what's going well. When the purpose of your meeting is to face a challenge, begin by identifying everything that is good and positive related to what you'll be discussing. What we focus on grows. There's no room in the discovery stage to focus on the negative reasons you're meeting. Only determine all the good things that you have to work with. Regardless of the size of the challenge, you can always find positive elements.

For example, let's say you're in the boardroom with your managers and site supervisors. Prior to the meeting, everyone was up in arms about delays and cost overruns on one of the biggest jobs you've ever been awarded. Appreciative questions to lower the tension in the discovery stage could include:

- What's good about this situation?
- What elements of this job are we doing well?
- Where are we winning?
- What have we learned so far that will help us get this job back on track?
- Where are our strengths?

To avoid meetings that go over and drag on, you can state clear expectations of how you'd like your questions answered. For example, each staff member gets one or two minutes to answer. Be consistent. Set and keep the same expectation for each stage of your meeting.

Appreciative Inquiry Stage Two: Dream

Next we enter the dream stage. Imagine what could be and discuss your preferred future with your team. The dream stage has no limitations. If you could have anything you want in this situation, what would it be? Assume no idea is "dumb." Imagine all the possibilities in a positive future. Describe them in detail. AI questions to guide your team in the dream stage include:

- What are all the resolution options for this challenge?

- What is an ideal outcome?

- What could it look like?

- What individual contributions can we make to improve this situation?

- What else do we need to think about?

- What best practices can we adopt to move us forward?

- What support do you need to get this done?

- What are we proud of that we can build on?

- What does getting this job completed successfully look like?

Notice you're not asking accusatory questions like, "Why didn't you do that already?" or "What are you going to do about it?" Instead, you're asking, "What do we want the solution to look like?" and "What systems could we build or improve on that would alleviate this problem and give you the support you need?"

Let's take one of my favorite examples: bathrooms that need to be cleaned. If the owner finds herself going in to scrub toilets, sinks, and floors every night, the owner can call a special meeting. She can ask, "What do we all want the bathrooms to look like?" and "What would be an ideal system that would ensure the bathrooms get cleaned so I don't have to stay till ten every night?"

During COVID-19, a client had this exact situation. Sales of their hand sanitizers exploded. Business was great, and no one had time to clean the bathrooms. The resolution was simple—bring someone in temporarily every night to clean the bathrooms. Just like that, a huge daily stress on the owner was gone. All it took was an appreciative meeting.

Appreciative Inquiry Stage Three: Design

In the design stage, you determine what needs to happen and decide the direction to go. Using your ideas from the dream stage, choose actions that will move you forward. This is where you'll want to identify and design any new systems to support your ideal future. Take everyone's voices into account when designing the future. Design questions could include:

- Which idea(s) will we choose to move forward with?

- What specific actions will we take to complete this job profitably as planned?

- What systems do we need to strengthen to ensure our desired outcomes? What does that look like?

- What are the exact steps to build an ideal system?

Appreciative Inquiry Stage Four: Destiny

In the destiny stage, create what your future will be. You and your team have a dream. You've made the decision to make it happen. This is the "just do it" phase of AI. You're giving everyone a shared responsibility to put a plan together and holding them accountable to get it done, rather than berating them over unaccomplished tasks or humiliating them over unsolved problems. To commit to your shared destiny, ask:

- What needs to happen now to put this into practice?

- What can everyone commit to doing?

- What support can we give each other?

Wrap up every appreciative meeting with a call to action—tell employees they have the authority and responsibility to do what was decided during the meeting and report back.

Appreciative Meeting Structures: My Two Recommendations

How long your meetings are or when you hold them matters much less than how you run them. Appreciative inquiry covers the how. That said, I'm a fan of two meeting structures: **scrums** and **huddles**.

Scrums

Scrums are thirty-minute meetings dedicated to getting projects that are close to being done actually done. Scrums give employees the authority to tell you what they need to close the loop. The last thing you want is more work to come back to you. It's their job. Ask them what they need to do it.

At Systems Business Coach, we hold two scrum meetings a week. Because we're a small team, we meet every Monday and Thursday for a short thirty minutes. Expectations are clear. We don't have a huge infrastructure. We're innovating, and we have a lot of things coming our way. What we were going to do three months ago is different from what we're doing now. We go in knowing the outcome we want from each scrum. Appreciative inquiry allows us to do just that.

Daily Huddle

I learned about the daily huddle meeting framework from Brian Scudamore of 1-800-GOT-JUNK. At their head office, called the Junktion, they call a company-wide daily meeting at ten minutes after ten for ten minutes. (10/10/10). Based on a framework they learned from Verne Harnish of *Mastering the Rockefeller Habits*,[18] it's a collaborative structure deeply rooted in appreciative inquiry and gives everyone a voice to help move everyone forward.

The first question they ask is "Who has good news?" They shout out company-wide wins, positive sales reports, and what's going on in employees' lives (e.g., somebody had a baby). Then they move to briefly discuss the current top priorities and highlights of what individuals or teams are working on toward company goals. At the Junktion, they include a question about any missing or broken systems that are in the process of being resolved. The entire meeting lasts only ten minutes and puts everyone in an appreciative mood.

If your business employs a large team and it's not possible to fit every report into ten minutes, create a huddle system for each department or team separately. Use the same framework so everyone gets on the same page. Even a team of three can benefit from a daily huddle.

That brings us to another essential system that complements appreciative inquiry–driven meetings.

---

18   Verne Harnish, *Mastering the Rockefeller Habits: What You Must Do to Increase the Value of Your Growing Firm* (Ashburn, VA: Gazelle's Inc., 2002).

Reporting: A System to Make Sure Things Get Done

Reporting is an essential activity that's part of every good meeting system. Appreciative inquiry includes creating robust reporting systems, whether verbal or written, so that you get real-time feedback. Reports allow you to see where the challenges are and what the solution may be. For example, maybe the latest sales report you have from your sales team is from last quarter. How can you shift production based on what's happening right now if you don't know what's happening?

When I wrote this chapter, I was working with the CEO of a small business who didn't seem concerned that he couldn't produce the previous month's financial reports. Two years prior, he had shared with me that he knew he needed a financial system. Still, nothing changed. Rather than knowing his numbers by the seventh of every month, he reviewed the books once a year. Then he found out in April that $16,000 wasn't billed back in October. That finally convinced him to implement a billing reports system to prevent this from happening again. Learning the hard way is overrated.

Reporting is a great add-on to regular staff meetings. Start by looking at all the positions in your company. What do you need from each of them to effectively understand what's going on in your company? What do you need to know every day? What do you need to know every week, every month, every quarter, and every year? And what tools do employees need to quickly compile these reports for you so they're easy to read? Once you know what you need from each individual, communicate to them what you need, when you need it, and why.

Let's say your bank accounts aren't reconciled: a big (and common) issue. If the system for reviewing your bank statements is scheduled six months from now, no one is going to remember what happened. It will be too late to get any money back if there was fraud.

Instead, the owner needs a reporting system. By the seventh of every month, you schedule a check-in meeting with your bookkeeper. The bookkeeper knows about the meeting, they know it's going to last fifteen minutes, and they know they have to report on the accounts receivable and payable and show proof that all the bank accounts are reconciled. They also have to report the trends, what's going well, what could be better, and what's missing.

Some owners—restaurateurs, for example—need reports to monitor daily wage expenses and/or supplier costs related to cost of goods sold. Current market conditions around supply chains affect pricing and resource availability. Here's how. Let's say you own a remodeling company and priced a big job using lights from China. Now, those bulbs were first delayed because of a coronavirus factory shutdown and are on a slow boat way past your promised deadline.

Nothing can be taken for granted. When you don't have information, you can't make decisions. It's that simple. Reporting allows you to fix problems in real time, significantly reducing business failure, especially in today's fast market.

What if you've designed a reporting system, you've communicated it to your team, and your team isn't following it? An installation company client had a problem with their foreman not submitting reports, so his data was always inaccurate. The owner could have spent time yelling at the foreman for not doing the reports. Instead, the owner took an appreciative approach and went back to the drawing board, taking into consideration the parts of the system that were working well and then adding in some new features including a new app that eventually solved the problem.

Whether you call for scrums, hold huddle meetings, or rely on regular reports, Appreciative inquiry will keep expectations clear and responsibility equal. Instead of feeling like the big bad boss who reprimands employees, you'll be the leader who inspires every team member to do better. And instead of employees complaining, they will feel empowered to solve their own problems. As a consequence, you'll have that much more freedom.

CHAPTER 9

COMMUNICATION SYSTEMS:
SPEAK UP AND LISTEN

I love cheese bread. There's a local bakery a dangerously short walk from my house that sells it. Their cheese bread is soft, chewy, and warm—the way cheese bread should be. I'm getting hungry just thinking about it as I often do when I pass by their shop. I take in that fresh-baked aroma and find myself standing in front of the counter before I realize it.

The last three times I've paid this bakery a visit, they were out of cheese bread.

The first time I saw their cheese bread basket empty except for crumbs, I asked the cashier, "When will you be baking more?" I had hoped to pick some up for dinner.

"We make six loaves every morning," she said. "Usually by ten we're sold out."

"Everyone in this town talks about your delicious cheese bread. If you made twenty loaves, they would buy them all," I said. I noticed the basket beside the cheese bread looked untouched. A towering pile of gluten-free oat muffins. Right at eye-level.

"Yeah, you're actually the third person to say that. I guess they're a hot commodity."

"I guess I have to stop by earlier in the day then," I said.

"You could, yeah," the cashier said. "I'll let the owner know. She plans our menu and does all the shopping."

I thanked the employee and left empty handed. I took her at her word and made plans to stop in a few days later before 10:00. Unfortunately, a meeting kept me busy until 10:15. When I raced to the bakery, what do you think I found?

"Oh, I'm so sorry. We just sold the last two."

"How many were there?"

"Six loaves."

Maybe the owner had not ordered the ingredients for a larger batch of cheese bread yet. Still, beside the empty bread basket was a bountiful supply of oat muffins. Once again, I left without buying anything.

About a month later, I stopped by the bakery bright and early, just after 8:30 a.m. Two cheese bread loaves left. I grabbed them both. A different employee rang me out at the register.

"Just curious. How many loaves of cheese bread were made today?" I asked.

"Six."

I stared down at yet another fresh basket of plain oat muffins along with a similar-size pile of day olds offered at 50 percent off. Then and there I decided to write this chapter. The bakery's owner, the cashiers, or possibly both are not listening to their customers. How many cheese bread sales have they lost out on? How much money have they wasted on those damn oat muffins nobody wants? How much profit could they have gathered over the years, and how much will they fail to gather over the years ahead?

Failing to act on repeated customer feedback is evidence of a systemic issue that many small business owners fail to deal with—broken or missing communication systems for both customers and employees. If there's no communication between the bakery owner and their customers, imagine the chaos behind the scenes. A business owner and employees who deal with each other every day yet are unable to clearly share information is a recipe for disaster. And unsatisfied customers who want more cheese bread!

The ability to communicate is among a business owner's greatest leadership strengths. Do it well, and everything falls into place. Do it poorly, and you'd best grab some aspirin for the headaches. Many small business owners think they don't have time to communicate. Or they think they're communicating well, but they're too overwhelmed to realize they're not.

In a fight-or-flight state, it's easy to be short with people, say the wrong thing, regret it afterward, and have no time to go back and fix it. A quick text to a client here, a burst of emails to staff there, and in the absence of body language, the recipient takes away an entirely different message than the one you intended.

Or you're so busy that you forget to communicate, and you miss an important deadline—like submitting paperwork for the grant you hoped would get your business back on its feet. I had one client who forgot to ask his bookkeeper to send invoices for over $80,000 worth of work. Meanwhile, there's always something new vying for your attention. Most people get three hundred emails a day. Is that frenzied, rushed state the best place to write back from?

Poor communication is often why small business owners lose loyal customers, damage employee morale, and fall into the trap of doing everything themselves. They convince themselves it's easier than spending time explaining the why, what, and how of a task. Do this every day with every task, and before you know it, you are your busiest and lowest-paid employee.

Effective Communication Systems

System 1: Active Listening

Do you ever feel like your employees, vendors, customers, or partners are not listening to you? How does that make you feel? When you don't feel seen, heard, or understood, you may feel rejected. Like what you have to say doesn't matter. It doesn't make you feel like helping them succeed, does it?

Fail to listen to others in your business, and you'll make them feel the same. Effective communications systems start with simply learning how to listen. Using active listening with employees, suppliers, shareholders, and most importantly the customers you serve is like having a superpower. Small business entrepreneurs can use active listening to make their conversation partners feel seen, heard, and understood.

Stop What You're Doing

For many business owners, it's a challenge to stay present—to stop talking, start listening, and trust that by making others feel heard, things will get done. In our fast-paced technology-driven world, it's rare to have a completely distraction-free conversation. Being present means stopping whatever else you're doing, turning off screens and notifications, and focusing on the individual you're engaging with. Great leaders are great listeners. When they do talk, they ask solution-focused questions to understand what the other person is saying to drive results.

Listening is just good business sense. Your front-line people know more about what's going on in your business than anyone. They'll tell you what you need to know. Don't talk to the general manager and be done. Ask the janitor. Reach out to your junior salesperson. The new hires. The student intern. The person at the front desk. When you make an effort to listen to everyone, you'll get more information and move forward much faster. And it's OK if you don't always agree with or like what you hear. You're gathering information, and you're making the other person feel valued. Remember, acknowledgment is not the same as agreement. Nod and say something like, "I hear you. Thank you for sharing." This takes the pressure off having to respond in agreement or tell them why they're wrong.

Listen 80, Talk 20

Active listening is about looking for specific details in the other person's message to understand their intent. You're not just listening for words. You're listening for feelings. For tone. For themes. For images. For what's not being said.

In every interaction, aim to listen 80 percent of the time and talk 20 percent. Here's a tactic I use to get myself into active listening mode. I take a breath and tell myself, *Stand down, Beverlee. What do you need to learn?* As the other person speaks, I ask myself, *What else do you need to ask about? What are they thinking? How are they feeling at this moment? What system might need to be further developed?*

Communicate Their Way

In our age of digital communication, active listening doesn't always refer to a face-to-face conversation. Be aware of the other person's communication preferences. Senior employees may prefer a phone call to written communication or a cubicle drive-by. Staff who are fifteen to twenty-five years into their careers often tend toward email. For anyone younger, a text or direct message is the best way to start or continue a conversation. The same applies to your target market. Yes, customers are people too.

Collect Feedback Regularly

If customers feel you are not listening to their needs, your reputation and your margins will suffer. I recommend surveying a segment of your customers via text, email, or phone call at least once a quarter. Ask what is going well and be curious about any changes you need to make. Any time a customer says, "I want this," consider that feedback a gift. Don't wait until you get a bad review to ask customers what they need. If you do receive critical feedback from a customer via a survey or review or from a conversation with an employee, always be polite—even if they're not. Whether you or your employees are actually at fault or not doesn't matter. Always tell an unhappy customer, "You're right. I hear you. I apologize for the impact that had on you." A gracious response turns a terrible experience into a remarkable one that most customers won't soon forget.

Feedback is hard to receive; it's also gold. I once recommended a lawyer I'd had a good experience with to a girlfriend. After meeting with him, my friend called me to complain about their awful process and begged me to never recommend another company like them. I was surprised because I thought the lawyer knew better. He clearly wasn't listening. I called the lawyer to share my friend's feedback, and he didn't want to hear it. I never recommended him again.

Humans don't like bad feedback. If you don't acknowledge it, you don't have to deal with it, right? Wrong. Yes, feedback can be painful. Accept it anyway. We don't want to feel bad, yet if we ignore bad feedback, we lower our odds of future success. In a successful business, feedback is an essential communication loop. An employee or customer shares their negative experience with you, you actively listen, you redesign the affected system, and the experience is improved for next time.

Maybe you pick up the phone, and the first thing a new customer says is they couldn't find your phone number on your website. What does that tell you? To add it to your site in an obvious place. If one or two customers share feedback with you, chances are hundreds of others have had (or will have) a similar experience.

Record All Feedback in One Place

You need a systematic way to collect both feedback and suggestions, especially those your employees hear off the cuff from customers mid-conversation. Obey the one-book rule—record all customer feedback in one place. For customer surveys, keep all answers in the same document, spreadsheet, or folder. For day-to-day feedback, log customer complaints and suggestions in one easy-to-access location. For my retail clients, I suggest a notebook they keep at the checkout counter. For example, if a customer says they're disappointed you ran out of a product, the employee or manager (or you) talking to the customer writes it down on the spot.

"Thank you, I appreciate you telling me that," the attending team member can say. "Let me write that down, and I'll bring it up in our next meeting."

That's a customer service home run—so long as the book of feedback actually makes it to the meeting and affects change. Acknowledging is not necessarily agreement when it comes to employees, yet with customers, it usually is. And writing down their feedback in front of them makes them feel heard more than anything else will.

System 2: Coaching

Listening to your company's stakeholders and doing something with that information are essential in any small business. What about when it's your turn to do the talking? A top-down, tell-you-what-to-do communication style is the default in companies that make employees feel ignored, dismissed, and misunderstood. People don't like to be told what to do or that they're doing something wrong. People do best when they're guided by their own influence, understanding, knowledge, and horsepower.

The solution is coaching. You are the coach. Similar to mentorship, coaching is a form of communication in which a leader supports another person in achieving a goal. Knowing how to coach is an essential leadership skill every owner must master. Coaching drives performance and builds a healthier culture. It creates an environment for understanding, learning, change, and action.

Question, Not Command

While coaching is a powerful tool for meaningful and productive conversations, it must not be driven by your agenda. Your job as coach is to ensure your employees' needs are met by discussing what they want to talk about. That's where the first communication system, active listening, comes in. Think of coaching as the opposite of command-and-control communication. Remember, people don't learn when you just tell them what to do.

Famous coach and author David Rock created the SCARF model,[19] in which he uses neuroscience research to show how to work effectively with others. The SCARF model was developed in 2008 in Rock's paper "SCARF: A Brain-Based Model for Collaborating with and Influencing Others." SCARF stands for the five key "domains" that influence our behavior in social situations. These five social domains activate the same threat-and-reward responses in our brain that we rely on for physical survival. They are:

Status: our relative importance to others

Certainty: our ability to predict the future

Autonomy: our sense of control over events

Relatedness: how safe we feel with others

Fairness: how fair we perceive the exchanges between people to be

In fact, we're physically wired to challenge any new situation to protect us from the potentially harmful unknown. When we're told something rather than asked, that order enters the fight-or-flight center of our brain. We can't help but unconsciously resist the command until we're sure it is safe.

Only when a person is asked a question and generates the possibilities for themselves does learning take place. When we're asked a question, our brain is wired to process our thoughts based on what we know, what we're curious about, and what we care about. We have no choice but to think about what was just asked, so we become inquisitive rather than defensive. A good coach listens and asks questions objectively without solving peoples' problems for them. They're also curious and nonjudgmental. Yet that's easier said than done.

Be Curious

Curiosity is thinking, *What is this person really saying? What is my part? What don't I know? What do I need to learn?*

Curiosity means saying, "Tell me more about what that means to you."

Curiosity is more than hearing; it's paying attention. Watch for cues, emotions, and voice modulation that give you clues into what the other

---

19   Gin Lalli, "David Rock's SCARF Model: Social Threats in the World of Work," World of Work Project, July 8, 2019, https://worldofwork.io/2019/07/david-rocks-scarf-model/.

person is feeling. Ask thinking questions—"What do you think?" This is a powerful entry into a constructive dialogue.

Acknowledge What Others Say

When listening to someone else speak, it's natural to judge what they say. When we hear something we don't agree with, our judge's gavel comes out, and our mind shuts down. How do we get around this instinctive response? Remind yourself: acknowledgment is not agreement. When we acknowledge what others are saying, we make them feel seen, heard, and understood. In a coaching conversation, it doesn't matter if you agree with anything that is being said. Your job is to ask questions that get to the root of whatever the other person is thinking. As the leader of your small business, take some time later to reflect on what you heard to determine what if anything needs to be done. For now, just listen and learn.

Keep Advice to Yourself

Contrary to popular belief, and as difficult as it is to keep quiet, a coaching conversation is not about giving advice. Even if you think you have the perfect solution to another's challenge, this is not the time or place to give it. The individual being coached has the wisdom, power, and desire to talk things out so that they can resolve their own challenges. Your coaching gives them the opportunity to do so. If our goal is to empower our employees and support their growth, then we need to give them the space to think. Asking powerful, thought-provoking questions is a skill you can develop through practice.

Consider how sports coaches ask questions. How did that work? What did you notice? How did it feel doing it that way? What would a better performance look like? What's your next goal? What do you need to be successful? What do you need to solve this problem? How can I help? What does that look like? What would be a win for you today? What's our plan to tackle this? What do we need to learn today?

Contrast this approach with command-and-control leadership. Every coaching question elicits an answer. It empowers the other person to take ownership of their problems and their outcomes. Each follow-up question digs deeper. Often, in a coaching conversation, the first idea that's brought up is only at the surface of what that individual really wants to talk about. Your job is to keep asking open-ended questions until they've found the root of the issue. It's also valuable to inquire about the impact this challenge is having on the employee now, and what will happen if it's not resolved. Steer away from blaming others. Instead, ask how the person you are coaching has tried to resolve the situation thus far.

What if you're in a situation in which a task absolutely has to get done? Can coaching communication still be used? When my cousin worked at that insurance company, she was assigned the task of evaluating a new payroll software—on top of her usual forty-hour-a-week work. Of course, she had to complete the new payroll system training first. To do so, she would have to work eleven hours a day, six days a week, and there was a ban on overtime. She was completely set up to fail.

What if her supervisor had used a coaching system to communicate her new payroll responsibilities? She might have said, "I understand these are really challenging times. What have you got on your plate? What's realistic? What's your deadline for getting this done? What other help do you need?"

This communication is far better than burning out your employees and having them quit. You as the boss might think something has to get done. If it does, wouldn't it be better to know as soon as possible whether or not your expectations are realistic? Then, if needed, you can assign the additional support the employee needs before it's too late. You'll be amazed at how motivated employees feel when you ask, rather than telling.

Make coaching a company-wide system, and you create an almost metaphysical state of cooperation without backstabbing, infighting, or quitting. This applies to personal relationships as well. In our family, we don't fight because we just ask. Asking eliminates all the conflict. When you have the opportunity to tell your side of the story, you feel understood. It's safe to disagree. It's like the Serenity Prayer.

> God, grant me the serenity to accept the things I cannot change, courage to change the things I can, and wisdom to know the difference.

Coaching communication lets you live these words day in and day out. When you are the boss, there are some things you don't need to be in the middle of. That means not everything is going to be your version of perfect. Pick your battles. Know when to acknowledge and when to agree. If something just isn't that important, can an employee lead the way? Even if it's not exactly how you would do it, if it's working for them, great. Don't change it. You'll likely have a new and improved system on your hands if you stay curious.

Be more than a small business owner. Be a coach, and you'll lead your team to business victory.

System 3: Delegating

Remember when you wrote "and any other duties" in your position agreements? Tasks come up along the way that you shouldn't be doing yourself. As your business grows and changes with the times, there's always something new to delegate. Delegation is a communication system to give others the authority and responsibility to act on your behalf. Along with delegation comes accountability for the results. This is why you must always delegate results, not tasks.

Delegate Results, Not Tasks

Just like the other forms of communication, delegation is a two-way communication. You tell the employee what to do and how, and you must ensure they receive your instructions. And vice versa—the delegate gives you feedback on the work you expect them to do, and you receive feedback on whether your instructions were clear or not. Then it's their responsibility to report back to you. This builds on the reporting system we discussed in the previous chapter.

I'm not saying delegating is easy. Sometimes it's painful to learn how to delegate. However, the longer you hold off on learning how to delegate, the longer you have to do everything yourself. And the longer you're trapped. Most humans find it far more difficult to articulate what they want than just to do it themselves. You may not even know how to do the task yourself, yet it still needs to be done. Most small business owners will figure it out and do it themselves or not do it at all. Anything before delegation.

This is why we need a delegation system. Effective delegation reduces burnout, helps you scale faster, inspires others, saves money, and gives you time back for family and other priorities. How? Delegation allows you to get work done through your team. Delegating to your team builds valuable experience and skills. It also helps reduce your own stress of feeling like you have to do everything yourself.

Ideally, the person you're delegating to will complete the task with as much effort and skill as you would. In a small business, however, there are often skills, training, and resource gaps that make this a challenge. Luckily, you have started on your procedures manual, allowing for others to do things the way you want and expect them to be done. Remember to breathe; the task often doesn't need to be done as perfectly as you did it.

Follow the Five Delegation Steps

Step 1: Evaluate

With so much on a business owner's plate every single day, it's ridiculously challenging to even think about what to delegate. Here are some ideas to start with:

- Routine tasks
- Tasks that are low priority but still need to be done
- Tasks that someone on your team can do as well or better than you
- Tasks that will help train your employee and further develop their skills
- Tasks that are fun, interesting, or appeal to others on your team
- Tasks that you don't know how to do
- Tasks that must be done because a system is missing or broken
- Tasks that are faster to do yourself than asking a team member

And anything else you're willing to let someone else do.

Step 2: Select

For each task to be delegated, choose someone on your team or hire a contractor with the capabilities of doing a competent job. Can't afford to hire someone? Think again. What is the lost opportunity cost of you not having time to build and grow your company? Consider the long-term value of selecting and training the most competent candidate. Refer back to Chapter 5 for your essential hiring system.

Step 3: Define

Brief the delegate on your requirements and expectations. Be very clear on the overall objective and required outcome. Include all available resources and determine the deadline and method to complete the task.

If you have yet to document a process for this task, include creating one in your instructions so you'll have it the next time this task needs to be done. Ask questions of the delegate to confirm you've communicated your request clearly.

Step 4: Monitor

As I've mentioned, there's a difference between delegation and abdication. Abdication is dumping and running. Share with your delegate how you can support them and identify any possible red flags to watch for, which is when you'll want to be notified. Monitoring progress is an important step to help the delegate be successful. This does not mean micromanaging the task or interfering with their getting it done. It does mean being available for questions, providing additional resources if needed, and agreeing on regular times to check in. If you see things going sideways, don't jump in and take over. Work together by asking questions to determine the next steps.

Step 5: Review

Always provide positive feedback on a task well done. If needed, ask the delegate for feedback on how they think they could have performed better. Review the documented process you asked them to create. Ask questions about anything you feel is unclear, make any necessary changes, and sign off on it together. If appropriate, have the delegate show others on the team how to do the task by reviewing the process document. We learn best by teaching, so delegating is giving this individual another opportunity to grow in their confidence and skills.

Getting comfortable delegating tasks to others may take time. It is, however, essential to getting free of your daily operations. And the more you do it with the small, easy projects, the easier it will be when it comes to the big things.

By actively listening to everyone involved in your organization, from the customer to the janitor to the largest stakeholder, you'll enjoy a happier, more relaxed workplace as well as a business that practically scales itself. And when you use coaching questions to empower employees to solve their own problems, you'll feel a huge weight lift off your shoulders, bringing you that much closer to freedom.

CHAPTER 10

WHAT EMPLOYEES WANT:

CREATING A CULTURE THAT MOTIVATES

Culture is a shared set of attitudes, values, goals, and practices that characterize an organization. It's a human operating system designed by the way people work in a company. Any culture, good or bad, is downstream of leadership's decisions: decisions about how to lead, how to organize the team, how to compensate people, how to deliver bad news, how to delegate and train, and how to systematize. The founder decides (or allows) the way employees work long before the employees experience the consequences.

Everything you've learned about designing systems to unlock prosperity and freedom affects your culture. The systems you have or don't have, the goals you pursue or abandon, and the decisions you do or don't make collectively contribute to each employee's experience.

Choosing to make your culture the best it can be will earn you more money while also making the world a better place. Positive, empowering, vibrant small business cultures reduce anxiety and ambiguity, provide employees and customers a predictable experience, and help ensure stable profits. This team cohesiveness means everyone rows in the same direction. A company with such a great culture can achieve anything together.

So how do you build an amazing culture?

Five Culture Experiences Employees Want

Even though you, your customers, and the world will benefit from your great culture, the truth is that a culture is for the people working in it. Your employees are working hard for you. So what's important to them? As much as you, the leader, matter to the business, what they want and need is equally important. They are there for themselves, not for you. Your company can't exist just to make you and your family rich. A company like that won't grow. Your people are always wondering, *What's in it for me?*

When I was in graduate school, I was given an assignment to seek out answers to this question. All twenty students in my class interviewed both corporate and small business employees to learn what was important to them in a work environment.

Surprisingly, compensation was hardly mentioned. Yet most small business owners I coach think they have to pay huge salaries to keep their employees motivated. Money does not make a culture great. Overcompensating staff can actually drive employees to compete for higher pay. This can damage your culture because employees fight each other to "win" more money. A culture of wage competitiveness is not a productive culture. Rather than money, my employee survey findings (along with hundreds of interviews with my clients' employees over the years) have shown me that most people want to work somewhere motivating.

People don't want to feel like another cog in the machine. They want good communication from leadership that shows respect and transparency. They want to know the company vision matches their personal values. People want to be part of something that matters. Words like *trust, contribution, belonging,* and *consistency* were stated more often and rated higher as personal needs than *more money*. Because when put together, these positive elements create a motivating environment.

How does employee motivation affect a business? Think about a time when you were in a store, and you needed the help of a retail clerk. Odds are good that when you finally found one, you got the sense they just didn't care about your needs. How did you feel about that company? Compare this to a time when you experienced amazing service from an employee who went above and beyond to help you. How did you feel then?

The risks of having an unmotivated team are huge. They include poor customer service, loss of reputation, theft, and huge turnover costs because of constantly hiring and training new employees. The distractions alone in dealing with unhappy, unmotivated people keep business owners from growing and improving their companies.

However, motivated employees are like gold in the bank. They work hard, they care about your customers, and they consistently contribute to building and growing your company. A motivated team generously uses their talents and skills to contribute to the organization. Motivated people feel seen, heard, and understood and are genuinely happy to come to work each day. They don't feel like just a number, even in very large corporations. Motivated employees enable you to free yourself from day-to-day operations.

Even the busiest small business owner can strive to offer employee experiences that result in a motivated workforce. Based on my survey and interviews, here are the five experiences you must offer your employees to build a great culture.

1. Trust

Trust is a feeling and a virtue in an organization. It is both given and received in relationships with your team, customers, and stakeholders. Trust is used to make decisions, build strong collaborative teams, and create great companies.

A lack of trust in a business can turn to chaos, lost revenue, lost productivity, and the lack of ability to retain good people. And this slide can happen fast. Lack of trust shows up as competition, individuals "doing their own thing," and poor team communication. The more your employees trust one another, the stronger and more productive your team will be. The less they trust each other, the weaker and less productive they'll be.

Small business owners are especially vulnerable to relationship dynamics because their businesses run on relationships. That's why every business owner needs strong trust-building skills. These skills include the ability to share a clear vision and strategy, the ability to articulate what they need, and the patience to listen carefully and understand the needs of others.

Trust is built or diminished by repeated behavior. Documented procedures help build consistency, which, in turn, builds trust with customers and teams. Employees knowing that they are doing their job in the way it was designed builds trust and confidence. It removes the fear of trying to figure it out on their own. The systems I'm teaching you in this book can build trust in your team if you build and stick to them.

As trust improves, teams can better cooperate and coordinate their efforts, especially during challenges. Employees look to you to lead in the good times and the bad. When your business bumps up against everyday chaos, deadline stress, or catastrophes like a pandemic, show some grit.

Let your team see your determination. Let them witness your desire to succeed and bring everyone with you into shared success. This builds trust. Gather employees together in times of trouble and remind everyone that the company vision, purpose, and mission never change. Your promise to your customers has no expiration date or contingencies. In fact, recommitting to the promise is more important than ever during hard times. Few things motivate employees like a business owner with passionate perseverance. This builds trust that you are an employer who keeps your word. That, in turn, brings job security and personal comfort that they won't be forgotten.

2. Contribution

As much as systems and structure strengthen the business, the people who operate in those systems need a voice in how they are created and improved.

People spend forty hours or more every week working for your company. Your company is a huge part of their lives. To feel motivated, they need the ability to contribute in a meaningful way: to feel they're a part of something bigger than themselves and can make a difference to their customers, their coworkers, and the purpose of the organization. As much as you chose them at their hiring, they also agreed to work for you—because doing so meant something to them.

Unhappy employees I have met are often frustrated with their bosses because they are not given the opportunity to contribute to solving problems with obvious solutions. It is discouraging to have to deal with the same complaints, frustrations, and broken systems every day while knowing if the boss would only ask and listen, those problems could go away.

Make continuous improvement to your systems and processes part of your culture. Promote training and education so everyone on the team can contribute new skills, experiences, and knowledge to make your company stronger.

3. Belonging

Rituals like birthday celebrations, holiday bonuses, and nice company uniforms can offer employees a sense of belonging. They bring people together and create a sense of purpose and family.

At the travel agency, my team loved the consistency of company uniforms. Nothing speaks of belonging more than seeing seven powerful women walking into a chamber of commerce meeting dressed in matching high-end designer suits. Twice a year, I bought employees quality company-branded swag like briefcases and matching sweaters. Even if you have a low budget, does everyone have the same t-shirt? Or a matching company apron? Or at least a pin or name tag they wear? These say a lot about your culture with very little cost. You may roll your eyes at a name tag changing your culture, but putting on any type of uniform makes part of the human brain say, *I've got my name tag. I belong here.*

Even with my family's investment properties, we've worked to build a culture of belonging. Every summer, we hold a barbecue for all our tenants. We bring the food and drinks, set up outside the building, and play music. That's also the day we check the smoke and carbon monoxide detectors in all the units. This one annual event means so much that tenants who moved out three or four years ago still attend.

Employees look forward to annual events. They become an important part of how they celebrate life. There are so many cost-effective activities that you can introduce to help bring your team together. Consider summer picnics and invite their families, host a movie night at the theater, or reserve a table at a restaurant they would look forward to going to. It's the small things done consistently that generate big feelings of belonging.

4. Team Spirit

If no man is an island, no employee is a department. People want to know they're part of a team they can count on. From the owner's viewpoint, this means you must carefully monitor developing subcultures. Remember your shared vision. You can have different departments and teams with their own hierarchies, provided they all have the same vision and can count on each other. Yes, you'll see employees cluster in groups based on role, seniority, and other factors. As long as everyone is pulling in the same direction, team spirit is alive, and you have a winning edge.

Different work groups only become toxic when their own subcultures evolve differently from the one you want everyone to experience. The result is misaligned priorities, different customer service standards, and inconsistent profits. If you see an emerging subculture behaving in a way that goes against your company vision, don't call a meeting with only those people. Bring up your vision at your next staff meeting. Say you're looking for new ways to make your vision come alive and ask for ideas. Uniting everyone in a motivating task will pull your deviating group back into the larger team.

One factor that leads to subculture deviation is boredom. Boredom kills cultures. And so does its opposite, overwork. Employees with too little variety or too little time to breathe aren't enjoying themselves.

What does it mean to your employees to have fun at work? Perhaps schedule mandatory breaks, provide access to healthy food, and include some physical activity for those who are desk bound. At the travel agency, I knew my girls wanted fun in their work, so I asked them how we could offer that. They suggested catered Friday lunches. So every Friday for seven straight years, we ordered and ate lunch together. We were a small team, so this investment added up to only a couple of hundred dollars a month. That money went a long way. We worked hard all week, and it was fun to sit down together and celebrate on the last day.

5. Rewards

The currency we use called "money" has emotional connections far beyond its value at the bank. While money is not the number-one motivator in creating an amazing company culture, you need to pay your people enough to take the issue of money off the table. How your employees feel about the amount of money they're making can have a significant impact on their motivation, regardless of the amount. So how should you reward employees to ensure they stay motivated?

Reward tenure to keep your long-term employees engaged. Employees also need to know the impact of their actions on the financial stability of the company. When they do well, be sure to reward them with something that matters to them. When you see waste or lost productivity, work with them to create a better system. Then reward them for positively contributing to a better outcome.

Make each and every employee feel like your business partner. Let them feel the experience of ownership by encouraging them to think like entrepreneurs. I did that with my travel agency. Most agencies pay incentives-based individual commissions, meaning the top sellers get the most bonus money. That's why my bonuses rewarded everyone. I structured it so the salespeople did the selling, and the behind-the-scenes administration team who provided all the backup and made them look good shared in the spoils. If the entire company did well, everyone on the team did well. We shared rewards equally. We didn't parse out percentages because I wanted everyone to feel like their contribution mattered. This went back to my vision of excellence for our clients. Everything was based on keeping our promise. To keep our promise, we need to work together. That created a culture of collaboration.

It's also smart to recognize individual contributions in some way. Without this, people can begin to feel taken for granted, and motivation wanes—or worse, your best people head out the door to another company. At the travel agency, we once had issues with sloppy client record keeping, leaving our database with missing and incorrect information. So I ran a one-month campaign offering a dollar for every perfectly done client file. I made it fun by handing out big yellow star stickers so employees could write the name of the client and stick it to my office wall. At the end of the month, I had a perfect database and over 1,200 yellow stars covering my office walls. Every employee earned several hundred dollars, and my complete database earned me more than that.

Still, rewards go beyond money. Get creative with principles borrowed from Gary Chapman's *The 5 Love Languages*.[20] Words of affirmation are a reward. Reward an above-and-beyond employee with an act of service, such as hiring a part-time contractor to help them complete tedious yet necessary administrative tasks. Gift giving is a common reward mechanism—offering an annual holiday dinner, summer picnics, fresh coffee for employees all day, and homemade cookies and milk in the break room. Employees who value quality time appreciate team-building outings and adventures outside the workplace, such as river kayaking or once-weekly optional in-office yoga. A sincere pat on the back; a firm, friendly handshake; and making eye contact with words of thanks are examples of touch—a real, physical way to show appreciation.

However you choose to reward employees, the goal is the same: to create an environment where people are supported in bringing their best selves to work. They're rewarded and recognized for continuously improving on the job and develop a sense that what they're doing is bigger than they are.

Culture is experienced primarily by employees and customers, but it's your job to build it. Each individual associated with your company can

---

20   Gary Chapman, *The 5 Love Languages: The Secret to Love That Lasts* (Chicago: Northfield Publishing, 1992).

affect the culture through their work, yet you personally have the biggest influence. If you give your employees the motivating culture they want, they'll work hard for you and enjoy it. If you are organized, focused and disciplined as a leader, your employees will be motivated to follow your example.

CHAPTER 11

MARKETING SYSTEMS THAT CREATE CUSTOMERS

One of my favorite activities as a Girl Guide was acting in skits. Whenever I'm coaching a business owner to help improve their marketing, a particular skit we put on as kids comes to mind. It started off with me crawling around onstage searching for something. After an awkward ten seconds or so, another Girl Guide entered from stage left.

"What are you looking for?"

"I lost a quarter and can't find it."

"Oh, let me help you." She got down on her hands and knees, and both of us crawled around looking for my lost coin.

The next girl walked onstage.

"What are you both doing?"

"I lost my quarter," I said. "We're trying to find it."

"I'll help." The third girl got down and searched too.

This routine repeated until six Girl Guides from our pack were wandering around the stage on hands and knees. The audience watched us all search for several minutes but still no quarter.

Finally, the last girl walked in.

"What are you all doing?"

"Beverlee lost her quarter."

"Come help us find it."

The last girl looked at me and asked, "Where did you lose it?"

I pointed way across the stage to a dark corner.

"I lost it over there, but the light is much better over here."

This is precisely how many entrepreneurs search for customers. They look where the lights are shining and ignore the spot where the money is likely to be.

That better lighting is any bright and distracting tactic—Facebook and Instagram advertising, blogging, YouTube videos, podcasting, Twitter thread writing, direct mail, newer platforms like TikTok and Clubhouse, website visitor retargeting. Anything that everyone else raves about.

When we see other entrepreneurs feasting, we want to join them. We feel like we've been crawling around for no reason. And too often, we shift our marketing practices to reflect their business instead of ours. If that successful competitor is collecting clients from Twitter, we think we should too—even if we don't have a Twitter account, and our target market doesn't tweet.

This "comparisonitis" distracts us from foundational questions that lead us right to the money. For example, where do your customers hang out? How do they make their purchase decisions? What websites do they surf? Do they read magazines? Do they cruise Amazon for products?

In my experience, many entrepreneurs have no idea what their customers are doing—because they are too busy crawling in circles under shiny lights to have any time for effective marketing strategy and execution. The good news is that answering the important questions empowers you to reverse engineer your customers' buying process so your marketing can match. And once you know where your quarter is, you can walk right over and pick it up.

Finding Your Quarter

Marketing is an intimidating word for many entrepreneurs. Just saying it out loud can raise blood pressure because many feel like they're terrible at it. Better to not market at all than to fail a campaign so badly they reveal themselves for the fraud they feel they are.

Fear is misleading. In reality, these business owners have no idea how to "do marketing" in the first place. Once they learn, marketing is as manageable and predictable as any other operation in the business. Then the shiny objects lose their appeal.

So let's end the intimidation, demystify marketing, and find your quarter.

Let's begin with a straightforward and complete definition of marketing. Marketing is a set of processes for creating, communicating, and delivering value to customers and for managing customer relationships. And marketing covers every aspect of convincing someone to buy from you, from knowing your customers to packaging and promoting your products and services in a way that makes them easy to find and buy.

Marketing is as much about the experience of doing business with you as it is the actual product or service you sell and for how much. People are less persuaded by price than they are by the perceived value they receive from your product. The more you understand your customers and what they want, need, and expect from you, the better your marketing will be and the faster your business will expand.

If a business isn't growing, it's dying. Stagnation isn't safety; it's decline. Marketing is essential, not optional, especially during years three through eight. Many business owners make the mistake of undermarketing and overservicing. The seemingly justifiable reason is supply and demand: time is in short supply, and their business is in high demand! During the first few years of growth, the typical small business entrepreneur gets busy serving influxes of new customers. Why waste time marketing when word-of-mouth referrals already cause you to be overwhelmed? When they hit 150 percent capacity, systems aren't in place, and things begin to fall through the cracks, but somehow, they make it work.

Until business slows down. Referrals cease suddenly and without explanation. Profit plateaus. Entrepreneurs aren't sure what to do next because they stopped doing what worked to get the first batch of customers that opened multiple streams of referrals. Revenue stagnates while marketing has stopped, and the business owner doesn't remember how to start it up again.

Throwing random tactics at the wall like spaghetti will not work. Marketing requires an educated approach to spending your company's money. You can't just toss up a website and hope people are going to find it. Many business owners operate on a thin budget and can't afford to dump thousands of dollars into marketing strategies that might not work. How can they figure out what's going to give the best return on their investment?

If that's where you're at, take a breath. Relax. I'm going to show you exactly how to generate tremendous attention for very little cost. Some of the strategies in this chapter only require a few hours of poking around online. Others will require some capital investment, sure. But if you're going to spend money, you want the best bang for your buck. I'll show you how to maximize lead generation and customer acquisition for the lowest cost possible. As you know, with me, there's always a system.

When I help clients turn their businesses around, I break marketing down into two distinct phases: **attract** and **convert**. First, you attract customers; then you convert their attention toward buying. To do both effectively, you need to know what you're selling.

To Attract and Convert, Know Your Product

Your product is what you sell to your customers in exchange for their money. Your product is the value you bring to the market. It is specific and clearly defined, and the customer who needs it must completely understand it.

Features, functions, and design all affect how your potential customers make buying decisions. The look and feel of your product, the words you use to describe it, and the experience consumers have of doing business with you are all components of your product offering.

Your product has a specific value and benefit to the consumer. For marketing purposes, you need to fully understand the value-to-benefit connection. Then you can leverage this connection to effectively communicate with your target market.

So ask yourself, *What exactly am I selling?* Anything you offer in the market is considered a product, whether that's a physical item like lumber or an intangible service like coaching. Even if you're helping people accomplish something rather than handing them a physical object in exchange for money, you need to define exactly what that "product" is.

In booking trips for people, I was really just the middle person, selling items (tickets, hotel reservations, etc.) from other providers. I wasn't generating a physical product; I was selling a service connecting customers with the items they wanted. I offered a streamlined experience that simplified an intimidating process for customers who were too busy to do the extensive coordination themselves. And by offering packages, I could help those customers reduce their overall costs. That was my product. By defining my exact product, I could market perfectly to my best-fit audience.

The same principle applies even if you do sell physical products. Former Harley Davidson Europe managing director John Russell once said that Harley Davidson doesn't sell motorcycles.[21] "Harley Davidson sells to 43-year-old accountants the ability to dress in leather, ride through small towns and have people be afraid of them." That's selling an experience to a specific niche audience. Knowing the experience they're selling has helped make Harley Davidson the number-one motorcycle manufacturer in the United States.

You may be surprised to learn that the majority of small business owners don't know exactly what it is they're offering. They have too many products, and they're trying to be all things to all people. Or maybe their offering isn't packaged in a cohesive easy-to-buy unit. If the company owner is confused about what they're selling, the customer is guaranteed to be even more confused. And when consumers are confused, they are less likely to buy. Products are available everywhere, and consumers have a choice who they do business with. The loudest pitch with the clearest value proposition usually wins.

To break the value-to-benefit communication barrier, I'm going to help you define your product.

Marketing Exercise 1: Write Your Value Proposition

How well do you know your product? Consider the following questions.

1. What are your product's three best features (what the product does)?

2. What are your product's three best benefits (why that matters)?

3. How will your product either (a) increase pleasure or (b) decrease pain?

4. What differentiates you from other companies that try to solve this same problem?

---

21   David Fairhurst, "Harley Davidson Is Very Clear about What It Is Selling to Its Customers—And It Isn't Motorcycles," *HR Magazine*, August 3, 2011, https://www.hrmagazine.co.uk/content/features/harley-davidson-is-very-clear-about-what-it-is-selling-to-its-customers-and-it-isnt-motorcycles/.

5.   What one thing makes you the preferred provider of this solution?

What you've just created is called a **value proposition**, the primary reason customers will give you money. And the better your value proposition is, the more justified you are in raising your prices. It's a deal for everyone. Offering tremendous value means customers are more likely to hand you larger sums of cash to increase pleasure or avoid pain. The greater the pleasure you provide or the harsher the pain you relieve, the more your product is worth.

Let's distill your product's value even further. If you had ten words or fewer to describe why people should buy your thing from your company instead of another thing from somewhere else, what would you say? For my travel agency, I might have written something like *Responsive, resourceful travel planners who save you time and money.*

This ten-words-or-fewer summary of your value proposition is often called an **elevator pitch**. Boiling your entire service down to an elevator pitch and then being able to roll into a full value proposition once you've hooked your customer's attention are key to attract-and-convert marketing.

Now that you know what to say to get a customer's attention, let's figure out who you need to be talking to.

Who Needs Your Product?

It's normal to be biased in favor of your own company and to know in your heart why people should buy from you. It's a completely separate matter to be able to convey that value to customers and understand what they're really looking for. Getting inside your customer's head shows you what your business looks like to those who aren't the CEO.

There's a reason undercover bosses learn so much about their business by pretending to be a customer. There are some things you just don't understand until you see the customer experience firsthand. An owner may spend a fortune improving the interior of their restaurant, but if they don't take the time to walk out into the street and look at the front of their building, they'll never notice the bad paint job. Hanging crystal chandeliers over every table won't make up for a burned-out sign and broken windows if customers won't walk inside.

Once you understand how potential customers are seeing your product from the outside, you need to decide who is best served by your product. Someone out there has the exact problem you're offering to solve and the cash to pay you what your solution is worth. It's time to reveal who your exact target market should be.

No, not everyone in the world is your market. Trying to attract a general audience is a great way to spend all your marketing budget with little return. Any customers you do attract may be unhappy with your product because it doesn't match their specific needs. Learning the warning signs of a bad product-market fit is as important as understanding your perfect match. Instead of trying to sell to everyone, reduce the work and cost by building a **target customer profile**.

What is your most-frequented store or service provider? Think about your own reasons for choosing to do business with them. What is it about this vendor that appeals to you? Is it their location or convenience? Do they "speak your language"? Are they a similar age group or the same social circle? Segmenting a population with **demographics** lets you determine the size of your potential market.

While demographics describe who your buyer is, **psychographics** describe why they buy. These are feelings, interests, and opinions. Think of yourself again. What emotional connections do you have with companies you do business with? How do you feel when you buy from them? What are you thinking when you decide to buy from *them*? What interests and values do you share?

To market effectively, get inside your customer's head and see your business from the outside.

Marketing Exercise 2: Know Your Audience

To understand your target market is to influence them. The more precisely you can describe your ideal buyer, the more persuasive your marketing messages will be because your product will be the exact solution your customers have been seeking.

The following demographic and psychographic questions will help you deepen your understanding of your target market:

1. What problem does your product solve?

2. Who is most likely to have that problem (age, sex, occupation, education level, etc.)?

3. How often will customers need to buy your product/service?

4. Is there a specific time of day, month, or year it is purchased?

5. What main factor triggers customers' decision to buy?

6. Where did they buy a similar product before they found you?

7. Where do customers use your product (home, car, office, etc.)?

8. What is the consumer's decision-making process (price first, speed first, etc.)?

9. What influences spark their interest (friends, ads, etc.)?

10. Is buying your product a big decision that requires a lot of thought?

11. What are they thinking and feeling after they buy?

This exercise gives you the makings of a customer profile—a detailed understanding of who is most likely to purchase from you. This crucial information enables you to tailor your marketing to your chosen demographic and psychographic population. Attracting and converting *only* your ideal customers means you maximize returns on your efforts. Instead of spending thousands of dollars on Facebook ads selling your laser hair removal service to a general audience that includes single men of all ages and orientations, for example, your laser-focused campaign can reach your real market—single gay men in their thirties. Dialed-in marketing results in more sales and satisfied customers. And you don't waste money advertising to people who will never buy.

The customer profile exercise tells you who your core audience is. Once you get their attention and earn their business once, you want to do so again and again. It's infinitely easier to sell a previous customer on your product than to bring more new people through your doors.

So let's design a remarkable **customer experience** that turns new customers into "evangelists" for your business—people who buy from you again and again while referring family, friends, and even strangers to you.

Marketing Exercise 3: Create a Memorable Customer Experience

In web design, the term *user experience* refers to how easily a person can navigate a website and find what they are looking for. Customer experience is similar. It encompasses every stage of the buying process, from the first advertisement they see on through to the receipt your cashier hands them.

A positive experience gives customers a reason to rave about you. And happy customers are the best salespeople. Check your systems to ensure the customer experience you offer supports your value proposition. The following questions will help:

1. Why do existing customers buy from you?

2. How did customers first hear about you?

3. Why do customers stop buying from you?

4. How does your target market find out about your competitors?

5. What is it your customers like about your competitors?

6. What do your customers dislike about your competitors?

7. What would it take for your buyers to buy more or more often?

8. Do your customers find your sales staff helpful and service satisfactory?

9. What could make your service better for customers?

10. What are the last three compliments you received from a customer?

11. What reputation does your business have in the local/online space?

12. What reputation does your product/service have?

13. How do your past/current customers feel about the price of what you sell?

You might feel discouraged by your honest answers to some of these questions. That's perfectly OK for now. You've just identified tangible ways to improve your customers' experience. Finding what isn't working is how you build systems into every operation within your business.

The experience of doing business with you is as important as the value of your product. You can have the best product in the world and still not retain customers. When I work with entrepreneurs whose sales have stalled, we review their very first sales. What drove that initial business? Why were customers happy? What was different in the first few years that might be missing now? As a business grows, owners often tack on new models or distribution systems on the spur of the moment. These slapdash fixes are supposed to be temporary, but the owner never comes back and improves them. Worse, they often make the buying experience clunky for the customer.

No new customer is going to repeat-purchase if your buying process makes them unhappy. Declining sales are the natural result of increased friction in the customer experience. By assessing your customer experience, you can find where quick fixes have made the customer's experience worse—and driven away sales.

On the flip side, a frictionless buying experience is marketing in itself. Satisfied customers will share that experience with others in your target audience.

Think about that last twenty-seven-dollar course you bought online, primarily because of the slick sales process. Before you knew it, you had PayPal open, made two clicks, and owned a magical course that would solve all your problems. Frictionless.

While every interaction customers have with your business matters, by far the most important stage is the transaction itself. In marketing, this is called **place**. Place refers to where you convert potential buyers into actual customers.

The most obvious place where customers pay you and receive their product is the checkout counter or online sales page. Take the time to study what you've got now. How does a purchase really look from a customer perspective? You can even hire a marketing agency to perform an assessment for you. Or pick a business-savvy friend you know will give you the brutally honest truth. Have them go undercover on a day you're not in the office or browse your website and note how it feels to buy online.

Whatever it takes to improve customer experience, as long as it's within your budget, *do it*.

Distribute Your Product, Deliver on Your Promise

To increase the likelihood that a one-time buyer becomes a repeat customer, go beyond the purchase itself.

All the steps of getting your product to the purchase transaction are collectively called **distribution**. This can include the manufacturer, warehouse, shipping company, distributors, schedulers, material providers, and all players in between. Your company may be a part of someone else's distribution network. Your company might be the producer, the agent or broker, the wholesaler, or the retailer.

Wherever you are in the chain, distribution makes or breaks your marketing because it makes or breaks your company. If distribution falters, your value proposition can become a flat-out false claim. How your product gets made and delivered absolutely affects customer experience, which directly affects marketing. Price, delivery timing or wait time, stock availability, warranties, and return policies can all affect distribution.

Having full confidence that you can deliver on your promises to your customers depends on the strength of your distribution. Imagine a soap shop offering ethically sourced shea butter in their products. Because of a natural disaster, shea seeds are no longer available, or if they are, the prices have doubled. Supply chain management affects the shop's customer service and profitability. This distribution problem could put this small business out of business. Do they raise the price? Find an alternative material? Whatever they choose, they can leverage their decision in their marketing while being open and honest with their customers.

For example, consumers across many industries have pushed in recent years for products from moral, humane, and renewable sources. If certain steps in your distribution would encourage your target audience to feel even better about buying from you, leverage that fact for marketing.

Marketing Exercise 4: Market What You Can Deliver

How well do you know your distribution system? Consider the following questions:

1. Where is your product or service available to purchase?

2. Where else could you sell your product or service?

3. Who else do you count on to acquire and distribute your product?

4. Are your customers aware of the steps in your distribution system? How do they feel about them?

5. Who else could you source your products/supplies from? How could those relationships make your target market more likely to buy from you?

The goal here is not to rebuild your business model or part ways with your longtime manufacturer. The unprecedented global disruptions of

COVID-19 showed us the many weaknesses in every industry's distribution system. A lot of small companies went out of business because they could no longer source products. Prepare for interruption. Make sure you have backups in case one or more companies you rely on is no longer an option. Let's begin to lay those plans now.

Next up, we'll review the key elements of any distribution system so you'll always be able to give customers what you promise.

Supply Chain Management

Your supply chain includes all the other companies involved in creating your product or service. Supply chain is the piece of your distribution that relates to the actual completion of the product, from the raw materials, components, supplies, and parts that you may need to make your product to all the logistics of ensuring you have what you need when you need it. Supply chain management is the art of managing the flow between these companies to ensure profitability and service.

System breakdowns often happen outside your immediate control. The COVID pandemic shut down factories all over the world, and it will take years to recover from the resulting supply chain mess. Let's say you're a retailer, and you're told without notice that your most popular product is no longer available. If you're a broker, commissions and fees can change, having an immediate impact on your profit. Wholesalers often struggle with overgenerous return policies and returned stock. Each relationship needs to be carefully evaluated and adjusted when market conditions change.

One international jewelry company grew its business selling charms at local stores and nail salons. As they expanded, they stopped supplying to the lowest-producing and least-profitable outlets. A few years back—and seven weeks before Christmas, the most important time for a retail jewelry store—this major global charm distributor pulled inventory from 630 independent Canadian jewelry stores. The results were devastating, with most trying to figure out how to replace 40 to 70 percent of their Christmas revenue. While you can't always prepare for this kind of catastrophic blow, it does help if you avoid relying on just one vendor.

Coverage

Coverage refers to how much of your target market you're able to service.

Where will you distribute your product? In a global economy, the doors are wide open to explore selling to other markets. Governments encourage export of goods and offer incentives for small businesses to sell abroad. For example, the Canadian government will pay up to 50 percent of the cost of export marketing. These grants are not just for big businesses; they are designed for small businesses to encourage exports of Canadian goods and services.

Explore export grants offered by your local government. How well positioned are you to sell online? How will you distribute your product? Do you sell directly or partner with a distributor like Amazon to sell and ship for you?

Logistics and Order Processing

These are the steps you take to process your customers' orders, from when the order is placed to when it is out the door. Systems are needed for inventory management, record keeping, stock retrieval, packaging, order status communication, and delivery tracking. Elements in these processes include scheduling, database management, and customer follow-up.

Technology is quickly evolving to match the demand for accurate tracking and distribution. For example, Shopify exploded in the pandemic. They offer e-commerce websites with all the bells and whistles such as a POS system and inventory management, all connected to QuickBooks or other financial tracking software.

Warehousing

What do you need to keep on hand to maximize efficiency and deliver your product or service to your client? Location and costs are important factors in making warehousing decisions. Keeping too much inventory too far away with too many steps to retrieve it needs to be weighed against not having enough inventory and risking losing the sale.

What is the cost of handling your products as they move from being stored to being sold? Factor that into your prices without pricing yourself out of competition or cutting yourself out of the profit you deserve.

Transportation

Transportation costs also play an important role in distribution. Something as common as a postal strike or a car breaking down can seriously harm your ability to provide a product to your customer. What are your backup transportation plans?

Website

We briefly covered your website's checkout process earlier. Now let's go beyond the sales page and shopping cart. No small business today can ignore the requirements for a well-built and well-maintained website. Consider your website's user experience, from the home page and About Us to Blog, Contact, and Shop. From the second a page loads, how easy (and fast) is it for customers to get where they want to go? To browse and buy? Is your phone number on every page of your website? At least half the buying population still relies on talking to a real person if they have a question or are stuck and need help.

Whether it's making an appointment for a service, signing up for an online course, or buying a bar of soap, your website design must prioritize ease of purchase over digital bells and whistles. If it doesn't, customers will click away and find someone else who offers a better shopping experience.

Marketing Exercise 5: Make Your Website Work for You

The following twelve features are must-haves for any entrepreneur running a business. Visit your website right now and see if you pass these critical checks.

- The text is visually easy to read.
- The content can be easily understood.
- You use short paragraphs and sentences.
- Your contact information is easy to find.
- All links are working.
- You include calls to action (buy now, etc.).
- Your site is search engine optimized (SEO).
- It loads quickly.
- It includes prices or information on how to get the price.
- You display a clear place where customers can buy your product.
- Your site is updated regularly.

- You have a current SSL certificate.

These may seem basic. They are. They also determine every customer's experience. You don't want to rely on visitors to email you with questions because they hate having to do that. Why figure out your contact form when they can go back to their internet search and find another company with a more user-friendly site?

We've covered a lot in this chapter already, from value proposition and target audience to customer experience and distribution. That section on website optimization alone probably has your head spinning with ideas for improving your presence, online and off.

Let those wheels turn. You may have thought of several ways to attract new customers perfect for your product, as well as to reengage old ones. Excellent! Marketing is losing its mystery and may feel a lot more manageable already. After product and place come two more elements in your marketing system that you get to have complete control over—price and promotion.

Best Pricing Practices

First things first: price is the total monetary cost a product sells for. Your price must cover all your costs, pay you a fair market wage, and earn a reasonable profit. It must also appeal to buyers.

Pricing is a critical part of marketing for the simple reason that people can't decide to buy what you're selling if they don't know the price. Also, consumers will only pay for the value they see. When setting a price, be aware of the customer's perceived value for the product.

Consider the point at which price enters the buying process. Once a customer becomes aware of a problem or need, they research and gather information (including price), evaluate options, make a purchase, and then evaluate if that purchase was a good decision or not.

Pricing your product or service accurately is both an art and a science. Get it wrong, and you find yourself struggling. Get it right, and you can pay yourself and your team well.

So How Much Should I Charge?

Your price is a balance point between what *you* think your product is worth and what your *customer* thinks your product is worth. Here are a few considerations to help you achieve that balance.

Pricing Objective

What's your goal in selling your product? Since you're running a business, it's probably to grow your business and make a profit.

When you set your price, ask yourself how adjusting your price up or down will affect your market share. Yes, lower prices mean an initially lower profit on each sale, but will that help you capture a larger segment of the audience, thereby increasing your market share? Or are there ways you could increase market share without having to lower your price?

What rate of return do you want to achieve and why? Many small business owners start out by targeting their house payment, bills, and food costs. Figure out your current objective and write it down. You can create a business and personal operating budget to help make these pricing decisions.

As exciting as it is to get lots of new business, don't compromise all your profit for market share.

Environment

You live and work in a wider world. The truth is that there are political reactions to prices. When your government decides to add an environmental tax on the gas you need to run your company trucks, you need to respond to that increase by raising your prices. Doing business with consumers in other countries requires you to consider tariffs, taxes, and other costs associated with international trade.

What situations are your potential customers in when they are most likely to buy from you? If there's an ongoing unrest issue for your customers, they may be less likely to buy a luxury service. Then again, if you're selling home security products, dangerous situations may increase your profits.

What cultural influences affect who buys from you? Knowing this helps determine what physical environments are best for your marketing and selling. Think Christmas markets, Independence Day pop-up fireworks stores, and rainbow flag vendors at a pride parade.

What environmental factors influence your pricing decisions on your specific product? This may be simpler than you think. Entrepreneurs selling cold water on the hot tarmac of a midsummer air show are a perfect example of environmental pricing. Purchased for forty-three cents each, they sell these in-demand products to thirsty show watchers for five dollars. Sure, it's gouging, and everyone complains about it, but we all buy that expensive water when we're thirsty. The consumer's needs are met, and the seller earns a satisfying profit. Concert ticket resellers (often called scalpers) are an example of demand pricing.

Other environmental factors include climate change, trade agreements, and social pressure. Knowing your fixed and variable costs is essential to making good pricing decisions.

Supply and Demand

Sometimes you can charge more for a product because you either have no competitors or your customers' options are limited. The other side of the coin is that some markets are saturated and drive prices down. Look at the red-hot real estate market that swept the globe early in the 2020 pandemic and compare that to the devastating financial crisis in the US that decimated real estate values in 2008. That's supply and demand in action.

To find an ideal price, figure out what factors influence demand in your market. How does current demand influence your current pricing? Some populations are sensitive to price adjustment while others are fine with increases as long as perceived value increases accordingly.

Customer Influence

There is more to a consumer's decision to buy from you than price. These include sociocultural (*Everyone else is buying it*), psychological (*I had this as a kid and want to have it now*), and situational (*It's raining and cold at this sports event, and I need to buy a branded jacket*).

When setting your price, consider the customer's decision-making process. Are they aware of their own need? How pressing is their problem, and how fast do they need a solution? Are they going to do research first or just buy the first one they see?

Competition

Where is your price in comparison to your competitors'? If your competitors are all premium pricing, you could find a perfect niche offering a lower-price alternative. On the other hand, if your competition has driven the price into the dirt, you're going to need to justify charging more in exchange for a premium version of the product or service. You may also need to pair your product or service with an additional product or service that your competition isn't offering that makes you a unique choice.

Contractors who regularly have to do "bid" work (submit a bid to win a contract) need to pay attention to what others are charging. If you are not within 10 percent of others on most jobs, then something likely needs adjusting. Regularly review information on your won and lost bids to tighten up your bidding system based on facts. You don't want to find yourself in a situation in which you win the job by being the low bidder but now have to do that work at a loss. There is rarely a time when you want to win work just for the sake of winning.

Ask yourself the following:

Do I fully understand the scope of work?

Do I have the resources to perform this work?

Is my material pricing accurate, and can I change it if the price escalates?

Are the products needed for the project available?

Can I trust this customer to pay me, or do I need to factor in the cost of waiting for money?

These questions will put you in the right state of mind for what comes next—the definitive answer to all pricing uncertainties.

The Best Pricing Equation (A Seventh Grader Can Understand)

While there may be times you have to just put a price out there and see what happens, most often you don't need to guess. Once you've taken these factors into consideration, use the following equation. I call this **Grade 7 Math Pricing**:

$$\frac{1}{2} = 2/4$$

I remember the day in grade seven when I was first introduced to fractions. I was fascinated by the example Mr. Bolton shared on the old chalkboard, where he cleverly pointed out that one half is equal to two fourths. That one example has stuck with me and helps me teach pricing to my clients.

Your pricing equation has to balance. If your costs (of goods and running the business) divided by the number of products/services you sell is higher than your price, then you will go out of business. If the cost of fuel (or any other operating cost) goes up and nothing else changes, your profit will go down.

When pricing your product, consider two sets of clearly distinct expenses. The first is the cost to produce and provide your product to your customer. The second is the cost to run your business, including your own compensation.

Do you have to pay the credit card merchant a fee to use their service? That 2.5 percent cost needs to be accounted for in your price. Did the cost of your raw materials go up this month? That, too, needs to be continuously monitored so that you don't erode your profit by being too late to raise your own prices.

How about the cost of the heat to keep your office warm or the cost of hosting your website?

Earlier, you learned about the cost of goods sold (COGS). Add that to operating costs to cover everything. Or go broke and get stuck in a cycle of making just enough to cover last month's bills. Profit is the goal. Costs need to cover your wages; profit is what comes after your wages are paid.

COGS are your expenses accrued while serving a customer. If your product is a massage and you need to wash the sheets afterward, laundry soap is included in COGS because washing the sheets is not free, and you wouldn't have to wash them if you didn't serve a customer. Operating costs are expenses that exist whether you serve a customer or not, including the rent, the heat, the lights, your car, your cell phone, manufacturing, or a website. Learn what the average operating cost percentage is for your industry. Shipping is also a consideration, both the cost to acquire what you need to sell your product or service (operating cost) and the cost to ship that product to your customer (COGS).

There are a host of industry-specific expenses too. If you sell food, consider spoilage. If in retail, remember that people are going to steal. For service providers with teams traveling from job site to job site in a single day, you need to factor in travel time to pay your employees. If you need to offer a discount to your customers because that is what your target market clientele expects, add that discount to the price so you are not working for free.

Consider what all of your operating costs are to create a price that profits. These may include the car you can write off, the cost of social media marketing, your rotary membership dues, and the costs of interest on business loans or credit cards. Again, these costs are in addition to COGS, which includes all the supplies you bought to make the product or deliver the service.

Sadly, many small business owners don't factor in everything when they price their product, and they certainly don't factor in their time and possible development costs. Knowing all your expenses enables you to cover all your costs and then some.

Marketing Exercise 6: Price to Sell

To set a marketable price that converts the customers you attract, consider the following questions:

1. What research have you done to determine the price of your product?
2. Are your prices higher or lower than those of your competition?
3. Does your product offer a higher quality or better service than your competitors for a similar price? If yes, describe the differences you offer.
4. What would happen if you raised your prices?
5. Have you discussed prices with your customers? What feedback did you get?
6. What reasons could you give your customers for a price increase?
7. Could you sell a lot more if you lowered your prices? How would that affect profit?
8. If you operate in different geographical locations, are your prices adjusted accordingly?

9. What options do you have to bundle/unbundle your products to create different price points?

10. Does your price cover all your costs, including a wage for yourself?

The Danger of Bait-and-Switch Pricing

Have you ever followed up on an advertised great deal only to find the actual sale price much higher? How did that feel?

A young couple went out and bought their very first brand-new family minivan. They carefully went over the price with the salesperson to make sure they fully understood what they were paying. Two weeks later, they headed over to the dealer to pick up their brand-new vehicle. As they were signing the papers, they were bombarded with extra fees, some of them required, others optional. This major purchase was already at the maximum limit of what they were comfortable spending. These "extras" felt like a sucker punch in the gut. They no longer trusted the car dealership. Whatever goodwill had been developed was gone.

Don't repeat this mistake with your customers. When quoting prices to your prospective clients, consider the value in full transparency up front. You can do this by including *all* the costs in a price or quote, including taxes, fees, insurance, and any other add-ons.

When Should You Change Your Prices?

The warning about dishonest pricing raises a reasonable question: What if you need to raise your prices? What about running special offers and discounts?

I recommend monitoring and changing your prices as needed to ensure they generate the most value to your business relative to what customers are willing and able to afford. The global marketplace is constantly changing with cost increases, new competitors and consumer interests, disruptive technologies, et cetera. Your pricing should respond flexibly to any and all shifts.

Inflation is an economic factor that affects both your business and your personal finances. If you are paying 40 percent more for fuel because of inflation, your prices need to rise accordingly. As minimum wages increase globally, adjustments to your own team's wages will go up. Inflation over the next few years as we come out of the pandemic will touch every business.

Keep in mind your fixed and variable costs. Never charge so little you make nothing—unless you're going to recoup that loss with some special offer at a higher profit margin that will bring in repeat customers. Business for the sake of business is exhausting, frustrating, and a game you cannot win in the long term.

Also ask yourself if you're revising prices for the short term or long term. Increasing prices during times of disruption might make sense if your production costs have increased, and reducing prices again once the market stabilizes could rebuild trust with customers.

One tactic that can work in any economy is discounting. Just know how much you are giving away. A local gift shop owner started giving friends, family, and her best customers 10 percent off every time they visited the store. A 10 percent discount equaled a 20 percent reduction in gross profit. Ouch. Over time, the consequences of that small discount added up until she had to close her doors.

Now that you know how to price your product to sell, let's get it in front of the people who will buy it.

Promotional Mix

Marketing techniques that motivate customers to buy are called your **promotional mix**. They fall into five categories: **advertising**, **personal selling**, **direct marketing**, **sales promotions**, and **public relations**. Let's review each.

Advertising

This is all your nonpersonal communication via every form of media. Your message targets an identifiable market and pumps out advertisements to potential customers, often in the form of digital ads in their apps, on the sides of web pages, or as pop-ups during videos. Other examples include:

- Newspaper ads
- TV commercials
- Radio commercials
- Magazine ads
- Billboards

- Direct mail
- Direct email
- Web banners
- Targeted web campaigns

You can usually buy these ads straight from platforms where your customers hang out. Facebook, for example, has an entire advertisement section to help companies target their exact audience.

Personal Selling

The face-to-face promotion of goods and services. This is you speaking straight to your customer about why they want to buy your service. Examples include:

- Networking (in person or virtual)
- Live webinars
- Volunteering
- Door knocking
- Discovery calls (in person or via video online)
- Friends and family
- Special events
- Trade shows
- Other direct selling online (e.g., Clubhouse, Facebook Live, Twitter Spaces)

Anything that is directly communicating with potential customers gives you real-time feedback so you can tailor your marketing to their personal needs.

Direct Marketing

Marketing messages that are sent directly to consumers and target specific prospects. That means your customers get personalized messages instead of generic sales emails. This method is used mostly for announcements, special offers, order confirmation, and customer feedback. Examples include:

- Text messages

- Direct emails
- Targeted mail drops

This is a great way to follow up with existing customers after their purchases and continue the relationship. A tactic used by a new real estate agent I met made me smile. She decided to choose one condo building and "own" it. She got the list of owners and sent each a personal note in the mail saying she was "the real estate agent" for that building. She made a point to send notices every time a unit was sold with another targeted postcard. Within a year, she and her clients were buying and selling 80 percent of all units in that complex. She rocked direct marketing!

Sales Promotions

Use special promotions to stimulate consumer purchases. These cover a range of activities that you might engage in to promote your business and encourage potential customers to get off the fence and buy. Examples include:

- Exclusive deals
- Limited-time offers
- Catalogs and brochures
- Coupons
- Samples
- Contests
- Bonuses

Another term for sales promotions that professional salespeople use is **lead generation**. A lead generator is anything that pulls customers into your store and gets them looking at your products. Some companies offer a free incentive to sign up for offers, which, in turn, opens up the customer's email or social media to more targeted advertising in the future. A car repair shop may email coupons for cheap oil changes, then offer additional useful services when the customer comes in. A common lead generator is a free download, whether a free coupon or a free e-book with useful how-to information.

I recommend making a list of the highest-return lead-generating activities you've engaged in so far. What's worked? Why? What about that lead created more value for both the customer and your company?

One of my clients was complaining that business had slowed. He owned a roofing company and couldn't figure out how to pick things back up again. I asked him to think back to when he first started the business and tell me what he did to generate those first few sales. He shared that he would go door to door after completing a job and leave a flyer with the company phone number on it. He was smiling as he remembered how well that worked. I asked why he had stopped doing such a successful lead generating activity, and he didn't have an answer.

Public Relations and Social Media

Good PR earns public understanding, acceptance, and trust. It's about you, your product, and how your company positively contributes to the world, to your specific industry, and to the consumer's daily life.

Social media plays a major role in modern public relations. Platforms like Twitter and Facebook offer companies the opportunity for customer engagement like never before in the history of business.

Through social media, you can also come to understand your customers more deeply than ever. Remember some of the marketing questions in earlier exercises (e.g., "Who does your customer talk to?")? Social media can identify your most engaged customers' closest connections and give you valuable new contact information for future customers.

Social media can also identify the unique value your company brings to the market. This happens with both customer compliments about your service and customer complaints about other companies. You can see in real time what customers hate most about your direct competition. You can also stay connected with everyone who has shown an interest in your product or service. This makes it effortless to inform past customers about new offers they're sure to love. That allows you to nurture the relationships you have with existing customers and bring in repeat business.

I'll give you an example of social media's power. My son's organization, ADHD Kids Rock, has 26,000 Facebook followers, 92 percent of whom are women. That implies moms are overwhelmingly more interested in joining a community of other moms to get support for their kids with ADHD. My son then figured out the engaged moms tended to be within a particular age group. Then he tracked other groups they were involved with to find cross-promotion opportunities. All this was entirely free.

Social media also offers the chance for traditional PR activities, such as making you, the owner, the public face of the company. Giving in-depth podcast interviews and publishing YouTube videos detailing your products' features and benefits, for example, set you up as a customer-friendly company with no secrets lurking behind your supply chain. They also give customers confidence to buy from you as they form an attachment to your cool, engaged personal brand.

Used properly, social media is a free marketing platform with unlimited opportunity to scale your lead generation, sales, and profit. It all depends on how much time you want to put into it or how much you're willing to pay someone to develop these platforms on your behalf.

Marketing Doesn't Have to Be Scary

One misconception I see a lot when coaching business owners is that most believe marketing comes first. Marketing is actually last, in my opinion, because only then can you bring in all the customers that you want and know you'll be able to keep them. If you do the marketing first before your core systems and structure are fully in place, you can spend all the money you have getting customers just to lose them. Then word gets out that you provide bad service. If your pricing and costs are off, you could be losing money with each sale. Then, no matter how much more marketing you do, those two stars that you got on Google and that bad Yelp review are going to limit your effectiveness for a long time.

Take the same approach that I do with my new clients. Do a full review of the systems in your organization, especially the client onboarding process and user experience on your website. Only once you've got your system fine-tuned to provide an excellent experience do you throw money into marketing. This approach generates tremendously positive word of mouth as your customers rave on social media about how wonderful your service was and how easy it was to buy from you. The goal is to turn your entire marketing approach into a system. That way, you're not manually marketing for every individual sale.

On time, every time, exactly as promised!

Feeling better about marketing yet? It's all about understanding what you're selling, who you're selling to, why they're going to buy, and how you're going to get it to them. Everything included in this chapter details those four essentials. From here, it's a process of refining what works until your marketing is organized—and profitable.

CHAPTER 12

ASK FOR THE SALE

Have you ever had a bad sales experience as a customer? Maybe you tried to buy from a terrible website that you couldn't figure out? What if your bad experience also shut down your business?

Roger, one of my contractor friends, received his standard license renewal notice in the mail like he has for the past thirty years. It's about $250 a year, so he's paid them $7,500 over his lifetime. They're still using 100 percent paper notices in the 2020s, but the notice directs you to their website. So he went to the site and tried to pay his renewal fee.

Roger signed in, made an account, and entered his billing code, plus a couple of additional steps. Somewhere along the line, the system kept messing up and forcing him onto dead-end pages that wouldn't accept information.

Poor Roger kept at it for weeks. He called their customer service number, but it was just an automated machine that redirected him back to the website. So he kept trying while searching desperately for another contact number.

Weeks went by, then two months. Roger got another notice, a nasty warning that his license would be discontinued if he didn't pay up. So he kept trying. He had other people try to help him, but the system didn't work.

I had lunch with him during this process and asked, "How's that licensing problem going?"

He stopped with a bite of food halfway to his mouth, then dropped his fork on his plate in disgust. "There goes my appetite."

"That bad?"

"I'm so mad, Beverlee. I'd love to get my hands on the numbskull who designed their renewal process."

I grimaced. "Some business owners act like they don't want your money."

"That's *exactly* what it's like! I've got to jump through all these hoops to prove I really want my license. Feels like I'm begging them to take my money, and they still won't. If I didn't need this license, I'd tell them where they can shove it."

A week later, Roger got a notice that his license had been canceled. His company couldn't get key contracts without that license, so he had to temporarily halt all related work. He then filed legal action against the licensing organization. All this lost time, wasted money, and unnecessary drama because of a broken sales system.

We've all experienced bad sales funnels. You might cruise a small artist's website and find a cool sculpture you'd like for your office. To buy it, you need to make an account. Then you need to verify your identity. Then you need to enter all your information in advance. And the payment options are really unusual. You're forced to create a second account on a payment processing platform you don't use and aren't sure you can trust.

If you were just casually shopping on your work break, you'd probably give up and abandon the sculpture in the shopping cart. You wanted to buy, but the business wouldn't let you.

Other problems arise when dealing with a human salesperson. I've had plenty of contractors I decided not to hire to work on my rental properties because they made the sales process too hard. We'd be on the phone, and I'd have my credit card in my hand ready to pay. Then they'd ask to call back on a different phone. Not right away, of course. They had to do something else first. So I'd wait for the return call . . . that never came.

Making the sale hard is death for any business. You as a customer prefer a frictionless buying experience. If that's your preference, offer it to your customers as well. Love your neighbor as you love yourself; sell to your neighbor the way you'd like to be sold. Here's how.

What Exactly Is Selling—And How Do You Do It Right?

Let's begin to answer this question by deepening our definition. **Selling is the process of exchanging your product for money.** It's the lifeblood of every business. To sell is to live.

While we've established that marketing is not selling, consider sales the final element of your marketing system. The last stage of a campaign. The bottom of the funnel. Whatever you call it, converting prospects into customers is the culmination of all the smart, hard work you learned about in the previous chapter.

Selling is also about helping. By selling the customer your product, you are solving a problem in their life. You, the seller, have something the buyer needs or wants. Selling is the transaction of fulfilling that need or want. Could there be anything more natural than this?

We all sell early in life. You've seen a hungry toddler in a grocery store demanding a treat. That's sales. If they're loud enough, persistent enough—sad, pouty, or whatever strategy happens to work on Dad that day—they close the sale.

The opposite of the high-pressure toddler is the entrepreneur with a great product. They've spent thousands of dollars on advertising yet are afraid to pick up the phone and follow up with a prospect. Selling feels uncomfortable, unnatural, because they feel like they're pressuring someone to buy something they don't need to survive. Sound familiar?

Entrepreneurs are brilliant dream-followers. They're talented technicians. Both brought about their business in the first place. Yet even experienced entrepreneurs will admit they're terrible salespeople. And they're terrified of sales.

This lack of sales know-how and confidence is normal, unfortunately, because we're taught to be humble. Don't brag, parents and teachers told us. Don't put yourself out there and talk about what you can do.

Resistance to selling goes deeper, from nurture to nature. We're human. Humans don't like rejection. Selling often means rejection. Don't sell; don't eat. Goodbye business, goodbye life. So if you want to survive, sell like your life and your family's lives depend on it.

Because they do.

The Difference between Marketing and Selling

When I coach small business entrepreneurs in building their sales system, they often ask me how marketing and sales feed off each other. I like to put it this way.

Marketing is lead generation. Sales is lead conversion. Marketing is not sales. It's the first half of every sale. Marketing brings attention to your offering so that consumers know what it is you're selling. Selling nurtures those prospects and makes it easy for them to buy.

Let's say you spend your weekend at a trade show promoting your company. Chances are you will have spent several thousand dollars and had to give up your precious weekend. In your marketing plan, you had a draw and collected names. By doing this, you were successful at lead generation. This is a great example of marketing.

Now what are you going to do with those names? Do you need to make some phone calls? Will you add them to your database and send them valuable information that you know will help them? How will you convert and make a sale? That shifts from marketing into the selling half of the process.

Your marketing and sales systems are deeply interconnected and need to be evaluated together. And every product has its own necessary sales process. For some, the sale is an automatic click from a marketing campaign. For other products and services, the sales process is longer and more complex.

Converting such browsers into buyers requires a follow-up, relationship-building stage. It takes strategy, action, and time. Often, small business owners don't ask for the sale in the first place. Or they neglect to stay with a prospect long enough to naturally allow the sales cycle to reach completion. Every small business owner needs a system that accounts for the entirety of this process, from first touch on through repeat business.

The Small Business Selling System

Selling takes time and effort; there is no getting around it. And it's all about personalization to the customer.

The sales systems you create should make it easy for a prospect to buy from you. That includes not only payment processing but also forming a relationship with the customer, understanding your consumers' buying patterns, and having the courage to stay engaged long enough to close the deal. No other system grows your revenue like a functional sales system, period.

What I say next should come as no surprise. The number-one mistake I see entrepreneurs make in their entire business is failing to follow up with prospects. These relationships could have led to a sale—or many. This doesn't mean you need to get aggressive or make anyone feel uncomfortable. Jeffrey Gitomer, North America's leading sales trainer and bestselling author, has famously said, "People don't like to be sold, but they love to buy!"[22] Jeff's right. No one likes in-your-face sales tactics. We *do* love to shop and buy. And we'd rather buy from someone we know and trust. That means your sales system needs to be built on relationships and trust.

Follow-up is crucial. This is sometimes a phone call or an abandoned cart system that contacts clients who didn't finalize a sale. Never assume that just because someone hasn't bought from you yet that they chose not to or never will. We are all busy. All a prospect may need is a little nudge from you in the form of a friendly text or email, especially if you know that what you're offering will help them.

When I ran the travel agency, clients often planned years in advance for special vacations, long before prices or airline seats were available to buy. Our sales system included a future travel registry that we reviewed daily to ensure our team was the first agency they heard from when products and better prices became available. Retailers do this well with regular discount coupons. Martial arts schools offer a free trial. And carpet cleaning companies offer to do extra work for the same price.

At some point, your prospect will be ready to buy, and if you are not in that relationship in some meaningful way, the sale will go to someone who is. For many service products, all your prospect wants is someone who is willing to sit with them long enough to help them buy what it is you are offering.

When building your lead conversion or sales system, include some way to stay in touch with customers. That way, when prospects are ready to buy what you sell, your company's name will be at the top of their minds.

---

22   Jeffrey Gitomer, "People Don't Like to Be Sold—But They Love to Buy." Gitomer, November 1, 2017, https://www.gitomer.com/people-dont-like-to-be-sold-but-they-love-to-buy/.

What Are Customers Thinking When They Buy?

Now you understand your goals, thoughts, and outlook on sales. Let's talk about what your potential customer is thinking as they wonder whether or not to swipe their card.

According to *ABCs of Relationship Selling*[23] by Charles Futrell, Raj Agnihotri, and Mark Valvasori, a prospect goes through five specific mental steps on their journey to making a purchase. These steps are also referred to as the sales funnel or buying process.[24] Here's each step and how to maximize your potential sale opportunity.

Step 1 Attention: *Obtain Your Prospect's Full Attention*

Start selling by grabbing your prospect's attention. This can be hard since you may be battling distractions, their lack of time, or their lack of interest. And no matter how good you are at grabbing attention, it's only a temporary effect. Once you've got that attention, move quickly to the next step in your sales system to sustain your prospect's interest.

Step 2 Interest: *Develop Your Prospect's Interest in Your Product*

You can maintain a prospect's interest by entering into a discussion with them. That could be face-to-face, through an ad, on your landing page, or via email. Listen to their problems and position your products as a solution. Connect your product's benefits to prospects' needs. Once you do this, they will desire your product because they understand how it can help solve their problem.

Step 3 Desire: *Create a Desire That Fulfills Your Prospect's Needs*

You know a prospect desires your product when they have clearly expressed a want or like for it. This doesn't have to be verbal. Prospects can express their desire by attending your webinars, booking free consultations, lingering in your store in front of a display, or signing up for your weekly newsletter. Maintain your prospects' desire by offering information that combats their objections and answers their questions before they even ask them.

Step 4 Conviction: *Prove Your Product Can Meet Your Prospect's Needs*

---

23   Charles Futrell, Raj Agnihotri, and Mark Valvasori, *ABCs of Relationship Selling Through Service*, 6th ed. (Whitby, Ont.: McGraw Hill Ryerson, 2015).

24   Corporate Finance Institute, "AIDA Model," November 26, 2022, https://corporatefinanceinstitute.com/resources/management/aida-model-marketing/.

Even though a prospect desires your product, they might not buy it because there are a lot of other options out there. Your prospect needs a strong belief that your product is the best for them. You can provide this by sharing testimonials, case studies, or other social or scientific proof. Establishing conviction removes all doubts your potential client has about the benefits of the purchase.

Step 5 Purchase: *Prompt Action from Your Prospect That Ends in a Purchase*

Once the prospect is convinced, you just need to ask them to buy or act. Plan the most appropriate method for them to purchase—perhaps an online purchase—or direct them to book an appointment. Closing the sale is actually the easiest part of the whole process when your system works correctly. If you implemented the earlier steps, your prospect will be happy to make a purchase.

Now let's look at the five mental steps in action!

Let's say you own a bakery and sell cookies. You capture a potential customer's **attention** by placing your chocolate chip cookies in a window display. They stop and look at the cookies and feel hungry.

You have a sign in the window that says *Want a snack?* Your sign opens up a discussion in their head that keeps them **interested** because they are hungry, and a snack will satisfy their need.

They don't know for sure if your cookie has chocolate chips or raisins in it. Then they see a label by the cookies that has all the ingredients on it, including chocolate chips. By listing the ingredients, you anticipated their objections and maintained their **desire**.

One of your most loyal customers walks out of your bakery and sees them looking. "Those are the best chocolate chip cookies in town," they say. This word-of-mouth testimonial establishes **conviction** in your potential buyer. No doubts about your cookies remain.

Your potential customer decides they will buy a cookie. They open the door to your bakery and see a sign at the register that says *Order here.* This directs them to the method they need to use to make a **purchase**.

This is a finely tuned selling system. To build your own selling system, consider the following points.

Eight Tips to Building Your Selling System

1. Get Clear

What are you selling? What does it do? How much does it cost?

One of the worst things you can do is confuse your customers or force them to ask clarifying questions. Make it easy for people to buy from you.

2. Sell What People Want to Buy

Have you ever walked into a health food store looking for zinc and had the salespeople yammer on about their vitamin C sale? You knew what you wanted to buy. You just wanted to get in and out. You wanted to give the business your money. Hearing about vitamin C three times made you wish you'd just ordered online from someone else.

Your customers feel the same way when pushed too hard. Once you get the sale, *shut up*. When they tell you what they want to buy, sell it to them. Don't talk them out of buying. Yes, you may be able to offer an upsell, but listen to what your customer is telling you. You're almost guaranteed to get their cash at that point. Don't screw it up by adding friction to their process.

3. Do the Math

How many customer conversions do you need? Figure out how many sales you require to meet your business goals. To do this, work backward from your gross revenue goal and break it down.

For example, say your company needs to earn $6 million. Assume that you have a big product that costs $1,200. That means you need to make 5,000 sales to reach your goal. If you assume that about 20 percent of customers will buy from you, you need to reach out to 25,000 customers in your marketing campaign.

Base this sales formula on your own business. This tells you exactly what your target conversion is not only to stay open but also to start growing as a company. Over time, you can increase your customer outreach numbers to boost sales.

4. Remain Responsive

Customers want to know you'll still be around after the sale. And they like feeling valuable enough to earn your attention.

Pay attention to phone calls and emails. Don't let customer communications pile up unanswered. Respond to your customers so they feel valuable to you. Each positive, uplifting interaction makes the sale all the more likely. People like buying from people who make them feel good.

5. Make a Compelling Offer

Sometimes a bit of urgency pushes resistant customers into action.

You've seen this in practice. Some companies give a deadline for a sale price or promise delivery by a certain date with a countdown clock. Others stir up a sense of scarcity by announcing only a certain number of products remain in stock.

Even service providers can capture this compelling urgency by allowing customers to book appointments online instead of waiting for a callback after they might lose interest.

Create compelling urgency in the sale—ethically, of course—and your more resistant customers may just push that buy button, sign off on the proposal, or put your product in their shopping cart.

6. Cross-Sell and Upsell

It's important to have an additional product on hand for customers willing to pay a little more. But you need to do this tastefully.

Don't bait and switch. Rental car salespeople are notorious for this tactic. Customers come in with one specific need; the salesperson introduces dozens of extra options and then packs on the fees and upgrades after the sale.

You want a little urgency to buy, but you don't want your customers to feel pressured or tricked. And don't be an airline that charges extra for everything, so the customer feels robbed. Only offer upgrades at the right time and be tactful about it.

7. Never Sell out of Your Own Pocketbook

Don't assume that just because you can't afford the products and services your company sells that others have the same limitations. What is expensive to one person is nothing to someone else. You may be tempted to offer a discount to make it feel better for your pocketbook; take a step back to ensure your own financial bias is not influencing the decision. A great offering at a price your ideal customers will pay is what we are looking for.

8. Keep Testing Your System

How well are your lead conversion strategies working? Your sales system can always be improved to better meet the needs of your customers and prospects. Here are a few ways you can measure the effectiveness of your systems:

A/B split testing. This means you have two versions of the same conversion strategy. For example, one version of your website might feature an option to buy right at the top of the website. The other version describes the product in detail first, then offers the option to purchase at the bottom. You run both pages and see which one sells more and adjust accordingly.

Yes or no. Does your sales system ask until your prospect says yes or no? Or do you stop before you get an answer? Most salespeople (a.k.a. small business owners) give up too soon. They ask once, "Do you want to buy?" And when they don't get a positive reply or they get no reply, they give up.

If there has been any interest at all from the prospect, it is especially important to stay in the conversation long enough for them to say yes. Stay in touch, keep asking questions, and keep listening and building trust and solving their problems.

Listening. You will sell more by listening than talking. Selling doesn't mean doing all the talking. In fact, you will likely lose a sale by dominating the conversation. The most successful salespeople ask questions and listen for a response.

Four Steps to Building Your Sales Confidence

You have a great product. You are super proud of what you are offering. Your prospects need you and your service. You have spent hundreds of hours and thousands of dollars on a beautiful website and social media marketing. And yet you are scared to ask for the sale. Why?

Reluctance to ask for a sale is a common experience. You are not alone! In fact, according to sales trainer and *Entrepreneur* magazine columnist Barry Farber[25], salespeople cause prospects to pull away from the sale for

---

25   Barry Farber, *12 Cliches of Selling (and Why They Work)* (New York: Workman Publishing Company, 2001).

one (or more) of twelve reasons. Ever noticed yourself or your salespeople acting this way?

1. **Yielder**: fears intruding on others or being pushy

2. **Overpreparer**: overanalyzes, underacts

3. **Emotionally unemancipated**: fears loss of family approval, resists mixing business and family

4. **Separationist**: fears loss of friends, resists prospecting among personal friends

5. **Hyper-pro**: obsessed with image, fears being humiliated

6. **Role rejector**: ashamed to be in sales

7. **Socially self-conscious**: fears intruding on others or being pushy, intimidated by upmarket customers

8. **Doomsayer**: worries, won't take risks

9. **Telephonic**: fears using the telephone for prospecting or selling; also refers to fear of using texting, social media, email, or any other device for selling

10. **Stage fright**: fears group presentations

11. **Referral aversions**: fears distributing existing business or client relationships

12. **Oppositional reflex**: rebuffs attempts to be coached

So what do you do when you meet resistance? The following four simple techniques will have you getting out of your own way, handling objections with ease, and closing with confidence.

Step 1 Admit and Acknowledge

Admitting and acknowledging your fear is the first major step in conquering sales reluctance. Just admit it. You don't need to take action yet because even when you acknowledge your reluctance to pursue sales, there will still be hesitancy to admit it out loud. Entrepreneurs deal with internal and external pressure to seem positive, knowledgeable, and successful at all times.

The first step in conquering your fear is not an easy one. You must admit to yourself what's holding you back. It will be OK. Give yourself patience as you work on yourself—and work through resistance to selling.

Step 2 Get Specific

Determine which of the twelve attributes contributes the most to your sales reluctance. All small business owners who close sales consistently once had to identify specific fears and negative thoughts around selling. Do the same. Once you've found your exact challenge, you can build a plan to beat it. For example, if you've suffered from stage fright, practice your pitch in front of family or friends you trust. Honest feedback and the choice to take yourself a lot less seriously will both go a long way.

Step 3 Break and Repeat

Tackling your sales reluctance is similar to breaking a bad habit. A habit is broken or maintained by repeated action and behavior. That means you'll have to make it a habit to force yourself to overcome that specific fear by doing it anyway. Eventually, it will get easier, but it's tough at the start. Some small business owners use a token reward system or rely on relaxation techniques early on when breaking a habit. Another counter-measure is replacing negative thoughts with positive ones. For example, when you are nervous about a sale, you can think back to the time you were in a similar situation and did well. My personal strategy to overcome sales reluctance fear is to ask myself, "What would I do if I were brave?" Works every time.

Step 4 Keep Going

Follow up! Keep emailing, posting, and making calls. It takes continual action for small business owners to overcome sales reluctance. It's not that you don't have the skills, prospects, or leads to make a sale; your results are most likely a reflection of your commitment to overcome your fear. If you want sales, you can get them.

Sales 2.0: Customer Retention

If you want to survive as a business, you'd best plan to keep your customers.

Ask any small business owner where they get the majority of their business from, and almost 100 percent of the time they will say, "Word of mouth." With the stakes that high, we can't ignore those existing customers who are referring new business our way. One of the most powerful and essential systems to grow your business is the way you take care of your existing customers.

It is way more expensive to acquire a new customer than it is to keep existing customers happy. Consider that the probability of a sale from a new customer is only 5 to 20 percent, whereas from an existing customer, it is between 60 and 70 percent. That means your past customers are the most likely people on earth to buy from you again. Eighty percent of your future profits could come from just 20 percent of your existing customers. You do not want to let them go without building a relationship.

It is common to take those deeply valuable relationships you have with your best customers for granted. Putting in place recognition systems that celebrate and support these relationships along with being open to constructive feedback will ensure that this lead generation tool stays strong. Happy customers will buy from you again and are most likely to tell others about the value your business provides. That's why customer retention strategies are so important.

Customer Retention Exercise

Do you know who your best customers are? Make a list of your top ten existing customers who appreciate and buy from you the most. Based on that list, what common attributes do those customers share? To answer that question, write down short answers to the following questions:

- What do they buy?
- How often do they buy it?
- How did you initially meet them?
- What do they love about you and your company?
- Why do they keep coming back?
- Who do they tell about your products or services?
- What words do they use?
- How long have they been a customer?
- How did you reward them?
- What was the total gross revenue from these top ten customers last year?
- What percentage of your business does this represent?

The Lifecycle of a Buyer

Assuming you have repeat customers, what does that relationship look like long term? You need to plan out how customers will experience your company over the years, not just at the first sale. Strategic approaches to lifelong customers can yield unlimited sales for barely any extra marketing cost.

Ask yourself what you can do specifically to delight and retain existing customers.

Remember that all customers you have now started out as strangers. Something you are doing attracted them to visit your place of business or website. From there, they became a lead and, after their first purchase, a customer. Some of them are so happy with you that they now promote your business.

When creating a marketing system for growing your revenue, ask if you are spending enough time delighting your existing customers versus trying to attract new ones. This will shift your mindset to making your current customers just as happy as new customers.

A good example *not* to follow is big banks. They are notorious for giving new customers lower rates, perks, and benefits that are often not available to existing customers. Don't make your existing customers feel bad for having signed up with you already. It's better to go in the other direction and make your existing customers feel like the stars. When new customers see that, they can anticipate the star treatment as their relationship with you grows.

When you plan out your strategies, ask yourself a few questions:

- What activities would resonate best with these customers and their needs?
- What would be the cost to me?
- When would I need to do this?
- How often?
- What results would I achieve?
- How would I measure those results?

Four Customer Retention Strategies That Work

Stumped for how to nurture existing customers so one-off purchases become recurring revenue? Check out these four strategies I've shared with other small business owners. Mix and match the tips and tactics into a personalized approach that works best for your industry.

1. Surprise and Delight

- Send a birthday card.
- Personally deliver a gift.
- Take them for lunch.
- Provide event tickets.
- Remember their kids' or grandkids' names.
- Buy them their favorite wine, chocolate, coffee, et cetera.

2. Show Appreciation

- Use your words to thank them.
- Check in on them for no reason other than to say hello.
- Call them right away when they give you a referral.
- Invite them to events, parties, or celebrations.
- Send a handwritten note or thank-you card.

3. Provide Memorable Service

- Give them referrals.
- Share helpful information specific to their needs.
- Offer to help.
- Offer to give their kid a job (if appropriate).
- Use your network to help solve a problem for them.
- Generously share information.

More practical advice on remarkable customer service coming up in the next chapter—stay tuned.

4. Be Personable

- Answer your phone.
- Call them back.

- Make it simple to buy.
- Have a stress-free return policy.
- Be transparent in your pricing.
- Talk to them.
- Use their name.
- Keep things simple.

Selling Is the Means and the Means to the End (And That's OK)

Small business owners are the most generous people on the planet. When they do well, the entire community benefits. New jobs are created, charities are supported, and families grow strong.

The goal of selling is to make money. There's no getting around that. With money, you have the freedom and power to contribute more generously to your own and others' lives. Selling makes community growth possible.

Don't be afraid of spending time on this part of the process. The average micro business owner (with fewer than five employees) may need to spend 60 percent of their time selling. With the right systems in place, the processes can be automated and done in less time. You'll just need some time to build those systems, and that starts by manually figuring out what works.

Remember that human beings are making the decision to buy from you. They need to feel seen, heard, and understood. Make it easy for them to buy, thank them, and give them business in return if you can. Every effective sales system puts relationships first. After all, you're not asking prospects to "marry" your business on the first date. So start where it makes sense to start. Ask for the first date—offer your solution—and see where it goes.

CHAPTER 13

GUARDING YOUR CUSTOMER SERVICE STANDARDS

Before I opened Somerville Travel, I had mastered customer service. Underperformance is not why I left my previous travel agency employer. We parted ways for reasons you already know, so I felt free to create a consistent customer experience across my own organization.

At first, the opposite happened. The travel agents I hired had their own understanding of service excellence. Each treated customers well yet differently. Everyone who walked through our doors received a unique experience based on who greeted them.

Why is that a problem? you may wonder. *Who cares if it's not uniform? After all, isn't good service all that matters?*

The answer may surprise you. As is the case with many small businesses, the majority of Somerville Travel business came by word of mouth. Our first customers had a delightful experience with me, then recommended us. If they came back and my staff didn't do things the way I did them, that word of mouth could turn sour, and we'd lose business. Even if my staff didn't provide bad service, it wasn't the same service. Maybe we didn't call to confirm at the same time during the process, or we offered different special options that didn't resonate. Customers didn't know what to expect.

Uncertainty could have crashed my business before we got off the ground. I quickly realized we had to unify our customer service standards so customers always knew what to expect and could recommend us with confidence. So I built a system around my own customer service standards and trained all my staff.

As a result, word of mouth exploded across British Columbia. Customers from all over the province rushed in the door to experience the Somerville Travel way.

Each time I've shared this story with entrepreneur clients, I've found that customer service, like marketing, is vaguely defined and poorly undefined. Every small business owner has their own definition yet confidently says, "Our service is the best!" Meanwhile, the company is disorganized and unprofitable.

It can't be true that every company provides the industry's best service. At the same time, I believe these owners honestly think that their service is the one thing that sets them apart from the competition. They just don't realize that discrepancies in their service model ruin the customer experience. After all, entrepreneurs tend to be technicians. Like me, they killed it on the job before starting their own company. Customers requested them specifically, so they turned their service into a business. As excellent technicians, they had certain service standards. Few technicians-turned-entrepreneurs realize that their previous standards aren't met by employees they've hired and trained. Often, they only realize this in a crisis, such as when a key employee leaves. Service standards change because that individual upheld your standards while other employees didn't. You just didn't notice.

That's why you need one overall company standard. Identify what "best service in the industry" actually looks like, how you can uniquely provide it, and what that requires of every employee. In this chapter, we'll do just that. And the resulting true excellence in service will save your business.

Live by Customer Service, Die by Customer Service

Put simply, customer service is consistent, excellent delivery of what is expected from your company to the customer. Ask anyone you know, "Where did you get the best customer service?" and they'll tell you a story about a hotel clerk who allowed them to check in early so they didn't have to wait hours at a diner. Maybe they'll recall an online store that refunded their money for an order because the item arrived a week late. Or an airline attendant saved the day by holding the flight a few minutes to allow an upset child time to use the restroom.

Then ask your friend, "Would you go back?" It's a silly question. Of course they would! Ask them why, and they'll likely explain their deep loyalty. They'll keep going back and always will because they know they'll get consistently excellent service.

To see the opposite effect, ask someone, "When did you receive terrible service?" The answer will be venom. They'll explain how a company wronged them, and it felt personal. Maybe an agent kept them on hold and couldn't answer their questions. They won't direct their anger at that one employee. No, they're angry at that company. And when you ask if they've ever gone back, they will explain the "burn notice" they put on that company. They're blacklisted for eternity—and they spread the word to everyone they know.

Customer service and the word of mouth that follows are the lifeblood of or death blow to your business. Good service makes you; bad service breaks you. Sure, people evangelize great customer service, but they also let anyone with ears and eyes know of the terrible customer service they received.

Great companies are built on a foundation of great reputation. And you want to be a company that people brag about because of how well you've done. That's how you stay in business, that's how you surpass your competition, and that's how you earn more money.

Your Brand Is Your Service; Your Service Is Your Brand

Brand is often associated with marketing. It's true that positive feelings about a brand are associated with customer attraction. That's not marketing or selling, though. Brand is the direct result of customer service. Consider this definition of branding: the process of creating a positive identity in the marketplace. Your product is what customers exchange money for, but the brand is what you actually sell. Your brand is the reputation and the experience you create in your customer's memory that keeps them coming back. It tells the world what they can expect from your company, you as the owner, and your products and services. And it's what inspires those recommendations customers give to family and friends that help your business expand.

It only takes a split second for consumers to make a judgment about your company based on what they see, hear, and feel. Because of that, all aspects of that experience need to be evaluated to systematize your brand. First impressions, previous experiences, the way your business looks, the tone your team uses to answer the phone or emails, and the energy in the environment all reflect how well you keep your promises to customers. They're also present in how you sell, how you market yourself, and how you treat one another behind the scenes every day. And they provide prospects and customers the ability to identify you in the market.

Imagine Joe's Java House sells the best organic coffee in town, but customers know that he may or may not be open early on Monday mornings. That experience of great coffee *and* the wait until Joe's Java opens are both part of that company's brand. If the coffeehouse is cluttered and has a funky pink logo, those, too, are part of their brand. Starbucks, on the other hand, has mostly good coffee. It's not necessarily the best, but they always open on time. Their facilities are clean, and their logo is recognized worldwide.

Humans like predictability, quality, and good experiences. As a small business owner, you can nurture these elements in your company, which, in turn, strengthens your brand. For that, you need a brand strategy. That may seem intimidating, but you've really got one already. You just don't know it.

Your brand strategy comes from your company promise, your values, and your purpose for owning this business in the first place. Ask yourself, *How do I want my clients and prospects to feel about doing business with my company?* That gets you started. Now consider these additional questions as small opportunities to improve your brand, resulting in better customer service.

What's your **company's promise** to customers? This is the one thing your company stands by. For my travel agency, that meant giving them the best possible price with the smoothest process to create the most relaxing experience.

What are your company **values**? Are honesty and integrity at the top of your list? Community? A shared identity? This informs your brand.

Does your **logo** reflect your promise and values? Customers should see your logo and connect some aspect of it to your business model. And it should be distinct enough that people could wear it on a T-shirt, which helps with word of mouth and brand recognition.

Let's talk about your **style guide**. What colors, fonts, and images do customers connect with your brand? What color dominates your website? Starbucks is noticeably green, for example. Maintaining a consistent style immerses customers in your brand.

What's your **communication strategy**? That includes communication with prospects, clients, vendors, and each other in your office. Is it always prompt and respectful? Do they believe that you value their time?

Last, consider **sensory environment standards**. How do the music, sights, smells, and tone of voice your clients encounter inform them about your brand? What memories do you create in their mind with tangible experiences?

When you design these with intention rather than letting them happen, you control how customers perceive your brand. So as you decide how you want your brand experienced, document the processes. This might mean having a checklist for staff that ensures the client area is clean or providing extra training on phone calls.

Remember that systems include three aspects: elements, interconnections, and purpose. A typical phone-based customer support system could be simply "How to answer your phone." The person answering the phone and the phone itself are the elements. The response script and how quickly the phone gets answered are the interconnections. The purpose is excellent customer service.

You might write a system that says, "In order to provide excellent customer service, every employee who answers a phone call from a customer should begin the phone call with the following greeting." Then you write out a specific greeting. You can model this on major companies: "Thank you for calling Amazon. This is Jorge. How can I help you?" Then you create a flowchart for directing calls to the right departments. This is a system that ensures your customers get the best phone experience from your employees even if you, the owner, are not present.

Having well-thought-out systems in place ensures you are consistently able to provide your highest level of service, which, in turn, builds incredible trust with those you serve. This is how you create the kind of predictability that makes customers recommend you to their closest family and friends. And you, the owner, will not be blindsided with terrible customer reviews because your employees don't hold the same standards that you do.

When developing service systems, take into consideration what you, the provider, are willing to give. This is based on resources of time, money, and perceived value. It may even be preference and how you want things done. The primary consideration, of course, is what the customer wants and expects. Great service is about meeting or exceeding expectations.

Another example is consistency. Customers expect it. To that end, you might have your graphics specialist create a visual identity guide that you use for all marketing and external publications that incorporates several of the branding elements mentioned earlier.

You already know how important it is to have open communication with your employees about their jobs. Leverage that transparency for your customers' sake. After all, the world's best brand ambassadors are your employees. Check in with them on how they feel about working for your company. What are some improvements they would like to see in areas of customer service, the work space, and company reputation?

I suggest asking your employees for ideas and feedback as you build and document these essential service-related processes:

- How to easily contact your company
- How to quickly respond to incoming inquiries
- How to provide information
- How to clarify questions and expectations
- How to quote prices
- How to easily buy your product or service
- How to explain product use
- How to provide maintenance or support
- How to monitor and evaluate customer service standards
- How to continuously improve at all levels

These little systems keep your brand and, therefore, customer service consistent. They also support your capacity to provide a remarkable customer experience they won't ever forget. Fulfilling a promise of value made to customers is more than what you do. It's how you make customers feel. Let's discuss that next.

The Next Level of Systematized Customer Service

"They may forget what you said, but they will never forget how you made them feel."[26]

Carl W. Buehner's famous line tells the difference between sales and service: between pitching your offer and meeting the customers' needs. I say *needs* here, not *wants*, because that's a useful way to think about doing business with your customer. You're not just there to sell; you're there to serve—to meet real human needs in the way only you can.

Maslow's Hierarchy of Needs for Customers

In 1943, psychologist Abraham Maslow proposed that humans require basic needs like physical safety and access to food to be met before they can focus on greater needs like education, relationships, and self-actualization.

Each level of the pyramid is a need that must be met, from bottom to top, to "unlock" higher needs and increased human potential. This maps onto the experience your business provides. Customers aren't going to care about how polite you are, for example, if your restaurant is filthy, and they're afraid you're going to make them sick. Each need must be met first before you can ascend to the next level. And the highest-quality companies that make the most money are the ones that meet all five levels of needs. Here's how.

Physical Customer Service

Maslow would say that a child can't focus on meeting their academic needs if they don't have adequate access to food and shelter. Basic human needs must be met first. How do your service levels meet basic human needs like using the restroom? Is yours clean and open? If yours requires a key, is the key clean and easy to access? Does a real human answer the phone? If not, is there a voice mail system employees are trained to respond to within minutes? Is *that* voice mail recording friendly and professional?

Physical customer service may not seem like it applies to every business model, but consider a hotel. Your job is to provide shelter. A restaurant provides food. Are you meeting those basic human needs consistently? A customer getting bad experiences at these basic levels is not happy.

---

26   Carl W. Buehner, quoted in Richard L. Evans, *Richard Evans' Quote Book* (Lebanon Junction, KY: Publishers Press, 1971).

This may even be the reason you keep a refrigerator of cold-water bottles available in the waiting area. Customers who show up early on a hot day and wait for fifteen minutes may feel dehydrated by the time they get to their appointment and may leave early.

Even providing snacks can help meet this service level. Maintaining a comfortable room temperature prevents clients from feeling miserable in your office. And comfortable chairs that keep your clients free from pain will prevent them from associating that pain with your company.

Whether you provide basic human needs as a service or not, incorporating this first level of needs into your business is a great way to build a positive brand reputation. Even something as simple as handing a free bottle of water to your customer on a hot day can give them positive feelings about your company and make them more likely to recommend your service.

Safe Customer Service

Maslow[27] stated that safety covers a range of topics including personal safety, employment, resources, health, and property. What service systems do you have in place to satisfy your customers' feelings of security? This question seems deceptively simple on the surface. You might answer, "We give them a receipt for everything we charge!"

Receipts are great, and that's one answer to a part of the question. Let's also consider a few other perspectives.

Is your office in an area that could make clients feel unsafe? Is your parking lot dark and ominous? Do they have to walk down a deserted alley to reach your front door? Is there a danger of getting robbed on their way in from their car? Some customers would rather order online and wait a couple of days than walk down to the corner store in downtown LA and get their items immediately because of safety concerns.

Inclusiveness is also important under safety concerns. If you're part of an organization that may historically have rejected certain groups, do those groups now feel safe coming into your company? Psychological safety is as important as physical safety.

---

27   Abraham Maslow, "A Theory of Human Motivation," *Psychological Review* 50, no. 4 (1943): 370–396, https://doi.org/https://doi.org/10.1037/h0054346.

Are your products safe from a health perspective? Even major corporations like McDonalds and Taco Bell have had to overhaul their offerings and images because public perception of the safety of their products was called into question.

Are your bathrooms clean? Is everything in your office orderly? Are customers afraid they'll slip and fall or get sick? Or are they just afraid you'll lose their order because your desk is a mess? Safety is about so much more than not getting robbed in the parking lot.

Does your website *feel* safe and secure? Do you have a current SSL certificate? If not, the visitor will receive a warning that your site is not safe. Is your website professional and orderly so the visitor feels confident inputting their credit card information, or are they wondering what scam artist threw this awful website together? Look at your website from a customer perspective and ask yourself if you'd rather put your sensitive information into your website or your competitor's website.

This level may seem silly to you if your company is in a safe area. Even so, make sure your customers feel totally and completely safe at every level. If you don't, you might be leaving money on the table and not even know it because those customers just won't come to you.

Customer Service for Belonging

Maslow defined belonging as friendship, intimacy, family, and connectedness. Through your service, how do your prospects and customers feel included and part of your mission? This is where clients begin to think of your brand as their brand. That's how you create repeat customers.

Clients want to feel cared for, valued, and respected. They also don't want to feel like you're just taking their money, and then you're done with them. They're looking to build a relationship that lasts beyond the cash. Are you providing that?

Even something as simple as adding them to an email list so they receive promotions in the future can help clients feel like they're a part of your business. So do special offers targeted at existing customers, rewards for repeat business, and special package deals just for clients you trust. Making them feel valued is a great way to get them hooked on your business.

Do you personalize your thank-yous to clients? Some online stores report great success and increased repeat business with something as simple as a hand-written thank-you note included with each item. Customers love that they took the time to write the note themselves by hand. It shows you care about the client even after they've handed you their money. Take it a step further and send them a birthday card. How could anyone not be impressed with this gesture?

You don't need to go overboard and offer clients free products that put you into the red. This isn't about breaking the bank because then you're wasting your repeat business profits. Instead, find simple ways to help your customers feel engaged.

Some companies even send out notifications as they grow to thank past customers for contributing. Maybe you send out an email when you open a new branch or expand your online store. You could say something like, "Your support helped make our growth possible." This gives clients a personal stake in your business.

Finding a way to make clients feel like they belong is how you shift from meeting the minimum expectations to building a positive reputation.

Customer Service for Esteem

The fourth level of needs on Maslow's hierarchy covers respect, self-esteem, status, and recognition. Forget about your product's features for a moment. How does your product make your customers feel about themselves?

Say you run a coffee shop with pastries and sandwiches. You're in a safe area, so customers aren't going to get robbed on the way in. You keep the food prep areas clean, so they know they won't get sick. And you help them feel like part of your culture by signing them up for exclusive deals and posting signs thanking them for their help in growing your business.

Then it comes out that your company gets your coffee beans through a distributor that benefits from child labor. Eating and drinking your products makes them feel like they're contributing to harmful and unethical activities. Do you think your customers are more or less likely to come back when they learn these secrets?

On the flip side, you can address these concerns in advance by sourcing products from ethical distributors and creators. You can make sure you're only offering products that clients feel good consuming.

What does your product say about a client's status? Are you the broke alternative to a better competitor? Or do you make your clients feel proud to set your product on their desks? You want customers to feel good enough about your company brand that they'd be happy to have your cup or paperweight or whatever product visible during Zoom meetings or YouTube videos they record.

The bottom line is that you want customers to feel proud at all levels to support your business. This transcends just the product itself and incorporates even aspects you may not consider, like how you treat your employees. If your company has an excellent reputation on employment sites like Glassdoor, you may want to capitalize on that and share with customers how genuinely satisfied your employees are. No one wants to buy from a sweatshop, but everyone feels good knowing their purchase improves not only the owner's life but also those of the employees.

Make sure your brand makes customers feel proud to be your customers. That keeps them coming back and gives you a buffer in case one bad experience slips through the cracks. A customer who loves your brand will often give you a second chance or write off the rare negative experience as a fluke.

Self-Actualizing Customer Service

Maslow said that humans who achieve all the previous need levels are then free to explore how to become the best version of themselves they can possibly be. This is the ultimate in self-expression and fulfillment. So what is it about your service that has turned some of your customers into evangelists for your company?

Many times, the pathway to this level of fulfillment is helping your customers feel like doing business with you is a way to improve the rest of the world. This is especially true if they feel that buying your product will help improve Maslow's hierarchy of needs for other people in their community.

I'll use my own family as an example. My father was one of the first people to buy a Tesla in Canada. He felt he could make a positive impact on the environment. That, in turn, would reduce the impact of harmful environmental damage on people in poorer communities. Did he feel like he got a status boost from driving a Tesla? Absolutely, and I won't pretend he didn't. Buying a Tesla made him feel great! It also entered him into an exclusive community, providing a sense of belonging.

Tesla charges premium prices because their product also meets this fifth level of human actualization. Owning a Tesla makes you feel like you're making the world a better place while keeping poor communities safe from oil and gas industry exploitation.

You as a company may feel challenged to apply this fifth bracket, especially if you're struggling to make ends meet right now. You might ask how you're able to help your customers change the world if you're just selling plastic molded parts for machinery or cooking up hamburgers in your small diner.

The answer is that maybe you can't. Maybe your product itself isn't the answer here. Your company is the answer. It could be that you solve this customer need by entering your company in charity and volunteer causes. Maybe you participate in Relay for Life and get matching company T-shirts with your logo. You take pictures at the event, raise money for the cause, and then share that information with your customers via email or in-store displays. You can run the charity drive inside your store and allow clients to donate to the cause too.

Then you follow up with emails. "Thanks to you, our company was able to participate in this event! We raised this much for charity! Thank you so much for being our customers and helping us assist these people in need!" That makes your customers feel like they belong, raises their self-esteem for supporting you, and helps them feel like they're changing the world. All by eating at your diner, buying your plastic parts, or booking vacations through your agency.

The *Next* Next Level of Service: Guarantees

Branding. Systems. Customer needs. Together, we've looked at these best practices of memorable service. Still, there's more. A promise made must be a promise kept. Everything you do in your business, from product sourcing through price negotiating, is meant to close the sale. Your operations systems are intended to make that sale as profitable as possible. Yet profitability is not the most important value. Integrity is. And sometimes, having integrity means losing the sale after you've made it—or at least being willing to risk just that.

I'm talking about product guarantees. A product as simple as a sandwich comes with a guarantee. The assumption baked into the product is that it tastes good and makes the customer feel full. If the sandwich tastes terrible or if the package presents a load of veggies but a tiny sliver of deceptive lettuce is all there is, a promise has been broken. Not only is the brand shattered, but integrity is also lost.

Unless the company is willing to do the right thing. So what is that right thing? A free sandwich? A full refund? And what does this sandwich have to do with your product or service?

Let's assume you're doing business with integrity, and your goal is to meet or exceed customer expectations. Complete the following two prompts.

Our company promise is:

We guarantee that:

You might hang your promise and guarantee in your shop or post them on your website. They build customers' confidence. Just remember that you need an adequate system to address these guarantees in a uniform manner. Design processes for taking returns, giving unhappy clients a discount, refunding shipping, or even refusing returns under certain circumstances if that's untenable for whatever reason. Make everything a clear and consistent practice.

Many major retailers post customer service guidelines at their front service desk. This sets expectations, gives employees a unified message, and gives the company a clear guideline to point to and say, "This is how our company operates. Here's what we can offer you to make this right."

Make sure your guarantees aren't going to drive you into the red just to make customers happy. You've got to draw the line somewhere. At the same time, know what you're promising and how to make things right if you ever fall short. That helps you address negative customer experiences and resolve those concerns before they become angry social media posts, harm your profits, or keep you up at night.

Customers may forget what you promised, but they will never forget how your promise made them feel.

How You Know You're Providing the Best Service Possible

When your customer service system is functioning well, you'll know. Customer enthusiasm for your brand will be high. Higher than you've ever seen. You'll be selling high volume, customers will have smiles on their faces after the transaction is complete, and social media will be buzzing with testimonials.

Your organization will stand out from competitors in the marketplace with a noticeable and defined brand. Everything you display and sell will be physically branded with colors and logos. The experience of doing business with you will consistently be at the level you set.

Your employees will be glad to work for you. They'll have genuine smiles on their faces even in the break room and while clocking in. They'll be some of your biggest sources of positive PR because they'll talk about how much they love working for you. Happy workers make for happy customers.

And word of mouth will be your biggest advertising. Clients will refer others to your company. When your customers are bringing the most important people in their lives in to see you so you can take care of them, you'll know you've done service right.

For you, the owner, customer service excellence means you can rest easy. You can take days off knowing customers will be treated as well as if you'd been there yourself. You won't need to wonder what headaches your inconsistent employees might create for you. And if you ever want to step away from your business, your reliable service ensures it can run without you and without any single employee you may have come to rely on.

You're organized, profitable, and above all . . . *free*.

CHAPTER 14
REWARD:
FINDING YOUR FUEL

Raj started his company at age thirty-two. For the first two years, he worked eighteen hours a day, six days a week. Over that period, business stabilized. There was money in the bank. He'd hired a competent team. And he started to work "normal" hours again. At that point, you'd think he might be happy.

"Beverlee . . . I just have to say . . . I'm miserable. Absolutely miserable." Raj, now a coaching client of mine, sat staring into his cup of plain black coffee. We'd met in a coffee shop known locally for blended drinks you can't find at the chains. He'd ordered the cheapest thing on the menu.

"What's going on, Raj?"

"Most days I just wonder, what's the point? When I make money, I have to surrender the taxes. When I lose money, I have to borrow against my house to pay the loss. Either way, there's nothing left for me. I barely have enough money in my pocket to buy myself a coffee."

I thought about Raj's business as he rubbed his eyes. I'd seen his financial statements already. He wasn't in danger of going under; in fact, he was doing pretty well. Yet talking about money made this thirty-five-year-old look his grandfather's age.

"Raj, why are you working so hard? What is one thing that would make you happy about being the owner of this business?"

He heaved a sigh. "I guess—I guess I'd have some cash to spend. And the time to enjoy spending it. I don't need fancy suits or a chandelier over my dining room table. I just want to be able to buy my wife flowers once in a while or, heaven forbid, buy that secondhand motorbike my neighbor is selling."

"How much are we talking about?"

"Maybe five hundred a month." He cringed. "That's a lot."

I took another sip. Five hundred was easily doable on his current earnings. The problem wasn't the bank account.

"What is keeping you from doing that now?"

"Well, I'm not sure. I'm constantly worrying about making sure we cover rent and payroll with money left over to feed my kids. I guess that makes me feel really guilty about spending any money at all on myself."

"Sounds like a no-win scenario. You, the leader, have to contribute the most effort. Everyone else gets to enjoy the fruits of your labor. And you force yourself to work harder without any reward. If you did that to an employee, they'd quit on the spot. You've been doing it to yourself for three years. No wonder you want to quit."

"Wow . . . Beverlee . . . You're right. I'd never tolerate that from anyone else."

"How are you supposed to run a business that takes care of everyone else if you starve your own needs in the process?"

It clicked. Raj made the decision to pay himself as we discussed: the $500 a month he wanted above the money he needed to bring home to the family to pay the bills. This was, for the first time in forever, money just for him to do whatever he wanted. That meant rewarding himself, the owner and technician in chief. True to his word, he didn't buy a chandelier. He spent that money on flowers for his partner and bought himself a motorcycle. He was happy.

The little things are always the big things. That few extra hundred a month—and what it meant to Raj—gave him all the energy he needed to further systematize his business into even greater profitability.

What Do You Want from Your Business Anyway?

Have you ever stopped to consider why you're working so hard? Yes, there's a lot to do. Yes, people are counting on you. And yes, you have bills to pay. And yet something about this business is serving you at a deeper level. At least it should be.

By years three through five, business owners who've survived that long typically see some revenue consistency. The initial madness has settled

REWARD: FINDING YOUR FUEL | 205

into a routine. For most business owners, that looks like a lot more work and a lot less life. They start to question what they're doing it all for. Is it really worth all this extra work just to say you own a business? All your friends who work a standard eight-to-five job get to check out at the end of the day. And they get paid for overtime and holidays and have benefits. Where's your reward for working double the hours?

The problem is, at the start, you don't mind working seven days a week. You love your business. Maybe your business feeds your family, even feeds your soul in some way. You pour your heart into your company. Then, one day, you realize you feel tired. And trapped. And you don't have the energy to build the systems that set you free because the reward of doing a good job has worn off. It wasn't enough to sustain your energy long term. You need more.

We business owners often don't think about what *we* need. We're too busy thinking about what the *business* needs instead, from customers and vendors to employees and interns. When you board an airplane, they tell you that in the event of an emergency, you need to put your oxygen mask on first before you put one on your child so that you, the adult, are clear and rational as you're taking care of others. You can't take care of the child if you try to put their oxygen mask on, can't figure it out, and pass out halfway through. Then you're both in danger. Put on your own mask first so you're able to take your time rescuing others.

It's the same in business. You're the leader. If you don't get your mask on first, you're frantic and fumbling as you attempt to care for others. You won't think clearly, you'll make mistakes, and you'll end up failing everyone involved. You'll be like Raj when we met, about ready to close up shop and send everyone home because he felt so miserable.

It's normal to forget your big *why*. I often ask entrepreneurs, "What made you believe it was important to own your business instead of working for someone else? What was your *why*?" If we haven't yet begun to organize their operations, I get a blank stare. And a confession.

"I don't remember. What the f— was I thinking?"

It's time to remember.

Your Reward Is Still There

With a strong enough reward driving you, you can endure through the years and build a thriving business. We've established that it's not enough to show a profit on the books at year's end if you, the owner, feel broke in bank, body, and spirit. There is no reason to work twice the hours of a full-time employee, earn less money, and have no fun.

It's all too common to be paid less than market wage or no wage at all when you own a business. Even worse, many business owners never take any substantial time off. They never rest, never earn, and then wonder why they burn out and feel like giving up.

At the very least, you need to be getting *something* of personal value as a reward for all your hard work. That reward may be owning the car of your dreams, taking annual vacations with your family, or even just being able to take a week off every Christmas holiday season. Saving money in your own account for your personal future use can be a great motivator for days when things are hard. As long as you keep a good record of it. Never underestimate the power of watching your personal fortune grow.

When talking about personal motivation in business, entrepreneurs like Raj have admitted how rewarding themselves worsens the misery.

"But Beverlee, how does this even apply to me?" they'll say. "There is no money. I can't take a bonus. I can't even cash my own paychecks!"

If this is the case for you, I encourage you to decide if how you are spending your time is worth the effort. If you're truly miserable and turning zero profit after many years of investment, you may be happier working for someone else.

However, chances are, the money *is* there. It's just being spent on other things that may be perceived as more important. Maybe you're pouring your paychecks back into the system to pay out employee bonuses or fund your advertising. Refer back to Chapter 5. Take a second look at your books—find where your paychecks are going. You can only go so long without getting paid or having time off. Your company is only as strong as you feel. And we want you to feel happy, healthy, and well compensated.

Owning a small business is one of the most demanding jobs on the planet. There's no getting around that truth. It is essential to decide what you want to get out of owning this company, or you will end up resenting it.

What's that for you? We began this book with prompts to help you put your values, goals, and purpose into words. Let's refresh your memory as we refuel your entrepreneurial spirit.

Six Steps to Claiming Your Reward

There's a standard operating procedure for everything. Here's one to find what will motivate you all over again to keep your business going.

1. Remember What Drives You

There was a reason you made the choice to become a business owner. What made you start your business in the first place? Why did you decide working for someone else wasn't going to meet your needs? What did you need to prove to yourself? Were you looking for freedom? Was it your passion for your industry?

What makes you wake up feeling energetic? What tasks or events or relationships make you feel enthusiastic about the day? What or who ignites your fire?

Beyond that, what makes you happy? If you're not happy, what specific change would it take to become happy?

I asked Raj, "How would your life change if your company was consistently turning a bigger profit every month?"

His answer told him what he needed. He'd have enough money and time to enjoy the fruits of his labor by caring for his family and himself. In the same way, ask yourself what would change if you suddenly had ample money flowing in. What would you do differently? That answer is what motivates you.

If you are honest with yourself, you will be able to find the things that make you happy, give you energy, and keep you going. Find your motivators first.

2. Reintegrate Company and Personal Goals

Aligning your business purpose with your life purpose brings the greatest rewards of all. If your personal goal is to spend as much time at home with your children as possible but your business keeps you at the office sixteen hours a day, your two goals are in opposition. You can only succeed in business at the expense of your personal goals.

Finding ways to align your personal and business goals is key for long-term sustainability. That doesn't mean everything is perfectly balanced; it just means you're working toward your personal goals by way of your business goals.

Maybe you're working more than you'd like now, and your personal goals are suffering. Take a step back with a coach or friend to honestly look at your current business model. What needs to shift? What system changes would give you more time off and more money to spend with your family while you're together so that you can unify your personal and business goals?

Some people also include personal causes and community drives in their business. They want to make money, and they also want to help people while they're doing it. If that's you, it might help your overall motivation to figure out how your business is helping people. You might need to make some changes or even add community events you haven't thought of yet as a way of including your personal need to help others.

3. Redefine What You Want

Now is not the time to be shy. Your business success is counting on you. List what you personally want to have from being the owner of your company.

If you were happy right now, what would that look like? For Raj, that was an extra $500 per month to spend on himself and save toward little things that made him happy.

Describe your perfect life. What does that feel like? What do you need? How will you know when you've "made it"? What will be different from how things are right now? Use phrases like "I have," "I am," and "I get to." These give clear present-tense directions.

- "I am spending time with my children."
- "I am saving money from the business so my kids won't need to take out huge student loans."
- "I get to help my community by providing low-cost service alternatives."

Your answers are your goals. These are what you're trying to achieve.

4. Tell Yourself the Truth

Now that you know your goals, can your current situation meet them? Does running a business in your current industry allow for the possibility of meeting those goals better than working a standard job? If the answer is no, then talk to someone who can help you decide if you should even be doing this.

Let's say you want to keep running your own business, but in your current situation, it looks impossible to ever meet your goals. You can't keep living at cross-purposes. What needs to change about your company? Maybe the company needs to go in a different direction. Or maybe you need to find a place where you can meet your own goals, even if that means working for someone else for a while.

Be honest with yourself. What changes need to happen to clear the obstacles from your path?

5. Design a Personal Reward System

To keep running this business, you need to have the energy and enthusiasm to keep going. And you have to find a way to make your own dreams come true. After all, you are the boss.

Write down the steps you'll need to take for those two things to happen. If your goal is to build a nest egg to buy a home, you might start with opening a business savings account and putting money aside every week for a dream house. Think of it like a lease payment to a supplier. Make it a fixed cost, put that money away no matter what, and watch it grow.

If money is not the issue and you need time away, then book that time off. Don't wait and find a way to make it work. Schedule the time off and start putting things in place right now so that you can get away.

Figure out the steps you need to make your goals come to life. Write them down, then start doing them.

6. Accept Your Reward

This is the part when you actually put yourself first. Too many business owners write themselves a paycheck but refuse to cash it.

It's time to start cashing your personal checks to yourself. Try it. You will be surprised at how much better you will feel after a holiday with your family or a whole weekend off to do one of your hobbies. A business owner who resents their own business is not going to grow that business to its fullest potential. You are a better businessperson when you're happy, rested, and fulfilled. You'll make more money by spending money on yourself than you will by cutting every pleasure out of your life.

Whatever it is that you need to be happy in this life, make sure you include it in your business plan. This will help you earn more in the long run.

Whatever You Want . . . *Go Get It*

You don't have to cut back from sixty hours to thirty next week or plan to take next month entirely off. Rewarding yourself could start with something as simple as taking every Friday afternoon off to hang out with your kids or go golfing with old buddies. Or setting aside money to get out of the apartment you hate and buy your dream home. Maybe even owning that 1968 Chevelle convertible you have always dreamed of. That could require raising prices or lowering other nonessential costs so that some of your hard-earned revenue can actually land in your wallet. If that's what it takes, make it happen.

Decide what you personally want to receive from being the owner of your company. And it doesn't have to be huge goals. You can have lots of small goals too. Experiment with small and large reward ideas. For example, if the thought of a month away from your business sends you into a panic, plan for one week. One week of no customer emails, employee phone calls, or fires to put out. Just rest and relaxation.

When you define your goals, describe how you and your family benefit from your rewards. When you imagine this personal goal achieved, how do you feel? What does that motivate you to do in your business? Do you feel that old fire waking up again? That's the power of rewards.

Whatever reward you want—whether that's taking August off two years from now or saving enough cash for the purchase of a lifetime—you can plan your personal reward so it becomes a reality. Pick your goal and then prepare, prepare, prepare. Ask lots of questions.

- When do you want to achieve it?
- What tasks do you need to delegate?
- What systems do you need to build?
- How much cash do you need to set aside for yourself? How will you measure your progress to ensure you are rewarded as needed?
- Who will keep you accountable for rewarding yourself when you get wrapped up in the business and feel like you can't cash your own paycheck?

Building your rewards into your company will ensure you actually want to run your company. If you never paid an employee, they'd never come back. So treat yourself like a valuable employee. Motivate yourself with the rewards you need to feel fulfilled.

And once you start rewarding yourself, get ready. Because your motivation will go through the roof. That means increased energy at work, accelerated company growth, and bigger profits.

When you think about it like that, you can't afford *not* to reward yourself.

CHAPTER 15

BE PREPARED FOR CHANGE

"People don't resist change. They resist *being* changed!"

That line from systems scientist and MIT lecturer Peter Senge has stayed with me for over twenty years because coaching hundreds of business owners during that time proved Peter true. Business owners enjoy change—when it's their own idea. When changes are forced on them, they often panic.

Not reacting quickly enough to these changes causes more business failures than any other factor. While it is essential to create a stable, systematic operating environment in your business, it's equally important to become a master of change. It may sound like a paradox to be both stable and flexible. We'll discuss this in a moment.

The word *change* is loaded with emotion. Why? Change simply means that something is becoming different than it was. That difference can be good or bad for a small business owner. And it usually depends on how prepared they are to weather those changes and adapt to the difference.

Change can happen to us, or we can make it happen. We call these planned and unplanned. Planned change includes making strategic staff cuts or deciding to expand. Unplanned change includes key employees leaving without notice or the world economy collapsing.

Both people and processes can be affected by change. It isn't just you or your business or your team; it's often all three that are affected at the same time. Change could come from your employees, your industry, the market, or the world.

As you might know, there are a wide array of possible changes that can influence your business. For example, social, political, economic, environmental, legal, and technological changes have all taken place just within the last two years (as of this writing) since COVID-19 arrived on the globe. Business owners in every industry have had to adapt on the fly. Some of these changes altered the way business owners could run their companies.

The key thing to remember about change is that it's inevitable, so it's best to prepare for it ahead of time. I'll show you how in this chapter.

Why Is Change So Difficult?

Even the idea of change creates anxiety for many entrepreneurs. Why? We don't like the unpredictable. We resist change because of fear: fear that we'll lose something, or we won't be able to adjust. If you and your family rely on your business to pay for your home and food, it can be scary when sudden instability threatens your household. Even if you're not reliant on your business for basic survival, losing money or adapting to changes is often enough to send a business owner scurrying to their favorite sugary snack for comfort. Change scares us because it *is* scary. We worry about looking bad, about losing our home, and about disappointing the people who rely on us.

Think of a small child who's never seen a thunderstorm before. Suddenly, their dark bedroom lights up with an unexpected flash from the window, followed by a tremendous crash. Even though the thunderstorm is outside, they don't know what to expect. Their world has changed, and they don't like it. If you're a parent, you probably remember many midnight invasions by terrified kids who worried a storm was coming to get them.

The same is true with business owners. For all our strength, skill, and poise, we hate the loud noises we hear outside our shop. We wonder if all that flashing light and crashing thunder are going to knock down our business. Sometimes all that noise comes to nothing, while other times we *do* need to adapt and change.

Business owners primarily fear change because of the risk of being overwhelmed. They started a business, so they know they can learn and grow with the market. After all, they've done it before. The sheer amount of time and energy required to both run that business and make changes can feel like a burden. The status quo is often easier and less painful to accept, even when business is dwindling. Many business owners forgo extra earnings because they don't have the energy to put in the work to change.

Fear of change can get in the way of our adapting effectively. Many restaurant owners who spent those crucial first six months of 2020 afraid of change ultimately went under because they failed to adapt to public concern over COVID-19. That thunderstorm really did invade their shop, and they needed to react. Some business owners had plans in place to push through that fear, and those were the owners who made it.

If you know you're going to have a fear response to impending change, you can manage that fear ahead of time. Prepare for change before it happens by laying out systems—systems that do the work for you, even when you're not at your best.

Let's talk about potential changes you might face and how to prepare for them.

What Causes Change?

Out of a million factors that can force change on a business, the most common ones are:

- When key employees leave
- When you lose your biggest customer
- When the government changes the rules
- When your lease runs out and the landlord won't renew
- When you change suppliers
- When the world economy shifts
- When you grow

Just thinking about some of these can keep you up at night. Still, they're considerations every business owner needs to plan for because change is inevitable. These changes will take place, and you will have to adapt to them.

And you don't have to let that worry you. As I always say, there's a system for everything. You just need a system for change.

Helping Employees through Change

In addition to owner challenges, there are a number of common changes that team members face. Yes, employees experience changes too. They probably won't be planning for them like you are, so here's a list of stressors to keep in mind when managing your team:

- When you, the owner, change the company vision
- When policies and procedures are absent
- When new people join the team
- When the technology systems are upgraded
- When you take on a big new client
- When someone quits
- When a personal crisis occurs

Think from the employee perspective for a moment. Instability in the owner means instability for the whole company. Everyone gets nervous that the changes you're implementing might cost them their jobs. When you make changes, or when changes happen to your company, it's important to assist your employees through those adaptations and address their concerns rather than dismissing them. And as we all know, personal changes at home can affect performance at work.

So what's the best way to address employee stressors and concerns? I'd like to present these useful change support systems identified by Edward Deevy in his 1995 book, *Creating the Resilient Organization:*[28]

- Create catharsis situations to help employees unload some of their emotional baggage.
- Provide evidence of why the change needs to occur.
- Share "business information" with staff so they understand what's happening and why.
- Treat employees like entrepreneurs.
- Stay focused on the big picture.
- Make the customer the focal point of all activity.
- Make sure your managers are on board with the change.
- Identify the most likely supporters and resisters early on in the process.
- Communicate that there is no going back.

---

28   Edward Deevy, *Creating the Resilient Organization: A Rapid Response Management Program* (Des Moines, IA: Prentice Hall Direct, 1995.

Most of this probably sounds like common sense. Because it is. But common sense often goes out the window when we're panicking about change. Writing down a procedure that lists commonsense approaches to change means you don't have to calm down enough to try to remember them in the heat of the moment. You can still be afraid, pop open your strategy binder, and just read what to do. Then you'll think, *That's common sense! I'd better go apply it.*

Notice that most of that list boils down to treating employees the way you'd want to be treated. Once again, if you're a parent, these may remind you of parenting strategies you used to get your children on board with tough changes. Humans of all ages get scared when authority figures in their lives force changes on them. While you're not your employees' parent, you're still an authority figure in their lives.

Taking the time to treat employees with respect, address their fears, and explain to them what's going on behind the scenes will show your workers that you value them. It can turn a difficult change into an opportunity to express appreciation. Handling change with care for your team can even deepen their loyalty to you as they recognize your respect for them.

There are often things in a company that, if changed, would significantly benefit all stakeholders. Your company is no exception. Can you think of one specific change you would like to see happen in your company in the next six months? Let's take a look at how to choose to change in a positive way.

Four Simple Steps to Managing Change the Deming Way

Remember W. E. Deming, the systems expert you met in Chapter 3? His process for successful change included four simple steps: plan, do, check, act.

Step 1. Plan

Look ahead to see how you want to improve your business. That could be identifying how you wish to adapt to a market change or figuring out how to grow your business. "Plan" is all about predicting outcomes and running through steps in advance. You can refer back to your change plan to complete this initial step.

I recommend naming the change in your plan. What one change would have a crucial impact on your company? What change have you been meaning to get around to? Or what have your best advisers been pushing you to do that you just haven't felt you had time for?

Now zoom out on your inquiry. Consider the big picture. How do you envision this change affecting the whole company? Identify the impact this will have on all the other elements of your business. What individual departments have to adapt? How will this change affect your earnings?

Next, identify how you feel about this change. What are your assumptions and beliefs? What scares you and excites you about it? What will it take to make you comfortable enough to move forward?

As you prepare for or respond to change, consider the support your managers and employees may need. Who on your team will need the most help related to this change? How can you provide that? How can you inspire others to want to make this change with you? What's in it for them? What actions can you take to ensure everyone affected by this change has the opportunity to express their concerns, contribute their ideas, and help implement this change?

Congratulations—you've just completed a change plan. This is how you identify improvements to be made and then make them. Now, let's bring this plan into the remaining three steps.

Step 2. Do

At Deming's second stage, implement your change on a small scale. Instead of rolling out the onboarding software to every client, you pick a small group for beta testing. Or you take employee volunteers to experiment with a commission-based pay system. You also document your steps as you go along so you know what changes actually took place.

Step 3. Check

Look over your results. Did your outcomes match your predictions? Did the change have the impact you were looking for? If so, move to Step 4. If not, go back to Plan and figure out new changes that account for what you learned during testing. Even failures are useful because they tell you what not to do, and they may even point you in a better direction.

Step 4. Act

Once your change is performing well in small tests, implement it with the whole company. Keep tracking data over time so you can see how your change continues to perform. If you're changing a sales system, keep a close eye on your sales numbers to see the effects of the change.

This four-step model lets you approach any change with confidence.

Transform Your Small Business into a Learning Organization

What if your company facilitated the learning of its members to continuously transform itself?

Learning is essential to successful change. When you not only support but also initiate building your employees' knowledge, you can leverage change into a positive experience for everyone involved. Change is no longer something to fear.

This means your company is always looking for changes coming over the horizon. Spot incoming trends from a distance, and you'll give your team time to adapt. And when you have to adapt quickly, you'll have the correct mindset to prevent panic because your team is already used to staying flexible.

Keeping your focus on learning means your team and company stay in a learning mindset. Learning organizations intentionally encourage and support continuous team learning and critical thinking, and they value employee contributions. A learning organization requires you and your team to be open to new ideas, communicate effectively, and understand the organization.

If you want to dive deeper into what it means to be a learning organization, check out Peter Senge's *The Fifth Discipline: The Art & Practice of the Learning Organization.*[29] I'll share five principles I've learned from him here so you can begin applying them to your work.

Systems thinking is all about understanding and addressing the big picture while examining the relationships between all related parts of that

---

29   Peter Senge, *The Fifth Discipline: The Art & Practice of the Learning Organization.* (New York: Doubleday, 1994).

picture. If you change one thing, what else will be affected? Sometimes smaller changes must be made to adapt to larger ones.

The discipline of **mental models** examines the impact of the deeply ingrained assumptions and generalizations that influence how we act. For example, change can be perceived as good or bad, depending on our individual life experience, power, and position in an organization. This is why those affected by change may need additional time, support, and input to feel reassured and ready.

The discipline of **shared vision** is the practice of finding "shared pictures of the future that foster genuine commitment and enrollment rather than compliance."[30] People change and learn not because they're told to, but because they want to. It's your role as business owner to find what motivates your team. That might include showing them how the business runs behind the scenes so they understand how their job might be in danger if this change isn't implemented. A more positive motivator could be shared performance-based bonuses for the whole team.

The discipline of **personal mastery** involves clarifying and deepening our personal vision. That means focusing our energies, practicing patience, and seeing reality objectively. We need to keep our heads and approach each situation realistically. People react differently to change, and learning to listen and understand is key. So are asking questions and taking the time to apply the answers you get.

The discipline of **team learning** starts with dialogue. Groups of people can look together for the larger picture beyond their individual perspectives. Change happens best when all stakeholders have the opportunity to contribute. Giving your employees the chance to voice concerns and share solutions can fill in gaps in your plan.

A Few Words on Grieving through Change

You've probably heard of the five stages of grief: denial, anger, bargaining, depression, and acceptance. Changes often follow the same pattern.

Business owners experience a cycle of grief when their business hits a major change. They can't just keep going the way they always have. If you feel some personal resistance, don't worry. The faster you work through

---

30   Senge, *The Fifth Discipline*, 9.

the stages of grief and change and the better you prepare in advance, the easier your adaptation will be.

If you suddenly lose revenue or a key employee quits, you'll grieve the change. You might first go into denial, refusing to accept the change and wishing it would just go away.

Realizing that the change isn't going away can make us angry. "How dare the government raise taxes! Don't they realize I'm trying to earn a living here?" Getting angry at the government really serves no purpose, and your only choice is to comply.

Realizing that leads us to the bargaining phase. "How can I minimize the damage without completely changing? Can I just give up some of my earnings? Maybe there's a tax loophole I need to find." Business owners will often go to great lengths to justify not changing. Some get stuck here, and their businesses suffer.

Then depression hits. When a business owner believes the change is just too big to adapt to or they feel too exhausted to make the change, they think about giving up. I see a lot of businesses go under during this phase because the business owner just gives up. They may be depressed for a day or for six months. A day is manageable, but six months can ruin your company. The key here is finding the drive to believe that the change can be managed and that you can still succeed.

This belief leads you into acceptance. "My world has changed, and I need to figure out how to keep up." Acceptance naturally leads to action. You embrace the change and dedicate yourself to your new course. That road leads you forward into the change and beyond.

And the changes never stop. In year five of owning my travel agency, the airlines decided to change the way we got paid. In one day, our revenue dropped by 70 percent! Over the next ninety days, 39 percent of all travel agencies in the US closed their doors. Many agency owners didn't get past the anger stage of the grief process. They spent their time writing to newspapers, begging the government to intervene, and crying on each other's shoulders in business meetings.

I also went through those emotions. I had a newborn baby at the time, and the last thing I needed was to change our entire revenue model. I went to one networking meeting with my newborn where there were about five hundred angry travel agency owners from various states. I was angry at first too. Then I accepted I had no control over the change. That meant I had to adapt or go out of business. Sink or swim. I chose to swim. Within three days, I changed our approach and charged a small fee for each ticket we issued. Within a week, I had a new financial model that included fees for hotel, car, and tour bookings.

My business was saved for the moment. The next step was to share this new model with every other agency I could talk to because if I couldn't convince other agencies to charge booking fees, we were all going to go out of business. We had to do this together. With babe in arms, I went from agency to agency, sharing my pricing and strategy.

The result? Our revenue went up 12 percent that year. Adapting to change was my only option. By embracing the challenge and changing to suit reality, we came out ahead.

When the changes come, and they will, don't throw a tantrum. Choose to win.

Remember, Change Doesn't Have to Be Awful

Yes, change is stressful. This stress is normal, and you may never reach a point where you feel zero anxiety over change. The systems in this chapter should take the edge off that stress and help you feel more confident. Writing down your change game plan allows you to communicate the next steps to others. And working with your team to embrace changes gives you the chance to grow closer to them while benefiting from their personal strengths.

If you approach change with a learning mindset and a plan, your company can thrive no matter what changes come your way.

CHAPTER 16

TAKING CARE OF YOURSELF

When I first met Lisa, I feared for her life.

Lisa ran a successful brick-and-mortar business that she had recently transitioned online. Her company had boomed so big that online sales accounted for the majority of revenue. Lisa kept the physical store open because customers traveled from out of province just to shop there. She even sold branded merchandise with her company logo to visitors as souvenirs.

From the outside, Lisa was thriving. She was a millionaire in her early forties, a single mom, and living the dream. But when she hired me as her business coach, I worried she might die before we could fix her issues.

At our first consultation, she had deep raccoon circles around her eyes. She laughed them off. "Sorry for looking so rough, Beverlee. I didn't sleep well last night."

"When was the last time you got good sleep?"

Her eyes glazed over as she thought. "Well, it's been a while. A long time. I think . . . at least a few months. Or years. Who has time to sleep when you run a business?" She laughed, but it sounded forced.

"Your money situation seems more than stable. You've posted profits for the last twelve months. What's keeping you awake at night?"

"Pain, mostly. And worrying about my son."

I did my best to keep the worry off my face. "What kind of pain?"

"Headaches. I'd guess you call them migraines, but I haven't gotten them checked out. Who's got time for doctor visits?"

"You get a lot of headaches?"

"Just once a day."

"*Only* one headache a day?"

"Yeah. Is that . . . like . . . a lot?"

"Well, some might think so. The pain keeps you awake. So you get them at night?"

"Usually around lunch, actually. But then my neck aches the rest of the day, right at the base of my skull. It's this constant throbbing pain."

"When was the last time you saw a doctor about this, Lisa?"

She laughed again. It sounded worse than fake. Closer to nervous. "I'm more worried about my son. He's always anxious and upset. When I come home, we get into arguments. He barely listens to me anymore. I don't know what to do."

"What have you tried so far? When was the last time you saw your family counselor?"

"I've definitely thought about calling her. My son means everything to me. He's the reason I work so hard. Gosh, we were so poor when I started, and I couldn't give him anything. Now he's got everything he could possibly want, but we're arguing more than ever. I'd love to fix our problems. But who has time for family therapy?"

I raised my hand and ticked off points. "So far you've asked, 'Who has time?' about sleep, your medical health, and your relationship with your son. If these aren't high enough priorities to warrant your time, what is?"

Lisa looked like I'd slapped her. "Beverlee, I do *everything* for my son!"

"I know you do. And are you taking care of the things that matter for the long term? You've given your son a financially stable life, and yourself as well. But are you giving your family a good life that you enjoy together?"

Lisa took my suggestions to heart. She went to see her doctor the very next week and was diagnosed not only with migraines but also with a slipped disc in her neck that pinched a nerve. She'd let it go on so long that she might need surgery to correct it. She cried when she told me the news.

As for her son, she scheduled family therapy the next month. Her son was diagnosed with anxiety and attachment issues. She and her son declined medication, and fixing the issues required months of focused relationship work.

Six months later, she confided in me, "Beverlee, I'm spending so much of the money I made in my business on solving these personal issues. I wish I'd been smarter about fixing them when they were small. Now they're huge and expensive. I may never get my full range of motion back in my neck, even with surgery. Why did I let it get this bad?"

Lisa Is All of Us

If Lisa's story sounds familiar to you as a business owner, it's because her story is not unique. Because there is no "Lisa." Unlike the previous true-to-life entrepreneurs you've met throughout this book, Lisa's story is a mashup of hundreds of real small business entrepreneurs I've worked with over the years. At one point or another, every owner feels like Lisa.

Running a business can suck the life out of you. Most people aren't trained to handle the pressures that come with starting a business. So many of us start out poor or undereducated or have challenging life circumstances we need to overcome while learning how to balance a budget, advertise, source cheap parts, and retain customers. The average person can't possibly do it all without sacrificing something important.

Too often, that sacrifice is made to our health and or personal relationships. The very things that inspired us to start the business then get pushed aside as we focus on making it work. By the time we realize how bad our health or relationships have become, the problems are incredibly costly to fix. We end up spending a huge chunk of our profits on fixing the issues that running a business have caused.

All business owners have felt the enormous pressure that comes along with the responsibilities of owning a company. Over time, this pressure often turns into feelings of anxiety, fear, and doubt that take their toll on the business owner's physical and emotional health. If you're a business owner, you know exactly what I'm talking about.

The Business Case for Self-Care

The number-one thing business owners neglect is themselves. Their physical and mental health often sits at the bottom of a long list of urgent priorities. The irony is that without your health, all the "priorities" become irrelevant. I've seen this time and again as I've coached entrepreneurs. Issues that come up are general health, exhaustion, no exercise, not taking prescribed medication, not taking time to go to a doctor, becoming overweight and feeling ashamed of it, no sleep, self-medicating with illegal or over-the-counter medications, and just not taking time to play.

Business owners who spend the better part of their lives working to increase their financial wealth at the expense of their health often turn around and spend their accrued wealth to heal their bodies from the damaging effects of stress and neglect of their fundamental needs. They may even be running inefficient companies in the meantime, businesses that suffer from their lack of energy and focus. Their best employees may leave them as the owner becomes bitter and resentful toward their own staff for making demands on their time. In the worst cases, when the health bills come due, they may have no one to turn to because they've already driven everyone away.

Healthy business owners, on the other hand, have more energy, are more focused, and make better business decisions. Their businesses run more smoothly over the decades, and they don't have that unexpected medical expense down the line because of years of medical neglect and high stress.

So how are you doing? "I'm fine, really," won't cut it. Let's take an assessment to find out the truth.

Your Self-Care Assessment

Are you taking care of yourself the way you deserve? Answer these questions—*Y* for yes or *N* for no.

- I eat breakfast most days.
- I eat five cups of fruit and vegetables every day.
- I exercise regularly, including strength training.
- I meditate daily.
- I sleep seven to eight hours per night.

- I experience little or no negative stress.
- I am happy most of the time.
- I see the doctor at least once a year.
- I am happy with my weight.
- I have a positive, loving relationship with my partner.
- I spend time with my family.
- I stop working when I'm overtired.
- I drink enough water to be well hydrated.
- I have someone to talk to about my business challenges.
- I have enough money in the bank not to worry excessively.
- I most often cook meals at home.
- My alcohol intake is low to moderate.
- I have time for friends.
- I manage my negative emotions well.
- I spend some time doing what I want.
- I make time for my hobbies.
- I say no to unhealthy foods.
- I keep my promises to myself.
- I feel good about my body.
- I take my medication as prescribed.
- I seek medical care when I have a health issue.
- I take time off when I'm sick.

Add up your answers. How many *yes* answers do you have? How many *no* answers? The *noes* you see are places you need to improve. If your answers are mostly *no*, consider this your warning.

To arrive at the place where you feel free to enjoy life and control your schedule requires structure. You are already working hard, so put yourself first on your list and work hard for you. Think of what you need to be healthy and happy.

Stuck? You're not alone. Most business owners I work with have no idea how to begin. So I've compiled a massive list of places to start, things to consider, and areas in which you can improve your health starting today.

Suggested Self-Care Systems

- Schedule your next vacation and put a line item on your budget for the owner's vacation.

- Freedom might even start with simply taking a proper lunch break while someone else answers the phones.

- Focus on results, not the work. There may be places to cut corners without cutting quality.

- Do one task at a time, prioritize what needs to be done first, and stay focused.

- Huddles or ten-minute daily meetings with your team are better than lengthy monthly meetings and can help you learn about problems faster. Your team can also help you solve them.

- Don't overbook. Be aggressive about protecting your calendar and your time. In the same way, practice delegation so you're not doing everything yourself.

- Establish a routine so you never wonder what you need to be doing. Build a rhythm that makes sense and refreshes you throughout the day and week.

- Engage in physical activities. A sedentary life can kill you, and it will make you miserable the whole time. Make sure you're getting some exercise in your life, even if that's a ten-minute walk during lunch. And stand up more often than you sit down.

- Create urgency to get tasks done faster instead of drawing them out and feeling stressed over them. Use deadlines, even if you have to create them for yourself.

- Divide and conquer big jobs. That means breaking tasks down into smaller components but also delegating pieces to other team members so you're not working alone.

- Have a scheduled "quiet time" to think. How can you assess your business if you never get a spare moment to think about it? You'll be amazed at the insights you receive just from taking a few scheduled minutes to ponder your life and business. Protect these times with a "do not disturb" message or a gatekeeper who deflects attention seekers.

- Schedule phone calls so they aren't constantly ambushing you throughout the day. Set one designated time to be on the phone and arrange your calls accordingly.

- There's an old saying: "If you have to eat a frog, do it in the morning so you don't spend all day dreading it." Don't postpone your "frogs." Get the bad stuff out of the way first. Then spend the rest of the day recharging instead of dreading.

- Take a lunch break. This is huge for most business owners. You need time to rest during a long day, or the second half will be terrible. Take your rest on purpose. Use this time to stretch and to think.

- Know when to stop working. You need a shutoff time where you're not available to customers. This ensures you're available to yourself and your family. Otherwise, your entire life is work.

- Figure out your best hour of the day and maximize productivity in that hour.

- Establish and commit to a note collection system like Notebook or Evernote so it's easier to document things. This will stop you from keeping a hundred mental notes open in your brain and feeling exhausted just trying to remember details.

- Your phone could be ruining your life. Turn off device alerts. You don't need to see every text message the moment it arrives. Schedule times to check your phone and free yourself from electronic distraction.

- Use your values to filter commitments. What deserves your time? What needs to be done? And what will get sacrificed if you overcommit in the wrong areas?

- Remember that "no" is a full sentence. You don't need to explain every decision you make. Learn to say "no" and move along.

- Make sure you're eating and sleeping appropriately. These are the building blocks of your health, but they're usually the first things to get sacrificed when business owners get stressed. Focus on repairing these two issues, and you'll find you have a wealth of new energy and focus like never before.

- Fix your desk and workspace. Clutter means you're going to stress out about the mess. It also means you're likely to misplace important documents. That could cost you even more money down the line. Invest in an organizational system and learn to prioritize using it even when you don't feel like you have time to file a letter. Or get someone to help you with this.

- Drink water. Lots of it.

- Start asking if you're happy and what would make you happier. Make sure you're getting time with the people you love. If you're not, what's the point? And make sure the people who love you are getting your undivided attention. If they're not, how will they feel about you? Make sure you aren't losing them as you provide for them.

Do these sound like hard work to implement? Well, they sort of are. They're definitely going to require energy to start doing. Consider the alternative—let me tell you about Bruce, another Systems Business Coach client. At the outset of one of our coaching sessions, the subject changed suddenly from an issue with a supplier to an intimate reflection on life priorities.

"I think I'm going to become my father," Bruce said, then explained what he meant.

His dad had passed away at age fifty-nine from a heart attack in the yard of the family equipment rental business. Bruce's father had smoked, drank daily, and ate fast food for lunch several times a week.

So did Bruce. Now fifty-seven, Bruce himself was a type 2 diabetic and forty pounds overweight.

Bruce then shared his vision—to play with his brand-new grandson at the park and to someday teach him how to drive.

"I'm so far off track," he said. "I don't even know where to start."

Family and friends had only nagged Bruce to stop smoking, eat better, and lose the weight.

"What would it mean to you to be healthy?" I asked.

That question and the literal days Bruce took to reflect on his answer changed everything.

Bruce's entire worldview changed, from health last and fear first to hope and a plan. To quote Mark 8:36, "For what shall it profit a man, if he shall gain the whole world, and lose his own health?"

Bruce decided he would not miss his grandson's formative years for the world. That little child was worth it; Bruce himself was worth it. He finally realized it. Goodbye, hamburgers and beer; hello, buddha bowls and sparkling water.

I hope you can see your dreams are worth it, too. Now scale that understanding of health to your entire organization. Even while you're building self-care into your own day, offer relief to your employees. It pays for you as a business owner to concern yourself with whatever takes a toll on employees' health. A business is only as healthy as its least-healthy workers. That includes you!

Simple Self-Care Tips for Your Team

Consider the following five sets of questions. These brief reflections will help you empower your employees to take care of themselves so they can take care of your customers.

1. How can you make time and space for everyone to have a healthy lunch in a healthy atmosphere? Does your place of business have such a place? If not, offer one. Are employees working from home taking lunch breaks?

2. What would it look like to offer a stress-release center in your building? This doesn't have to be a large gym. It can simply be an area where there is calming music or where several headsets are kept for people to listen to their music of choice. Provide large exercise balls, yoga mats for relaxation, small weights, a bar across a doorway to hang from and stretch, and other small items similar to these. Keep the area uncluttered, provide cleanliness wipes, put in a couple of very comfortable chairs, and get some magazines.

3. Where could you put up an employee bulletin board for posting special family events, family pictures of things done away from work, or notices about sponsored events that include families? Know your people. If someone is facing difficulties, there might be a way for the company to support them, such as supplying dinners or gift cards or doing a fun run for a charity. If you stay aware of your employees,

their needs, and their celebrations, it creates a healthier work atmosphere. When people know you care, it can make all the difference.

4. Who could you bring in for additional self-care? Consider hiring a nutritionist, a mental health professional, or a yoga instructor occasionally, giving you and your staff time to have a personal visit with them during the workday.

5. What if you encouraged everyone on your team (and yourself as well) to schedule a physical once a year and vision and dental appointments on a regular basis? You could host fitness challenges with prizes, walk/run marathons, or hold an annual employee health fair. Make sure you allow breaks for employees to take their prescription medicines appropriately, for breastfeeding mothers to pump, et cetera. Consider offering/approving mental health days off when needed.

Now let's go from thought to action. Which tips can you schedule to do this week? Today? Right now? I promise this book will be here when you come back. And you'll want to pick it back up, too, because chances are that the people you're looking out for feel like family. Or they *are* family.

As you can guess, I've learned a few things about running a successful family business. That's what we're covering next.

Family, Business, and Family Business

Behind the success of every small business, there is family. As a small business owner, you want a company that serves your family's interests above all else.

Your business has an impact on those closest to you, especially your family. Family is defined as the people in our lives with whom we are intimately connected. We may or may not live together or even be biologically related. In some circumstances, a family member may be either our boss or employee. Even when your family does not work in your business, they are affected by the business. Businesses involving family members can face some unique challenges, so the more prepared you are, the more successful your business will be.

What does it look like when family business goes wrong? Let's talk about an old client, Gerald.

Gerald, a shrewd businessman, is often described by others as a wheeler and dealer, always looking for a way to make a buck. His family uses other, less kind words to describe him. In order to finance some of his "deals," Gerald talked his mom into lending him money. He also convinced his wife to remortgage the family home with a large line of credit to fund one of his ventures. His children barely knew him as they grew up as he spent all his time at work. He was either chasing after the next big dream or putting out fires from the current one.

Gerald's mom had not been repaid, even though she desperately needed money for her own care. His children were now working in the family business, grateful to have a job. His daughter, however, would rather be doing something else, but she was the only one who knew how to run his software. Her brother also worked in the company. For some reason, Dad thought that men needed to be paid more than women, so his daughter made 30 percent less than her brother doing similar work. This caused even more family tension.

Gerald had stopped sharing anything about the business with his wife long ago. He was tired of the fighting and didn't agree with the advice she gave him on how to remedy problems. She therefore had no idea how bad things really were. They had even stopped sleeping in the same bed years ago because of the tension caused by the business. She was worried about his health and about their future as a couple and wished more than anything that he would just cash out and get a real job.

Can you relate?

Even profitable businesses can divide families. And functional families who all get along may turn chaotic amid day-to-day business stress.

We need to be honest about both your family and your business. Let's do that with a quick overview of the pros and cons of these unique creatures we call family businesses.

Ten Pros of a Family Business

1. Pride of ownership. Building a business from the ground up with a team of people who are related feels incredible. And you can share this pride with your children.

2. The ability to generate income and profits from the business and to share that income with your family.

3. Family members are usually more committed to the success of the business than regular employees as they each have a personal stake in its success.

4. The ability to be flexible in many cases, if situations arise that affect a family member's ability to work.

5. The opportunity to build a family empire with longevity, which can carry on for future generations.

6. The ability for smoother decision-making as outside shareholders or employees don't have to be consulted in making management policies.

7. Building a strong sense of camaraderie and unity among family members and strengthening family ties while working in a more relaxed atmosphere.

8. In some cases, there are tax advantages to employing family members. Profits and salaries can be adjusted to minimize certain tax situations.

9. Knowing the personality of the person you are hiring as often, an employee can hide their faults in an interview, which may lead to needing to fire them. Family is a known quantity.

10. Being able to adjust salaries and certain costs if there is a cash flow crisis or if funds are suddenly required for a capital investment.

Ten Cons of a Family Business

As wonderful as it sounds—and many people make the mistake of only looking at the positives—there are downsides to a family-operated business. To avoid the dream becoming a nightmare, you need to be fully aware of the common pitfalls. These include:

1. Having an inconsistent income, particularly during the start-up phase and early years. It can be boom or bust. Without the assurance of a regular income, the financial future of your family and home may be at risk.

2. A huge time commitment from family members, which means your personal lives can be affected, and time together is often mostly spent in the workplace.

3. Rarely having time to take vacations together or to celebrate special occasions.

4. If the business grows rapidly, the growth can change the whole family/employee dynamic and leave even less time for "fun things."

5. Walking a fine line in not showing favoritism to a family member over other employees or even other family members.

6. The fragility of the large financial investment that many families make in the business, expecting it to succeed.

7. Feeling an added pressure to succeed for the family, which, in turn, can be detrimental to the family lifestyle if the business takes up too much time or money.

8. More stress to get the business off the ground. This usually means less sleep, more worry, and missing children's events.

9. If the business fails, often the family financial structure is affected, and it leaves all members without an immediate replacement income.

10. Being more susceptible to family arguments. It is also more difficult to discipline or fire a family member should they not perform their work as expected.

Take Care of Business, Take Care of Family

You need not only business-related goals but also family goals. Having family working together means that as a cohesive unit, you all need to be working toward the same goals, within both the family and the business. You can't have any one person with strictly self-serving goals.

A business can grow quickly or flounder just as rapidly. Often, these situations are unforeseen and not in your plans. When family is involved, the ramifications of both affect everyone who works there.

To make a plan, answer the following questions:

1. What obvious changes do I need to make, or would I like to make?

2. Have we set goals together?

3. How is our current setup working for me?

4. How is it working for my family?

5. Is this what I had in mind when I went into this business?

6. Is the family unit stronger or under too much stress?

7. What would be our ideal business and family goals?

8. How many weeks of vacation do we all want?

9. How much money would we and the business like to earn each month?

10. What are my goals for acquiring a larger home or premises?

11. What amount of debt is the whole family comfortable carrying?

12. Who does which job, and is each family member competent at that work?

13. How much time does my family want to spend working each week?

14. What does my family need from the business, and can it meet those needs?

When you write down your answers to this analysis, it can open your eyes to situations you may have ignored—or not even realized. Carefully study these points and write down anything that applies to your situation.

How do these answers affect your family in particular? What has been the impact on you and your family of not having these things clearly defined? This could include changing family relationships and time, money, and health issues. You may think of others.

Now that you know the impact of the business on your family, there may be areas that require some changes to make both your business and your family unit operate more successfully.

My Favorite Family Business System: The Family Charter

I recommend creating a family charter to address any family business issues going forward. A family charter document makes all expectations clear and minimizes potential resentment or arguments. The guidelines of your charter might include:

- Discussing and making financial decisions together
- Not borrowing from family, no matter what
- Not hiring family members just to provide employment
- Protecting relationships over business
- Protecting health over wealth (time away and with each other, reducing stress)
- Where to draw the line where invested money is involved
- Which personal assets are not to be used for business
- A succession plan should a family member leave or become too ill to work

- Not talking about business at the dinner table

A family charter can be either a simple or a more complex document, depending on the business and family size. Whatever yours looks like, it should cover the rules relating to both family and business. Happy family, profitable business.

Remember the section in Chapter 9, System #2 on coaching? When it comes to family, it's even more important to take a coach approach in your communication. Ask, don't tell. This is by far the most powerful tool I have shared with you when it comes to building and protecting relationships. Remember, no one likes to be told what to do, and if a family member gets frustrated and leaves, the pain can be permanent. No business is worth losing a daughter's or a son's love because you didn't agree with the way they dealt with a new pricing policy.

When we are curious and nonjudgmental in our communications, we learn things we would otherwise miss. Maybe the only reason your family member is in the business is to make you happy. Maybe they're actually miserable and would rather be somewhere else. Release this sense of obligation. Find out what's really going on with your coach hat on. Protect the health of your family relationships first. Get that right, and your business will be all the better for it.

Good Health Doesn't Just Happen

A healthy lifestyle will not happen at all if you leave it to chance. You have to plan it within the structure of your day. Your quality of life improves with better health, less stress, and a company you are proud to call yours. And with healthy leadership, your business will operate more efficiently while generating more time and profit for you, the business owner.

So stop waiting. Make the time to build your systems and change your approach to health. Your future self will thank you for it.

CHAPTER 17

SELLING YOUR SMALL BUSINESS

Yay! It's time to cash out! You've built your business, worked hard, and are now ready for your next adventure. Or are you? The decision to sell your business isn't an easy one. And even when you make the decision to sell, there are a lot of steps to follow. How do you tell your staff? And how can you make your company attractive to buyers?

I've seen brilliant people fumble this process. In fact, this topic has been particularly on my mind lately as I've been looking over some listings for local businesses. One especially troubling example stood out to me. A husband and wife started a service company in the late 1980s that served other companies in the food industry. They built up a customer base with many longtime clients. After three decades running their company, they were looking to retire.

I flipped through the listing to see what was included. The husband listed his role as company president and also primary service technician. The wife had run the back office since they opened their doors over thirty years ago. They had a few contractors they'd maintained long-term relationships with. The price for this business totaled $300,000.

If you're selling any business for $300,000 and both owners are working multiple positions within the company, you're not selling a business. You're really selling a job. That's a situation in which one new owner will come in and have to pick up the slack from both previous working owners, on top of paying for the privilege of taking over.

I don't think anyone wants to pay $300,000 for a job. If both owners are working every day in major roles, that tells me they don't even have any systems that would be coming with the business. This listing didn't even say anything about office space coming with the business, or equipment, or if the owners would be willing to help with the business for a while to bring the new owner up to speed.

Several questions sprang to my mind as I read the listing. *What would I be buying, a customer list? How many customers? Do you even have a customer list? Are those customers as old as you are when you're retiring?*

The truth is that there are a lot of owners selling their businesses right now. A lot of people are retiring or getting out of their industry. Many of them are bleeding cash. And very few of them know how to make their business sellable and attractive to buyers.

Build to Sell

The best time to prepare to sell your business is the day you open it. The second-best time is today. The worst time is when you've decided you need to sell fast and get out.

The truth is that if your dream is to build a thriving business and sell it for top dollar, you can't start preparing at the end. Don't run it with zero systems and then try to hand it off to strangers upon retirement. No one will want it because they'd be buying your job.

When I talk to most business owners about the idea of selling their business, they scoff. "Well, Beverlee, I don't need to prepare because I'm never going to sell. I love my business. I'm never going to sell it."

That's great. You love it now. And at some point, you may want to sell it because you're going to get old or burned out or need the money. You are not going to want to work for the rest of your life. And even if you plan to hand it down to your children, they may have other ideas. Even if they don't, handing over an organized and systematized business is a much better gift to your kids than handing them a stressful job.

The biggest question I ask company owners is "Do you have a business, or do you have a job?" If you're working long hours every single day to keep things afloat, then you have a job. You're just the owner of your job. If you could step away and things would run just fine on their own with minimal input from you, then you've got a business. And a very attractive one to potential buyers. That's really what buyers want: to pay the ticket price, step into your shoes, and collect a check every month from their investment.

If you've just realized you're working a job instead of running a business, that's OK. Any enterprise can be turned into a real business.

Before we talk about how, let's examine what makes a business sellable.

Four Attributes of a Sellable Business

Is your business sellable right now? Let's find out.

1. It's Profitable

Buyers want to buy businesses that will make them money.

You're going to have an incredibly hard time convincing a buyer to take on a bleeding business. That's an ugly truth that many business owners need to face. Your debt, your dwindling customers, and your red financial status will work against you.

If you're struggling to keep your business afloat, you may feel the urge to just sell and escape. That might be a hasty decision that loses you the chance to make a lot of money off the work you've done. Instead of running, you might want to stick it out and work another year or two and bring your earnings up. Two years of consistent positive growth is a great incentive to convince buyers you've offered a viable company with room for expansion.

You don't even need to be operating poorly for this to affect you. If you've been writing everything off for years and your books look like you don't make any profits, that's still bad for buyers. Your car, your furniture, your kid's cell phone, even your home toilet paper: all those expenses add up, and if you're racking them up as business expenses, then you look broke on paper. You might need to take the tax hits for a year or two just to show that you actually are turning a significant profit.

2. It Has a Policy and Procedures Manual

Do you have a document that shows how your business operates at every level? A clear policy and procedures manual is worth $40,000 to $50,000 right out of the gate on any business evaluation. This is probably the biggest selling point to leverage in any business sale because it shows exactly how the company runs, what to expect, and how to reproduce your results without you.

If you've been working all this time with the policy and procedures manual in your head, that's a huge risk. That document is only alive as long as your memory stays intact and available to the people running your business. If something happens to you, your business is effectively gone.

And if you try to sell without writing it down, buyers are really purchasing a confusing mess with no instructions on how to make it work.

When I sold my travel agency, my policy and procedures manual was only twenty-seven pages. It was shocking that it was so small, but that was a major difference for the buyer. He bought mine because I didn't work in my business, and I had the whole system documented, so it ran independently of me. The other two owners whose businesses he looked at had the same gross revenue. They had the same number of staff. The primary difference was in mine, I was not considered; I did not generate that revenue. My staff did. And I had the instruction manual to show how he could too.

3. It Runs Separately from You

This sounds like a repeat of the last point but consider for a moment.

If you're selling a job that you have to work at every day, why would someone pay you for that? They could go get a job anywhere else without paying.

Would you pay your asking price for the privilege of doing the job you're doing now?

Also consider that people who buy businesses aren't looking for a job. If they wanted that, they'd start a business themselves. No, they're looking for a profitable investment that requires minimal input on their part. They want to collect a check every month and tell people they run a business in this industry.

You can't sell your own brain or your own time. You can only sell your company. You don't come with it. Remember that the only things you can sell are those that operate entirely independent of yourself. If nothing operates independently, you need to fix that before it's time to sell. And also so you can start taking vacations, as we discussed previously.

4. It Has Standards, Values, and a Company Promise

A company is an investment. A company's reputation tells buyers what to expect from future earnings.

If you've got standards, values, and a company promise, you can show buyers exactly what your reputation looks like in the marketplace. If people expect your product to be the very best in the industry because you've upheld that level of quality for twenty years, you can command a far higher price than someone with little or no reputation.

Your company's reputation is huge. It determines where the new buyer will start in the industry before they make positive changes. A strong reputation requires little work to boost profits.

Five Things to Do Before You Sell

Let's say you've looked over these four attributes and decided your company is sellable. And you're tired of your industry. You want to retire and travel the world for a year or two.

Great! Where do you start? You can't just pull up your anchor and sail away in a month. There's some prep work you need to engage in before your company is ready to be sold.

The good news is that when you're preparing to sell, you're probably going to hire a broker to help you. They'll recommend a lot of helpful suggestions on how to prep your business so it's ready to hand over to a potential buyer. The bad news is that if you wait until that moment to start getting your business ready, you'll be paying a broker extra just to sit there and advise you as you slowly bring your business up to par. That'll cost you money and time.

The best news is that you don't have to wait to begin improving your business. Whether you sell later or hand the business over to your children, the following suggestions will get your company into top shape and make life easier for whoever eventually takes over. Plus, it will make your life easier while you're running the business in the meantime because you'll be organized.

1. Talk to Your Partner

The last topic to discuss when selling a business is how to handle partners. This can be a huge complication in the process.

It is common to buy the business from or sell it to your partner. One of you wants out, and the other needs to pay them a fair share. In that case, you can bring in accountants to evaluate how much the company assets are worth and what an equitable distribution looks like. The goal is to make sure both sides feel like they got a good deal. The last thing you want is for that relationship to be ruined because one person paid too much or gave up too little.

Business partnerships can be a real challenge. I recommend avoiding them as often as possible just because they're so messy and easily wounded. Everyone has their own expectations, and when huge sums of money are involved, it's easy to spiral into anger and resentment over perceived slights.

When selling a business with a partner or when one of you is trying to sell your share, make sure it goes fairly for all involved. That might involve hiring a mediator before things get tense and frustrating. And make sure everything is documented: who owns what and how much each person can expect from a sale. Get everything clear on paper so expectations are objective rather than subjective.

2. Take Stock of Company Holdings

Remember the incomplete seller listing at the start of this chapter? They didn't even mention what came with the business! How is a buyer supposed to know what they're getting?

Consider it from this angle. Every Christmas season, millions of people go toy shopping for the kids in their lives. They head to the toy aisle and try to decide what gift matches that child. Every package lists every item that does and does not come inside the box, right down to the batteries. Because no one wants to give an incomplete gift that the child will open up and ask, "Where are the batteries? You mean I can't play with it yet?"

Your business works exactly the same way. Buyers want to know exactly what they're getting. They especially want to make sure the "batteries" come in the box. No one wants to buy a business and find out they can't run it. That costs time and money on top of the purchase price.

Take stock of every asset your company possesses. This may include but is not limited to furniture, land, property, rent agreements, contractor agreements, full-time employees, office equipment, intellectual property, and customer list. And the more detailed the customer list, the better.

You also need to decide what you own that does *not* go with the business. Some owners I know built their business on a plot of land near their house. When they sold, they kept the property and rented it back to the new owners. That decreased the selling price, but it was important to the owners not to give up their land. You may not be ready to part with your dream car that you bought with company money. If that is the case, now is the time to buy it from the company yourself.

To get your business ready, take a full inventory of every company asset you will and will not part with.

3. Get Your Books Updated (And Keep Them Up)

Imagine you want to buy a business. You ask how much they're making and how much they're spending each year. They open up their books, and there haven't been any entries in three years. Yet they assure you they know the numbers off the top of their head.

How do you feel about buying that business? How confident are you in the numbers coming from their memory?

Would *you* want to buy a business like that? Unless you're paying cash, lots of luck getting financing.

Keeping your books up to date helps you in your daily life so you see exactly how much is coming and going. It also helps if you get hurt and someone has to take over unexpectedly. And when you go to sell or hand the business over to someone, your books show them exactly what they're walking into.

This extends to taxes too. You need documented tax returns that show everything. These are official documents that inspire greater confidence in buyers because they were actually filed on time with the government. There's a level of assumed authority there that's not always present in personal books with no oversight.

If this is a struggle for you, hire someone to do it. There are accounting firms all over the globe, even tiny local ones who won't charge you much at all. Get them to do your dirty work for you. If you want to sell today but don't have updated books, they can help with that too. You just might need to wait a year or two to show consistent tracking for potential buyers.

And making sure your books stay updated may give you a shocking revelation about how much money is being spent. You might not think some of your expenses are a big deal, but you'd be surprised how much extra some owners spend without realizing it. Updating your books can help you shave off unnecessary expenses and increase your bottom line. That means more money in your pocket even if you aren't planning to sell.

To get your business ready, update your books and keep them updated.

4. Watch the Market

Selling a business is not like selling a house. It takes a long time. Much longer than selling a house does.

The truth is that it could take years to sell that business. If your lease is running out in two months, it may be too late to try to sell that business if you don't want to sign another lease. I've seen owners selling their equipment out their back door in a fire sale at the last minute the day before getting kicked out of their building because they didn't want to sign another lease. They had tens of thousands of dollars worth of equipment and had to sell it at a steep discount just to take what money they could from a desperate last-minute sale.

To get your business ready, keep an eye on the market. Plan to sell way in advance. Selling fast means leaving money on the table, and you don't want to miss out on reclaiming the fruits of your labor.

5. Keep Your Business Ready to Sell (Even if You Never Do)

Once you make these changes, keep them up. They're good practices for every business owner to bear in mind anyway. Knowing your company's assets, keeping your books updated, and knowing what the industry looks like and who's being bought and sold bring huge benefits to the savvy business owner.

And as I've said before, you never know what might happen tomorrow. You could be in a car accident, get a divorce, be diagnosed with cancer, or just wake up and decide you hate running your business. Keeping your business ready to hand off to someone else protects your family and yourself in the event of any unforeseen circumstances.

To get your business ready, keep it ready! Because you never know what life might throw at you.

Finding the Right Business Broker

When you sell your business, I recommend hiring a broker. They'll do so much of the heavy work for you, and they'll think of things you won't. If you're selling your first business, a broker is a must. Still, there are some things to consider when you hire a random person to sell your business for you.

Number one, don't just hire a random person. Always check references on brokers. If possible, use someone one of your friends or associates have used before and had a great experience with. Make sure you're not picking someone who's just starting out and doesn't know how your industry works.

Number two, check their energy level. Do they call you back right away? Are you a priority? Are they friendly, professional, and enthusiastic? Would you want to buy a business from this person, and are they going to represent you well to potential buyers?

Some of the best brokers will want to see a business evaluation before they take you on. You can get one of these done by an accountant. It might cost anywhere from $3,000 to $7,000, but at least you will have a breakdown of what your business is actually worth.

Remember that while your business may come back with a handsome evaluation, it is only worth what someone is willing to pay for it. That could be more, or that could be a lot less. Even with facts in front of a buyer, often the purchase is made on hope. Hope that they can do it better than you. Hope that this business will fit perfectly into their life.

The more time you have to sell your business, the better. Don't wait until two months before your lease is up or a week before your best employee retires. Watching clients close a perfectly good business because they waited too long to sell is heartbreaking.

When and How to Tell Your Staff

When I sold my travel agency, I wasn't sure when to tell my staff. Wait until the sale is almost final? Alert them right at the start? I decided to play it by ear and let them know once things were certain.

So, of course, things went as badly as possible. I was pregnant at the time, and I went to a prenatal visit. While I was there, a major airline company called my office and asked to speak to the new owner. My staff instantly went into panic mode. "What do you mean, new owner? What's happening? Where's Beverlee? We need her to explain this right now!"

I came out of my prenatal visit to a flood of missed calls. I hurried back to my travel agency and met an anxious crowd of employees. My cover was blown, and so was my chance to inform them myself of the coming changes. That was about the worst way it could have gone.

There's a balance here. If you inform your staff too early, they could leave you. That cuts into your business's assets because you're losing valuable trained staff. And it's not fun having to tell people there are changes coming because they get scared and may be upset. No one likes instability in their life.

At the same time, your new owner will need to set up connections with other businesses and get the ball rolling before the handover happens. That was the case in my situation, when the new owner needed to connect with authorities prior to his opening day. It couldn't wait any longer. I'd delayed too long.

Decide where and when to tell your staff, but make sure you're the one who tells them. Don't be like me and waddle in super pregnant from a prenatal visit with your cheeks red from embarrassment and tears and have to explain to your staff that they caught you.

Working for the New Owner (Or Not)

Selling your company often includes working for a while under the new owner so they have you on hand to answer questions.

When I sold my company, I agreed to work under the new owner for a while. That was awful. I'd been demoted from leader to employee. I had to sit there and watch him drop the ball and fumble his way through everyday activities that I could have handled in a snap. That's a normal part of getting the hang of a new business, but it was hard to watch the company I'd built be run in a way I didn't like.

I have not yet met a business owner that has liked staying or has in any way appreciated being there after they've sold. If there's some way you can get out and just stay out, do so. That's where the policy and procedures manual will save you. If you've got that manual, you can just teach them the manual. And then you leave, rather than being there, holding their hand, and still running this thing, but now you're not the boss.

In the end, this topic is one more reminder to get your policy and procedures manual up to date as soon as possible.

Saying Goodbye

Saying goodbye is messy. There's no way around that.

After I patched things up with my staff, we were happy together in our remaining time. When I left, everyone wished me luck. It was a great experience. At the same time, it included so many emotional moments.

I'd had seven years with these people. Seven years of relationships and personal talks and relying on each other. I won't say they were all my best friends, but they were my trusted allies in building and running the business.

Business owners care about their people. You try to maintain professional boundaries, but you do care. You don't like to see the people who trust you get scared about what might happen to their jobs after you leave. Their needs are important. And it can be tempting to make skewed decisions that leave you in the lurch just to take care of your employees. That includes you staying on for an extended time as an employee just to make things smooth for your staff.

Remember the oxygen masks on airplanes? You can't make every decision based on what's best for other people. As the business owner, you need to meet your needs first. Then you can make sure your people are taken care of as much as possible.

And once it's time to go, pack up and go. Say your goodbyes and mean them. Then move on. Life doesn't end, and this isn't the last job your employees will ever have. Look forward to what comes next in your life. Then go make it happen.

Finally Letting Go

You've heard of buyer's remorse, when a person regrets spending money after completing a purchase? Selling your company can bring on seller's remorse.

Some business owners lose their identity after making a sale. Or they think, *I should have stuck it out; I could have doubled my profits! I wish I had kept my business.* These thoughts aren't usually realistic because the owner forgets they were often fighting for their life to keep things as good as they were.

This can be a normal part of the process. There's a grief cycle to go through after you let go of a business.

When I sold my business, I was used to having a company car and a company phone and getting dressed up every day ready to go to important meetings. I liked my position in the community. Suddenly, I was a stay-at-home mom with three kids, including a newborn. Talk about an identity shift!

The status change can be a huge blow to business owners. You go from saying "I'm a business owner" to "I'm not really sure where I fit in anymore." It can feel like a loss to walk away from something your entire identity has been attached to. Some owners are almost embarrassed that they sold their businesses. They can pocket a fortune and still feel like a failure because they're not working, and they can't claim to own a business anymore.

On the other hand, you don't own a business anymore. You don't have livelihoods riding on your every decision. You aren't responsible for keeping a whole company afloat. There are no employees calling you with complications you need to fix right now. There's a tremendous amount of freedom in your new life.

And you don't have to sit around in sweatpants for a year wondering what to do with your life. Plenty of business owners take their experience from their first business and open a second one in a new industry. They use everything they learned to start their second business the right way. They automate as quickly as possible and make running their new business more like fun than work.

When you sell your business, it can feel like your life is over. In fact, that's just one chapter of your life. You get the chance to start over fresh with more money in your pocket than ever before. Now it's time to build the next thing that matters to you. And this time, you won't be a newbie flying by the seat of your pants. You're an educated business owner with a successful track record. Consider building, running, and selling a business your on-the-job MBA. You are more prepared than ever to do it again.

Imagine what you can build this time.

CHAPTER 18

SERIAL ENTREPRENEURSHIP:
STARTING UP AGAIN

"Beverlee, it looks like Canada is bouncing back from the pandemic."

It sure sounded like good news. And Janice, the Canadian politician who told me this on the phone, wasn't one to be overly optimistic.

As a small business coach, I've gotten to know several people in governments who influence the North American economies. They all want healthier small businesses that create the jobs that drive tax revenue, and when I help entrepreneurs keep their companies profitable and growing, it's a win for everyone.

"That's excellent to hear, Janice," I replied. "What are you basing that on?"

"I saw the numbers myself just this morning. Applications for incorporation were down in March. But April, May, and June are breaking records. And I mean records from even *before* the pandemic. Businesses are exploding all over the place at a faster rate than we've seen in decades."

"So . . . we're coming out of the COVID-19 winter?"

"Big time. Business is back!"

I laughed. "Give entrepreneurs a problem, and they will build a solution. It seems they're the ones carrying us through this economic downturn."

"Yes, I'd have to agree. I've seen a few new businesses that teach people about improved health guidelines. Trainers from these companies come into your organization and teach your employees how to social distance in tight spaces, how to maintain good hygiene protocols for your specific environment, things like that. Find a need and fulfill it with a new business. It's what our entrepreneurs do best."

Entrepreneurs really are the backbone of every economy. They can adapt and change faster than big corporations or governments. They see a problem and build a solution.

The 2020 shutdown crushed small businesses across the world—but you and I know there's no crushing the entrepreneurial spirit. Businesses are coming back now, and they're leveraging the very issues that shut them down to open new doors to financial opportunity.

The same is true of you as a business owner. Ending or selling a business does not have to mean ending your career as an entrepreneur. The last chapter talked about selling your business. So what comes after you sell? Or what if you don't want to sell? Maybe you just want to start a second company on the side. Most entrepreneurs start multiple businesses because that need to create is in their blood.

Or maybe, like 80 percent of all small businesses, yours couldn't keep its doors open. Maybe you lost your business in the pandemic, or maybe every business you've tried to start has failed.

Life after building a business usually means building more (and better) businesses. Regardless of how many failed businesses you've had, if you're an entrepreneur at heart, your career is far from over.

What Drives Serial Entrepreneurs?

The truth is that entrepreneurs are both born and made. To paraphrase William Shakespeare, some people are born for business, and others have it thrust upon them . . . often by necessity.

I was a single mom with zero control over my work environment. I needed more flexibility and time with my child. I needed a work environment that would be forgiving if I needed to step away and be a parent for a moment. I knew my family had to come first, and I couldn't make that happen working for someone else.

Other entrepreneurs start off miserable while working for their bosses. They despise working for rude owners and seek freedom from being yelled at. And some just plain can't handle having a boss at all.

It all boils down to freedom. Freedom is the ultimate reason most entrepreneurs start a business. Freedom *from* something or freedom to *do* something. Some crave it by nature; others require it to make their dreams come true. Entrepreneurship is all about freedom.

This need for freedom is why entrepreneurs are so resilient. When a business fails, entrepreneurs often pick themselves up and start a new one. When they sell a first business, they start a second, then often a third. When the economy drops, they dig deep to find ways to survive.

Is it easier to work for a big corporation during a bad economy? Probably, if you have job security. It's easier to let someone else take the risks. The thing is that every entrepreneur values something more than ease. That driving motivator forces us to make decisions others might call crazy. People gave me lists of reasons not to start my own travel agency. Freedom for my family was more important to me than an easy life. I *had* to start my travel agency. And once I sold it, I needed to keep going to create more freedom for myself and my family. I needed to embrace the new passion I'd found for creating and for helping people along the way.

Since you're reading this book, you probably feel a similar way. And you might be wondering about your next step.

To Serial or Not to Serial

We briefly mentioned in the last chapter that some entrepreneurs feel a sense of loss when they sell a company. Some even lose their identity. This can also happen if you keep your company and automate it so thoroughly that you don't have much left to do. We creators are so wrapped up in what we create. We need to continue creating, building, and contributing to work through this sense of loss.

Once you sell or decide to start a new company for other reasons, you might struggle to figure out what your next step should be.

To figure out your future, look at your past. Most entrepreneur life stories follow a path on which each new step connects to their previous work. An electrician may specialize in single-family homes, then start an electrical company with others working under them. Over time, they expanded their offerings to handle more and more of the whole construction process. After ten years, they have a construction company that can create a home from start to finish.

When they sell that company, they wonder what to do next. They could go into consulting and help other construction companies expand like they did. Or they could help entrepreneurs in general automate their businesses, like I do. They could even start a new company that helps fill in any gaps their previous company didn't fulfill, like a company that streamlines the construction permit process. Maybe their new company could end up doing business with the old company they sold.

That's what entrepreneurship is all about. Selling your business doesn't really end your connection to that industry. In fact, it cements your reputation within the industry in which you succeeded. Your next step will likely be to leverage that reputation in a new way that no one else in your industry has done. You can find a need that you as a business owner used to struggle with and develop a new company that would have made your old life a lot easier. And you can leverage your reputation as a success to attract all the business owners you used to compete against. Now they'll need your help to boost their profits.

After running a couple of businesses, you might feel more like a flipper than an entrepreneur. Remember that period from 2004 to 2007, when everyone became a house flipper? It was the hot new thing. That's what serial entrepreneurship may feel like.

The serial entrepreneur view looks at whole industries rather than individual companies. Instead of just building one company, you're filling gaps in your industry with multiple different companies, then handing off those new companies to other people to manage. Maybe you find another gap, and you build five interlocking companies that make your whole industry a well-oiled machine.

The companies working in these industries are just cogs that fit together, making the industry run. You might even buy a cog that's badly out of place just to adjust it, improving the overall industry. This even helps your other companies run more smoothly. This is what big corporations do when they buy smaller companies that affect their main industry.

Take Deborah, a fashion design consultant for women in the 90s, then a multilevel marketing guru selling juice in the 2000s, then an independent mortgage broker. After the 2008 housing crash, Deborah moved on to build courses online and is now a podcast host and TikTok seller of electronic art.

This is the spirit of the serial entrepreneur. You probably know someone who fits this bill.

My only other advice to serial entrepreneurs is to make sure you know the system behind what you are getting into. Don't get sucked into someone else's system where you do all the work, and they get all the money. That is not a business.

If this sounds overwhelming right now, it's important to remember that entrepreneurship gets easier and easier—because your skill set never goes away. It grows with each endeavor. You get better at building companies, and you do it faster. Then you automate the start-up steps by buying companies other people have started. Eventually, you don't even want to buy start-ups; you want to buy established companies in which you see potential for improvement using the skills you possess that the current owners don't.

And you don't have to sell your companies at all. You could build five companies, automate all of them, and just collect your paychecks as the owner. There's no sense selling if it earns you money for a lifetime. Plenty of people do this. You can too.

The entrepreneur's path is unique to each individual. When you're called to it, you can't really escape it because working a nine-to-five corporate job just isn't enough for you anymore. You don't want a job. You want freedom. You want to create. It's who you are.

Starting Up All Over Again

At some point, you'll wonder what this is all for. Why keep making money? The answer for me is legacy. The companies you build all employ people. Remember, small businesses employ 70 percent of the entire world's workforce! You're feeding families when you give others a job. You're making livelihoods for real human beings who can pay their bills because of the jobs you create.

Your legacy might also be your heirs. Maybe you have kids who will inherit your businesses. You could have four children and create four companies so each child gets one. Or maybe you take on a protege later in life and hand your businesses over to them.

Your impact on your industries and on the lives of the people you've helped employ are a lasting legacy that you create. Entrepreneurship leaves a path of humans behind you whose lives you have touched. If you do things right, those lives are all improved because of the work you did.

Entrepreneurship isn't just about money and freedom. It's about changing the world for the better, one life at a time.

CHAPTER 19
GIVING BACK

Small business owners are the most generous people on the planet. They build everything and donate to everyone. So why do they often underestimate their power when it comes to growing their own businesses?

Most small business owners feel tiny compared to the big corporations. They feel like a small fish in a huge pond, and they wonder what they could possibly offer that someone else couldn't do better.

It took a pandemic for most of the world to realize how important small businesses are. Governments shut down economies and strangled local companies—especially restaurants. They learned very quickly that small businesses not only employ but also provide for a ton of people and their neighborhoods. The big corporations could help keep society running, but it was the small businesses that connected the supply chains and filled the gaps. As the economy of each nation recovers, it's the adaptable small business owners who are identifying new needs, employing the unemployed, and finding ways to bring the world back online.

On a smaller, more personal scale, individual businesses provide jobs to people who live near them. When small businesses do well, more local jobs are created. Small business owners also take on students, give vocation nights to teach skills, and reinvest in their community.

Most corporations don't do that. Sure, they have flashy campaigns like "Do you want to add a $1 donation to your purchase?" That's the consumers' money they're donating, not their own. And when they do donate to some global cause, the money gets swallowed up by big bureaucracies. Small business owners, on the other hand, make donations out of their own profit. It's usually the generous small business owners donating that dollar at the checkout when the big corporations ask.

The small business spirit makes a difference in this world. That's the reason we start our own companies in the first place! The same drive that led us to create a business leads us to continue to help others once the money rolls in. Most business owners don't earn a profit just to sit back and hoard it. We want to change the world that gave us so much trouble when we were struggling.

And small business owners don't do this in a vacuum. We get our family and friends involved too. And our staff. Helping others becomes a company-wide endeavor. Business owners get involved on boards and committees to drive even greater change.

Do you remember when I mentioned Rotary International earlier in this book? In their own words:

> Rotary is a global network of 1.4 million neighbors, friends, leaders, and problem-solvers who see a world where people unite and take action to create lasting change—across the globe, in our communities, and in ourselves.[31]

Here's their mission statement:

> We provide service to others, promote integrity, and advance world understanding, goodwill, and peace through our fellowship of business, professional, and community leaders.

Did you catch who those 1.4 million people are? Mostly business owners! Rotary is one place where small business owners combine their strength to create enormous change in the world. They help fight disease, provide clean water, improve sanitation, support education, and assist mothers and small children living in poverty. All this is done by small business entrepreneurs. We grow our companies large enough and automate enough tasks so we have the money and the time to improve the world around us.

That's ultimately one of the best reasons to focus on systematizing (and system fine-tuning) your own company. Imagine the good you could do if all your bills were paid with money (and ten extra hours a week) left over. You could help shape the future into a better place.

Running your own company just got a lot more interesting, didn't it?

---

31   Rotary International, "About Rotary," accessed March 25, 2023, https://www.rotary.org/en/about-rotary.

At the Travel Agency . . .

Generosity and charity were driving forces in the travel agency that I built.

For example, we were a drop-off point for the Christmas Bureau, a Canadian nonprofit that allows you to adopt a family in need at Christmas time. The parents can't afford gifts, so the Christmas Bureau connects them with charitable people who buy items the kids asked for and then drop them off to be delivered to the families. It happens anonymously, and the parents get to wrap the gifts up themselves, so they keep the dignity of preparing each gift for their child.

Several of our staff would adopt families and buy every item they asked for. What a small price to pay to give children the gift of a real Christmas experience. And to give their parents the gift of seeing their children smiling instead of feeling left out. I cannot overstate the importance of this kind of giving. You provide toys and books, yes, and also joy, dignity, relief, and perhaps a restored faith in human goodness.

Apart from Christmas giving, we often took on student interns. It can be hard to find an internship that treats you well, and we wanted to educate students to give them the best chance at success. Thirty years later, I'm still in touch with many of these interns we trained.

As a company, we also adopted a World Vision child in Thailand. Our contributions made her life better, and I got a letter from her when she shared that she was able to go to college because of our support. That's real, tangible change.

For our company's fifth anniversary, I wanted to go all out. We put up an outdoor stage in front of our store and brought in balloons, doughnuts and games. We had a play area for kids. I bought four tickets to Disney so we could do a family trip giveaway. We brought in the local Hawaiian dance school and grade five ukulele band to perform. It was all travel themed, so it matched our company. We had neighbors talking, laughing, dancing, playing, and eating together. This was a great way to spread the word about our travel business and also a way to give back to the community.

Today, our anniversary party, first held in 1998, is an annual community event called Brookswood Days. Every business in our neighborhood comes together on this day once a year to celebrate our community.

The heart of the community is its business owners. They employ, supply, and give back to their neighbors. I embraced that with my travel agency, and I teach my coaching clients to embrace it in their own businesses.

Let's talk about some ways you can start giving back right now, even if your business isn't fully optimized yet.

How to Channel Your Generosity

In truth, you are already generous. Odds are that you're humble, and you often don't want people to know what you're doing. Maybe you cringe when you realize your attempts to be charitable could be misconstrued as attempts to boost your business.

First of all, it's OK to benefit from what you're doing. If you practice generosity and earn more money as a result, that just creates an infinite loop where you can be even more generous. When you justify benefitting from your charitable works, you can focus on increasing your giving as your business grows.

Second, it's OK to consider charitable acts as marketing opportunities. That protects you from the swarm of charity companies who may pounce on you once they hear you're giving away time and money. Make sure that what you're doing aligns with your company mission and values, and don't give unless it's directly tied to those goals. You don't want to get sucked into the "please please please" circle where everyone comes to you with their causes. You will get bombarded, and you'll need to draw a line. Be the one who chooses to give rather than the one being chosen by charity companies. If it fits your criteria, great. If not, move along and give where you feel it meets your personal and company vision.

It also helps keep your giving aligned with your company's main products. Let's say you specialize in fashion. It makes sense to give to charities that involve clothing. Maybe you work closely with companies who give clothes to children living in poverty. Your company can work to make sure these children have daily outfits they can wear with pride. That would make a lot more sense than your fashion business putting together care baskets for men with prostate cancer. Both causes are worthy, yet one aligns closely with your business. Let the gift basket companies focus on those men while you clothe the children.

You might be feeling inspired and convinced. It's time to let the generosity flow. So what are some specific things you can do right now?

1. Consider starting a **networking group**. Talk to a handful of other professionals and business owners you know and find others who would benefit from weekly or monthly networking meetings. Advertise your meetings to students, interns, and young professionals looking to connect. Or better yet, join your local rotary club and help them modernize this powerful organization. Gain an instant 1.4 million new connections. Networking can be one of the hardest parts of growing a career. Make it easier by creating networking opportunities that enhance the next generation of your industry. People remember who supported them, and you just might find a lifelong connection with the newcomers you assist.

2. Have a **raffle**, give away a bottle of wine, and donate the proceeds to a good charity. That means you pay for the (nice and expensive) wine yourself while encouraging your community to give to a charity. You can also offer to match raffle donations up to a certain amount if you've got surplus profits. This gets the word out about a cause and about your business at the same time.

3. Sponsor a golf hole for a high-profile charity golf tournament. Remember it's not who you know, it's who knows you. Join **civic organizations** (like Rotary International), where political and economic influencers help those in need and shape the future. At your networking meetings, find ways to pool your resources with other business owners to maximize your global impact.

4. Or take things in the other direction and **stay local** by giving as close to the individual as possible. Be generous on a personal level instead of giving money to a big charity. This ensures the people in need get the maximum benefit without charities peeling off a huge portion for administrative costs. Consider buying pajamas for the local transition house or socks for the homeless shelter. Share your plans on your company Facebook page; you will be delighted with the response.

5. Do you know the **local leaders** in your community? Introduce yourself. Get to know each other. Your phone number should be in their contacts if they have a favor to ask. That also keeps your local leaders accountable for their decisions. If they vote against small businesses, you can give them a call right away to make sure they think long and

hard about what they're doing for their community. That's the backbone of democratic government: accountability to the people.

Consider the charity that is employment. By employing people in your local community, you are changing lives. Just running your business is already changing the world. And the way you treat your employees can make the world even better. If you're adaptable and flexible for single moms, you're providing more care for their children than a corporate job would. That means healthier families, which are really the foundation of our community.

In small businesses, we actually are like family. Not so much in corporations that claim they're a family. You can give to your own family in ways that others can't. You can teach younger family members job skills, business ownership, ethics, and how to take care of themselves instead of looking to a corporation to do it for them. Business ownership is a unique way to strengthen your family and take care of all its members.

If you aren't sure where to start, that's OK. You can start anywhere. Maybe you have no extra money right now, so you decide to volunteer at a soup kitchen this weekend. While you're handing out hot meals, maybe you identify a need that your company could help fill. That gives you a chance to work with that soup kitchen, hand out products you make, and improve the lives of people in need.

No matter what level you're at or how your business is going right now, there's something you can do to get involved in your community. And more generosity will help your business, which means more opportunities for generosity later. It's a big circle that helps everyone involved, yourself included.

Two Generous Entrepreneurs

I'd like to share the stories of two business clients I've coached and how they blew me away with their charitable hearts.

Angie owns a food company with a retail store, a kitchen that offers cooking classes, and a catering service. When COVID-19 hit, her kitchen and catering services were forced to shut down. Instead of panicking, she started asking for donations, shifting her catering kitchen into a hub for feeding overworked hospital crews. Her company churned out thousands of meals in the opening months of the pandemic and fed countless nurses and doctors fighting to keep patients alive.

Since then, Angie has become involved with local community groups to keep independent restaurants afloat. When COVID got a high-priced hospice gala canceled, her team cooked the meals anyway, bagged them up, and delivered them to individual members who would have attended. By doing that, she helped raise $85,000 for the gala even after it was canceled.

Angie's company has thrived, and her community has benefited tremendously from her charity. That's the circle I was talking about. Everyone grows together.

Sasha owns a natural products company, and she hooked up with a local distillery at the beginning of the pandemic in March 2020. You probably remember that hand sanitizer disappeared from store shelves, and even front-line responders couldn't get any. Her company provided the bottles and basic materials for the gel and got the distillery to provide the alcohol, creating their own hand sanitizer. The first 5,000 bottles went to doctors, nurses, police, paramedics, and other front-line responders. For free. They gave away over $80,000 worth of hand sanitizer.

Because of their generosity and quick thinking, this company got featured on local and national news. Everyone knows who they are now. Their company is thriving because people want to support them. When you see someone doing good, you want them to have more resources to do even more good in the world.

If there's a need, an entrepreneur will come running. They don't whine about challenges. They buckle down and get the work done. If they make a dollar doing it, they give away a huge chunk of that dollar to their employees and their community. Some even save lives with the work they do.

Don't underestimate your global impact as a business owner. There is so much you can do to make the world a better place. So what impact do you want to make? Figure that out and start now. Your generosity will help create a better world.

CHAPTER 20
THE TYPE E PERSONALITY

My son Jeff was kicked out of school in grade seven at twelve years old.

Jeff was unable to pay attention the way teachers demanded. They told me he had "impulse problems." The teachers treated him like a bad kid. I was furious and heartbroken for him.

Soon after, Jeff was diagnosed with ADHD. A lot of kids who don't fit into boxes get that diagnosis, and just like Jeff, they face consequences for not being able to focus in school. Sitting behind a desk and listening to someone talk at them for six hours a day just doesn't work for everyone.

Jeff has gone on to start ADHD Kids Rock, as you know. He teaches kids and parents that the diagnosis they've been told is a financial death sentence is actually just a different way of thinking. And when they harness their powerful brains and embrace their strengths, kids with ADHD can achieve incredible things that no one else can match.

You know what population has a tremendous percentage of ADHD diagnoses? Entrepreneurs. Turns out the same kids who can't sit still in an archaic schoolroom also don't do well when shoved into cubicles. Those impulse spikes that teachers hate are actually fantastic leaps of insight that turn entrepreneurs into powerful innovators and community builders.

When I realized this connection, I took a different approach with coaching clients. I started having conversations with my clients about atypical neurologies like ADHD. Many of them were shocked and said, "That's me!" For the first time, a lot of them finally made sense to themselves. Many actually went and got diagnosed.

Don't take my word for it. Brian Scudamore from 1-800-GOT-JUNK was featured in a major ADHD magazine. And Richard Branson, the owner of Atlantic Airlines who also started Virgin Galactic for space-flights, has come out about his ADHD as well. A great number of famous

CEOs whom the whole world looks up to have opened up and said, "I couldn't focus in school, and my teachers hated me. Now I'm running a global company."

This chapter isn't all about ADHD. It's about what this sort of behavior, diagnosable or otherwise, means for entrepreneurs. Because even if you don't fit the full ADHD profile, it's likely that you have some of its features.

I call this personality Type E—for entrepreneur.

Type E Individuals: The Distracted Entrepreneur

A lot of entrepreneurs couldn't stay in school. Instead, they found they could build a business.

It's an old cliche that straight-A students work for C students. Some people focus on adhering to the system and doing what they're told, and those students score great on tests. Then they often struggle when they're left alone to plan their own way forward. The C students, on the other hand, have experience plotting their own course and only invest as much in the system as is necessary to get the job done.

Unfortunately, many are told this lack of conformity is a problem. Often, these people self-medicate with alcohol or drugs to conform rather than letting themselves be free.

The distinguishing difference between successful Type E personalities and unsuccessful ones is the ability to create focus through systems. Building systems that make up for their unique distractedness is the key to success. The entrepreneurial brain thrives in a systems environment where bills are paid on time, keys are always in the right place, et cetera so they can be the creator—not the doer of the boring task they're unable to focus on. Without systems, your brain scatters in too many directions to be productive. By focusing your energy into creating systems, you channel your enthusiasm to achieve success.

What if designing systems is hard for you? You can pay other people to create them. As an example, you can choose which software to use and decide your hiring questions, then have someone else configure the software and interview candidates for you. Don't rely on your own memory—for anything. Systems are what help Type E personalities flourish in the business world.

ADHD entrepreneurs in particular struggle with executive function. This could include adaptable thinking, planning, self-monitoring, self-control, working memory, time management, prioritization, and organization. These are weak points that can easily be addressed with systems and hired assistance.

Type E personalities are gamblers and risk-takers. It's fun to take leaps and find out what's at the bottom. When I started my travel agency, I remortgaged my house, hired an employee, rented a place for $2,000 per month, quit my job, and had no child support. I threw everything in before I was even sure it was stable! Even with everything I've learned since then, I'm still a risk-taker at heart. Every time I take a risk with another investment property, I love it. That kind of risk terrifies a lot of people. Not that I love losing, I just love the experience—the unknown, the tension, the discovery. And to be honest, I've made quite a bit more money by taking the leaps. Sure, you lose some. You also gain a tremendous amount in return.

Entrepreneurs are not as worried about safety and security because we believe we can make it. That confidence doesn't come from thinking we're invincible. We just know that we'll do whatever it takes to adapt and grow. We know we can survive and thrive, wherever we end up.

Most of the people who've created the greatest wealth in the world are Type E. That often coincides with a diagnosis of ADD, ADHD, or autism spectrum disorder. Elon Musk[32] has Asperger's syndrome, a form of ASD. Some of the most successful people in the world are neurologically atypical and have leveraged their unusual brain activity into incredible personal and financial success.

If you've always been told that you're a little weird, rejoice! That weirdness others perceive is what gives you the ability to break free from a standard life and create a successful business.

To do that, it's important to be aware of the common pitfalls we face along the way.

---

32   Denise Brodey, "How Elon Musk's Neurodiversity Comment Showed the Power of Getting Personal," *Forbes*, May 13, 2021, https://www.forbes.com/sites/denisebrodey/2021/05/13/how-elon-musks-neurodiversity-comment-showed-the-power-of-getting-personal/.

Challenges of the Type E Brain

Type E individuals are great at building businesses. However, they often create a disorganized, unprofitable business. Their brain doesn't want to focus on boring details like bookkeeping, ordering supplies, interviewing workers, and writing policy and procedures manuals. This overlooking of details often leads to feeling trapped as they watch their profits leak through the holes in their business.

Let's talk about the five key issues my business friends and coaching clients have faced and what you can do to overcome them on your way to being profitable and free.

1. Persistence That Doesn't Pay

Rebecca had opened a used furniture store. She struggled trying to find a way to compete against Craigslist and garage sales. She was losing $10,000 a year. Years later, she vented her frustration to me.

"I stayed in it for four years because I wanted to make my forty thousand dollars back! Then it was year seven, and I wanted to make my seventy thousand dollars back. After ten years and a hundred thousand dollars lost, I quit."

Some businesses don't work. Sometimes it's a bad personal fit, a dying industry, or a poor business model. Sticking with your first choice and persisting is sometimes the worst thing you can do. It's tough for some entrepreneurs to accept that because they're so eager to adapt and discover. Bailing out of a dying business feels like failing. It may even feel like accepting a lifetime of criticism from others. That need to prove everyone wrong can be an entrepreneur's downfall.

2. Self-Destruction

I've been guilty of this one. During the first month after opening the travel agency, my motto was "Feel the fear and do it anyway." I put that on my fridge so I'd see it every morning. I drove myself like a machine and prided myself on my dedication. Being that driven resulted in me getting no sleep for fourteen straight nights. And let me tell you, I didn't feel so smart after that.

I wrote an entire chapter in this book on the importance of self-care because so many entrepreneurs forget to do it. If that's you, go back and read that chapter again. If you don't take care of yourself, you'll destroy the business you're trying to build.

3. Broken Families

Entrepreneurs aren't the only ones who suffer from their own self-neglect.

When a business falls apart, family is often the first to suffer. Even focusing too intensely on a thriving company can make your family feel forgotten. I've seen marriages deteriorate and children feel alienated from parents. The entrepreneurial brain makes it too easy to focus on what's fun and avoid tricky relationships, especially when they need your focus the most. Remember that without your family, your business will bring you little joy.

Stop and ask yourself, "Why am I working so hard?"

4. No Failure Allowed

A lack of belief in failure can sometimes be a good thing. It motivates you to take risks, and you trust yourself to work it out no matter what. Or it can mean ruining your marriage because you refuse to listen when your spouse tells you there's a problem.

As an entrepreneur business coach, I've met people who felt enslaved to their chaotic, disorganized business. Too proud to quit, they gave up everything to make their business work. Their health, their family, and everything else that mattered was gone. Unless they were in a health industry and forced to embody their own advice, they surrendered everything in pursuit of success.

And the harsh truth is that those who sacrifice the most often still fail in business. It's important to remember that it's OK to let your business fail rather than losing everything else that you value more.

5. Operational Abdication

Entrepreneurs often abdicate things around money, books, and financial planning. No one likes these boring details, and Type E brains can't be forced to endure them. They tend to get into trouble with money for the same reason: "Details don't matter! Show me the fun stuff!"

Even if you don't know how to reconcile a bank statement, you need to know it has been done. And even if you can't identify your KPIs yourself, you need to know what they are.

If it can cost you money, you need to know about it. You need to know exactly what's being done and what needs to be done based on your goals. A system will take care of these details for you so that when you *do* delegate, you'll still be in the loop. Work with the people you're delegating to and say, "Let's create a system together so I can see a report once a month."

Most entrepreneurs don't want to do this. Instead of delegating, they abdicate. They hand over their money and say, "Tell me where to sign." If you don't really understand how you got to a certain point, you know you've abdicated. Leonard Cohen[33] didn't know his manager was embezzling millions from him. When that story broke, it derailed Leonard's career, and he barely turned this around before he passed away.

A simple system of regularly scheduled check-ins with your team will both keep you informed and free you up to do what you love most.

Fallout Prevention

Throughout this whole book, I've talked about the importance of systems. That's because systems are the only thing that's going to save you from the problems mentioned here. Bottom line: if you want to prevent fallout, you've got to systematize your whole business.

You need systems that work all the time, every time, especially when you're not there. Don't build systems that rely on your constant input. You'll hate it. That systems will crash, and you'll be trapped.

Follow the steps in this book to build systems that support your brain. If you hate some part of your process, automate it or pay someone else to do it for you. Get the awful stuff taken care of so it doesn't fall apart while you're doing the fun stuff.

Do all this in advance and you won't have to worry about explosions. Your systems will have your business running like a well-oiled machine, even in your absence. That's true fallout prevention.

---

33   Alan Light, "How an Embezzling Manager Caused Leonard Cohen's Late-Career Comeback," *Billboard*, November 17, 2016, https://www.billboard.com/music/features/leonard-cohen-embezzlement-career-comeback-7580545/.

A Type E Business Owner with a Systematized, Organized, Profitable Business

Once your business could run without you—if you decide you truly want that—life becomes sweet because you don't have to give up this business; you can simply do whatever you like. You can take a holiday whenever you like. Somewhere with a panoramic view of snowcapped mountains. Feel the warmth of the fire. Smell the sweet aroma of burning logs. Or you can treat yourself and your family to a tropical paradise. Coconut drinks, coconut snacks, coconut everything. Sunlight ripples across the pure blue waters of endless ocean. Wherever you go, you'll know things are just fine back at the office.

It took me two full years to fully systematize my business. That first summer I took a full six weeks off, traveled with my family to Disney World, and spent time at my childhood vacation cottage in Ontario. The business ran completely independent of me. Now that's freedom.

Sounds nice, doesn't it? The truth is that you can't relax (as a business owner or as a Type E personality) until you've got everything systematized. Once you do, relaxation becomes effortless. You can take plenty of time to refuel yourself. That makes you even better at building your business. Relaxation actually makes you more money! Build those systems to support your weak points, and this will be you.

There's a great Kenny Rogers song called *The Gambler*. The lyrics say, "You've got to know when to hold 'em, know when to fold 'em, know when to walk away, and know when to run."

When you know, you know.

CHAPTER 21

HOPE FOR THE FUTURE

Vincent heaved a sigh. He sat slumped in his chair with bags under his glazed eyes. "I'm making a lot of money. But despite having all the work we can handle, I'm miserable. How did things get so out of control?"

"That sounds exhausting," I said. "Is that what made you book a coaching session with me?"

"Actually, my wife decided it was best for me to meet you. She says there's got to be a better way to manage my business. One that doesn't suck the life out of me. But I've been looking for the answer for years on my own and I'm still more stressed than ever. Some days I want to throw in the towel."

"Before you give up, let me ask you a few questions. What does owning this business mean to you?"

We talked about Vincent's initial reasons for starting his business. Then we looked over his business assessment and identified challenging areas. Behind the scenes, he had more positives than problems. But his problems were big gaps that created a ton of extra work. Once we'd identified the missing or broken systems causing him the most grief, nearly all his remaining issues could be solved by applying more confident leadership.

The session began with Vincent slumped in his chair. As the session went on and we talked through his problems, he sat up straighter. His eyes grew sharper and more focused. He stopped sighing and started answering questions with greater attention to detail. And he started to see his business through a systems lens instead of his emotional command-and-control perspective.

After ninety minutes, Vincent had come back to life. He shook my hand so hard I thought it would pop off. "I can't believe you know how to fix all these problems. Are you some kind of genius?"

"I didn't do it. You did. I've just learned how to ask the right questions. It's all about perspective. In your case, you were missing a bunch of key systems. Once you've got them in place, your whole world will change."

"I can't wait."

"So, Vincent, what stuck with you the most today? What are you taking out of this meeting?"

Vincent smiled. "Hope. I finally feel like I have hope again."

That's the number-one thing business owners take away from their first conversation with me. Hope. It's the most important thing they've lost over the years as their business problems have beaten them down. Regaining that hope is crucial. Nothing can get better until they have hope again.

Hope can also make you overeager. A lot of business owners have been without hope for so long that once they taste it, they imagine everything fixed in a few weeks. They suddenly have a burst of energy and a burning desire to systematize their entire business right now. They pick ten problems and try to tackle them all at once.

As you probably expect, that goes terribly. They crash and burn, then they feel disappointed and lose hope again. "I tried and failed! I was wrong. Abandon ship!"

To prevent this kind of overwhelm, I ask my clients, "What one problem, if systematized, would make the biggest change in your life?"

My goal in this book has been to inspire you to fix the issues threatening your business and your personal life. Now it's time to translate that hope into action—without trying to do everything at once.

Pick one big fire in your business that you can put out with a system. Have a supplier who fails to deliver on time and causes you inventory headaches? Is your tech not up to par, or do you have equipment failing all the time? Are you spending too much time running IT and need to outsource to someone? Is hiring giving you a migraine, or do you keep hiring the wrong people? Maybe it's even more basic than that. Are you unsure of where your money's going?

You don't need to build twenty systems tomorrow and overhaul your entire company before you're allowed to take a weekend off. Focus on what will get you one more day off every week. After implementing just one new system to solve one of your biggest troubles, watch how it changes your life for the better.

It might cost you a little money up front. You may lose profits for a short time while you adapt. The goal is to make your life better in the long run, not make as much cash as you can right now while sacrificing your health. Eating properly is more important than making one extra sale. Prioritize yourself, your health, and your family. You don't need to be an entrepreneurial Hercules. You just need to start with one system.

The COVID-19 pandemic was a wake-up call for small business owners. Many of us found out how much control the government holds over our ability to earn money. We also discovered how fragile supply lines can be. And we learned the word *pivot*. Many business owners had to pivot into a new industry or into a new stance with their business. When your main source of income dries up, you need to take a step back and strategically look for ways to adapt.

We also learned that every business has value. Even the smallest little business can be sold. There are people out there right now who want what you've built. Once systems are in place, you can shop around for a new owner and hand off your optimized moneymaking business. Your future is wide open.

Protect Your Hope

Right now, you've got hope. You're dreaming of how good life can be. *You can do this.* You can take your business from chaos to calm, from messy to organized, from bad to good, from loss to profit. This change is a process. It might take you two months to wrap your head around what needs to be done. Don't focus on changing today; just start thinking today. Look at your business with fresh eyes and finally be honest with yourself. This honesty and perspective will show you what you need to do about your problems.

Most people understand the benefit of systems fairly quickly. Once in a while, though, someone struggles. Remember that business owner I told you about who insisted on cleaning every toilet herself? It took three years of coaching to break through her resistance to building systems. While she substantially grew her profit during those three years, she still wanted to do everything herself. She needed control and couldn't let go, using her own "it's in my head" manual. She didn't trust the systems.

Even while she checked and double-checked every employee's work, she wanted to be free. Childhood trauma had instilled patterns of belief, lack of worthiness, and a damaged ego, all of which needed to be worked through before she was willing to try trusting systems. One day, she finally broke down and couldn't keep going anymore. She gave the systems a chance, and everything changed. She was suddenly free. Relaxed. Her business was running better than ever. She just had to get out of her own way.

Since you've read this book, your process likely won't take nearly as long. But it will take as long as it takes. Remember this, and you won't lose hope. Look at your business as separate from you and treat it with respect. The faster you open your mind to thinking in terms of designing systems instead of doing manual labor, the faster you can build a business that pays you for taking time off.

Take Action One System at a Time

Many business owners despair at this point because they already feel worked to the bone. They throw up their hands and shout, "How am I going to find another forty hours a week to systematize this business?"

You don't need forty hours. You need about five hours per week to work on your systems, get organized, and stay (or become) profitable. And you can split them up however you like. The clients who do the best either block one hour of each workday, or five hours in a single day per week. Commit to setting aside five hours a week to improve your life. You'll see tremendous growth (and a chance for more time off) in a very short time.

Remember to apply one system at a time. Do not do everything at once because you will burn out and keep your miserable job. Chances are there are one or two main things you're doing that drain your time and energy. Solve those problems first.

Once you break free from that one big problem, finding time to solve the others will be easy. It all starts with that first victory. Your first successful system will give you such tremendous new hope, you'll wonder why it took you so long to begin!

Calm the Chaos with Coaching

Part of the problem with solving all your problems alone is that you're the one who created those problems in the first place. That's not to say that you're entirely to blame. Just about every business owner falls into the "I have to do everything myself" trap. It's a natural part of entrepreneurship because no one else shares our passion for what we're building. We have a vision, and we know how we want to execute it. And we rarely have time to refine the structures we build.

Then, eight years in, we feel trapped. We've dug a mine shaft into the earth looking for diamonds, and now the walls are closing in, and we can't find our way out.

If this initial trap is part of entrepreneurial life, then it's a good thing there's a second part: mentorship. Specifically, paid mentorship, in the form of coaching.

For many business owners, a coaching session is the first time they feel like they have a partner: a nonjudgmental partner who actually listens and can help draft a plan and prioritize steps. When you're alone, it's easy to get stuck on the problems. You focus on what's wrong, then you get too upset to focus on a solution. When you work with a coach, they listen to your frustration and still remain objective. You can get all fired up and convinced there's no way out, then your coach says, "Here's what you've told me; now let's talk about the way forward out of this mess."

Chances are you know what you need to do. It's just that there are so many competing priorities, so many things to learn, and so many people counting on you to get this right. In your coaching session, the world stops long enough for you to get some clarity. A good coach lets you drive the conversation toward the most important thing you want to talk about. You built this business, so you know what you want it to look like when fully developed. Imagine having both the confidence and a solid plan to get there. That is what coaching does. You have a vision and a laundry list of competing priorities and zero time to execute your great ideas. Taking the time to talk to a business coach takes you out of the chaos and into a calm, focused, strategic-thinking space where you can actually see the path forward. Someone needs to call you out on your oversights in a way that's both compassionate and enlightening.

If you feel like you've been going in circles, it's probably time to hire a coach. If your family knew how to solve the issues, they'd have stepped in long ago. And employees don't want to listen to the boss complain. Protect morale, defend your own mental health, and hire somebody to help you find the pieces you've been missing.

Now, you could just ask random business owners for their advice. Business mastermind groups are great except that now you have ten people telling you what to do who haven't figured it out themselves yet. Sure, they'll probably have a couple of helpful ideas. The thing is, understanding exactly how to help a business grow is a whole skill set that takes time to perfect. Find a coach who actually knows how to help you achieve long-term success.

Rather than just googling *business coach*, hire a business coach who knows where you're coming from. Systems Business Coach (SBC)–certified coaches know this book (and all my methods) like the back of their hand. They're trained to pinpoint exactly what applies to you and what doesn't. I built this certification program specifically to extend my help to business owners like you on the journey to freedom.

We aren't consultants. We don't come in and boss you around, demanding you change your business to our liking. Do you like being told what to do? Probably not. Entrepreneurs have their own vision. Even if you're looking for advice, you don't want to run someone else's company. You want *your* company. Just . . . better. And with more time off.

You want someone to talk to about your challenges. You want someone to ask your opinion and build solutions with you. You want someone to bounce ideas off so you know you're doing the right thing. SBC coaching provides just that, with you and your vision at the center. We're here to find your maximum potential and help you build a set of systems that makes sense for you. Most of all, an SBC coach is there for you. You finally aren't alone in your business anymore. You've got help, and it's going to be OK. Our job is to help you build the best possible version of your vision—the one that earns you the most money while giving you the maximum amount of time off to be home with your family. Prosperity and freedom.

The number-one most important thing we will support you with is that policy and procedures manual. The one that makes you aware of exactly what you're doing, helps you find better methods, and allows your business to run without you. When you see problems and gaps, you know you've identified the need for a system. That's why we start by assessing how things operate. And an SBC coach helps you stay objective during that process.

Not only do SBC coaches possess an expert understanding of small business needs, but they also have access to the database of over one hundred business tools I've created at Systems Business Coach. We believe that the client is the boss of their own learning journey, and only the client can decide what's best for them. That means selecting which business competency you need help with first. Those competencies may include running a debt reduction calculator, learning better hiring practices, or reevaluating your target market. Wherever you need help the most, we have a system for that. Surprised? Like Mary Poppins's carpetbag, our toolbox is deep and wide. It took a dozen years to build, test, rebuild, and test again to develop the exact systems that work. We don't offer anything fluffy, made up, or trendy. What we do offer is a way forward that's been proven to work in every corner of the globe and an experience that's customized to your needs. And if you aren't sure what your needs are, we've got you covered. Clients also receive my 350-page full-color *Small Business Field Guide*, which maps out all fifty-two small business competencies, what they are, what they mean to you, and how to master them in your own business.

Our coaching sessions offer a zero-risk introductory session when you reach out and ask for help. If you've never experienced real coaching before, you owe yourself the opportunity to be seen, heard, and understood. You'll get a full confidential and comprehensive business assessment with one of our certified Systems Business Coaches. If this book spoke to you and you want to implement it with professional assistance, schedule your assessment session with us at https://www.systemsbusinesscoach.com. Together with your coach, you can find your way forward to build that life of freedom you've always dreamed about.

Keep Going . . . One System at a Time

I've said it before, and I'll say it again. Please remember that you do not have to do everything at once. In fact, you can't. Instead, focus on that one first system to solve your biggest problem.

After you've solved the first problem, continue with building one more system at a time. Keep building systems (you guessed it, one at a time) until your whole company can run without you. Eventually, you and your family can take December off and go to Hawaii. You'll be earning profits while lounging on a sunny beach. That's the dream.

You can make all the money you've imagined if you have the right systems. With this book, you now have the tools and strategies to get you there. You can do anything you want—work whatever hours you want, live where you want, vacation how you want. You are the architect and designer of this business. And all it takes is stepping outside your day-to-day operations to build the business around yourself and your dreams.

What I've learned over my fifteen years of coaching small business owners is this: you are one of the most tenacious, giving, hardworking people on the planet. Small business owners are the backbone of our economy. They're also overworked, overwhelmed, overloaded, undervalued, and underappreciated. You create jobs in your community. You donate to Little League. You volunteer. You go to chamber of commerce meetings. You're the ones who bring the community together, often for little or no thanks.

You can be all that and still enjoy your life when you build your systems. And if that sounds like too big a task, hire a coach to help you. Life can be so much sweeter when your business runs on systems. Systems build wealth. They grant you prosperity and freedom. And they give you enough money so you don't have to worry—and also the time to enjoy the fruits of your labor.

You *can* make your business work for you. And I'm here to help.

What system will you build first?

ABOUT THE AUTHOR

Beverlee Rasmussen, MA, CEC, PCC, has devoted her entire professional and academic career to one cause: reducing the rate of small business failure. Why? Because she believes, fervently, that no entrepreneur should embark on a dream, only to watch it crumble. "Someone had to step up and help," she'd say with quiet intensity. In her eyes, each small business that closes its doors sends ripples through lives and communities. It's not just about lost revenue; it's about the human cost, the dreams shattered and the potential unrealized. And Beverlee, with her wealth of experience and deep empathy, has stood as a steadfast ally for these struggling businesses, offering meaningful assistance to those navigating the entrepreneurial journey.

For the past fifteen years as a Certified Executive Coach from Royal Roads University and a Professional Certified Coach from the International Coaching Federation (ICF), Beverlee has invested over twelve thousand hours in the development of The Small Business Field Guide, a roadmap to small business success. She meticulously broke down each challenge a typical business encounters and developed a framework for business success, encompassing fifty-two core business competencies, all written in plain language that any entrepreneur can easily understand and apply. This endeavor included pursuing a Graduate Certificate in Organizational Development from Royal Roads University and, most recently, earning a Master of Arts in Executive and Organizational Coaching, being one of only four individuals in Canada to have achieved this distinction.

After receiving the ICF Vancouver 2014 Business Coach of the Year award, Beverlee represented Canada at the Women in Business North America Summit at the invitation of the Canadian Business Women in International Trade commissioner. Beverlee was also the first female president of the Rotary Club of Langley Central, a multiple Paul Harris Fellow, and a rotary foundation major donor. Her speaking and facilitation talents earned her the position of rotary district trainer and president-elect training facilitator in Seattle, working with high-profile business leaders in rotary.

As the founder of the award-winning and internationally recognized Systems Business Coach (SBC), Beverlee has helped over four hundred small business owners document strategic business objectives and processes, break free from day-to-day operations, achieve consistent profitability, hire and train productive employees, attract and retain customers, and increase company value.

When not coaching clients one-on-one or holding business systems workshops, Beverlee shares her passion for helping small business owners by traveling the world training others to become small business coaches. Currently, there are SBC-licensed certified systems business coaches in Europe, the UK, Mexico, Malaysia, New Zealand, the US, and Canada.

Easy to talk to, with extensive knowledge and unmatched passion, Beverlee has rightfully earned the title of Small Business Thought Leader. She stands steadfastly beside small business owners worldwide, offering pragmatic help and real hope.

Helpful Links:

The Small Business Field Guide:

www.systemsbusinesscoach.com/systematize-your-business-guide

Elevate your next business event with Beverlee as your keynote speaker: admin@systemsbusinesscoach.com

Get help building your business:

www.systemsbusinesscoach.com

Become a Small Business Coach:

www.smallbusinesscoachtraining.com

Manufactured by Amazon.ca
Bolton, ON

36282654R00164